The Revolution of Self
The Three Keys to Personal Liberation

Shannon Graham

CONTENTS

PART I

Clarity

PART II

Inner Peace

PART III

<u>Tools</u>

Conclusion

Warning!

This is not a book! It might look like a book. It might feel like a book. And I may even call it a book at times. You may have found it at a bookstore. But this is not a book. This is a field guide. It is an instruction manual. This guide comes with rules and those rules are to be followed without fail. This guide concerns the most important of all subjects.

You must treat and view this book in a way unlike any other book you have ever read. It's simple. I am willing to guess that you have read more than one self-help book in your life and that you might have gotten some cool ideas from these past books. However, I'm also willing to bet that your life was not revolutionized by them. If it had been, I doubt you would be here with this book in your hands right now.

There is an epidemic in the self-help world. Consumers in this industry just can't get enough information. They buy book, after book, after book, in hopes that simply by reading them their lives will be magically changed. Well guess what. Their lives don't change. In fact, sometimes they get worse. The overload of data causes an affliction called information paralysis. I was in the same boat. I read hundreds of books and I didn't change. Until finally I realized that life-changing actions don't come from information but from decisions.

If you are not willing to roll up your sleeves and do some real work, then I would like you to put this book down right now and walk away. In the following pages, you will not read anything that will change your life. What!? Yes. As much as that sounds like the last thing an author should ever say, it's true. Learning new information is not what you need in order to change your life. Chances are you already have tons of information bouncing around in your head and it's not doing you any good.

You do not need a few tips or tricks to help you get by. You do not need tools to help you manage your stress. You do not need to awaken the giant within, because I can guarantee that the giant deep inside you is wide-awake and screaming to be let out. This is about seeing your life for what it really is - the good, bad, and ugly - and making a solemn promise to yourself that you are going to take control once and for all. You're going to live the life you are meant to live.

I tried my best to write this book in a manner that is conversational in nature. I will be making statements and asking you questions and I want you to think and act just as if you and I were having an actual conversation. At the end of each section, I am going to ask you to put the book down and work on the outlined action steps. Let's practice....put this book down right now. No really, put it down. If I am going to be asking you to do this later on, you'd better get used to it now. Put this book down.

I know I am totally sinking the chances of this book becoming a "page turner" but luckily, that is not the point. If you merely read this book and don't stop to do the exercises and take the action steps at the end of each section, then I can promise you that your life will hardly change at all. It's not about reading. It is about gaining a new perspective, asking new questions, making new decisions, and taking more action than you ever have before.

If you use this book as a field guide, then you will dramatically increase your chances of revolutionizing your world. Hold nothing back. Break out your highlighter and go to town. Tear pages out and post them on your wall. I don't care. Do whatever it takes to use this book as a tool that will renovate your life. Take everything you read as seriously as possible, as each chapter contains a very important piece of the entire puzzle. Each exercise is just as important as the next. Reread chapters. Find connections between chapters. And do your best to think of everything that is written in relation to your own life. Now, put this book down!

Good! You're getting the hang of it. I want to remind you that from here on out, things are going to get heavy. You are going to be facing your biggest fears. You are going to be

asking yourself some of life's greatest questions and you
may not know the answers to those questions right away.
You will discover sides of yourself that you didn't know you
had. Some of those faces will scare the heck out of you and
others will cause pure feelings of joy. However, before you
go any further, you need to ask yourself if this is what you
really truly want. Although in order to help you answer that,
let me ask you to stop and take a few minutes to answer each
one of these questions honestly.

Do you know exactly who you are?

Do you know exactly why you are here?

Do you completely love yourself?

Are you happy with your life?

Are you head over heels in love with your job?

Are you totally fulfilled in your relationships?

I told you it was going to get heavy. Fear not! Even if you
don't know the answers to any or all of these questions, you
will by the end of this book. But, the answers are not *in* this
book. What!? Am I bent on sabotaging my book sales or
something? Nope, I am just telling the truth. The answers are
within you, locked up. This book will act as a guide to show
you how to unlock them. Honestly, it would be even crazier
of me to think that I had the solutions to YOUR challenges
in life. I've never met you and even if I did work with you
personally, the best I could do was help you to achieve
clarity, give you some tools, and help you reframe your
beliefs about yourself. The combination of putting those
three together and making them work for you is what will set
you free. It's time to change your idea about from where the
answers are going to come.

Isn't it time you changed the things that really matter? The
big things. The things that have the most impact on your

life. See, I don't care about teaching you stress management techniques, because if you need all kinds of tools to simply make it through the day. then something's not right. Which would feel better? Squeezing a stress ball or having a life where you don't need one? I'm not into tips and tricks you can use to just get by. Forget that. To me that's like putting a Band-Aid on a broken leg. Real concrete solutions are necessary to obtain the life you really want. This is not about some life tune-ups. This is a damned revolution! Stop trying to learn tips and tricks in order to continue to hold it all together unsuccessfully. Chances are the things that scare you the most, the areas of your life in which you are most afraid to make radical changes, are exactly the areas where you need to triumph over the most. And, if your life feels like it's on the verge of falling apart, my guess is that it probably needs to.

You might not know it but the world needs you. No matter what you decide about your identity, as we move forward, remember that a part of that identity is being a hero. By becoming your ultimate-self, you become that hero. You show the rest of the world that you are not willing to back down to the mediocrity that exists all around you. You inspire each person you meet by showing him or her that you have stepped up to uncover your purpose in life and live each and every day at your peak. Your ultimate-self deserves a chance to stretch and live up to its full potential.

You do yourself and the rest of the world a great disservice by pretending you are a lamb, when in fact you are a lion. Whether you believe that right now or not doesn't matter. You will discover that. The world is full of cowards, and trust me, you do not need to remain one of them. There are far too many as it is. The world needs leaders, rebels, and revolutionists. This is the obligation that is thrust upon you when you decide to become who you are truly meant to be.

Why do we so willingly put ourselves in a cage? There is no genius in creating an unlimited world while admiring it from behind bars. The greatest good you can do mankind has nothing to do with building something, but it has everything to do with liberating yourself and contributing your time and love. The world doesn't need more stuff. It needs more of you.

Don't worry. No one expects you to go out and save the planet or end world hunger tomorrow. For now, this is about you and you only. Your focus must remain on yourself and how you can become your best self. Once you have unleashed yourself upon the world, being a hero will be automatic. And, although you may not move and breathe as that person yet, you have to at least believe that you can, will, and must.

I named this book *The Revolution of Self* for a reason. Evolution is too soft and takes too long. Your true self has been held captive for far too long as it is. Your time on this planet is much shorter than you think and to cross your fingers and hope that you will evolve into a new and better person is to waste the precious time you could be spending as that bigger and better person. Your true self lies within waiting to be unleashed, standing fast with its fist in the air. Now is the time for the greatest uprising of your life.

Take a moment now to prepare yourself for anything and everything that may come your way. Stop right now and get quiet. Get so quiet that you can hear the sound of your own heart beating. Hear that? That sound? ....bum bum....bum bum...bum bum... That is the universal call to arms. It is the battle drum each rebel hears as they charge full-heartedly into war. It is the sound of your destiny calling to you, beckoning you forth into a new world. It is the rhythm by which your life is meant to dance. As you move forward, in your times of doubt remember this sound. Let it forever more remind you that the heart knows no fear, and fears no death. Through your actions in this life, your heartbeat will manifest itself and go on to echo throughout the rest of time.

Heed this warning and go forth. It is your time to be great.

Call to Arms

Welcome to the resistance. The lines of battle are drawn and the trenches are dug within our minds and hearts. The gears of war will turn and minds of men and women will surely spin.

You will be a slave to the oppression until the shackles become too tight, and the pain will arise in you an undying need to fight. Remember though, in this conflict amidst all the chaos of this brawl, that love, my friend, is the greatest weapon of all.

Today, as you step out onto the front lines, fear and uncertainty run through your veins, yet your unshakeable soul has a firm grip upon the reins. You are outnumbered and your will shall certainly be worn thin. Your only saving grace is a little voice inside that says, "You can win."

Hold fast to that grand idea of victory, for as distant and invisible as it may be, it is the faith in that incredible dream that will one day make it the reality you seek. You have made your choice and you must now stand tall. You can no longer go back to living in a box that is two times too small. It is impossible to go back and change what now is. For that, it is too late. Taking control of today is your only means of rewriting your fate.

There will be pain and you will undoubtedly be sore. You will fight and you will fight and when you feel like giving up, you will fight some more. And, during the final battle, you will snap out of the trance and you will perceive this war as nothing more than a dance.

Though you may be on your knees and gasping for air from the very pits of your lungs, you will be filled with unlimited power and your victory song will be sung. You must now bide your time and not look back, until the garb of this endeavor can be laid on the shelf. Yet until that glorious day comes, welcome to the revolution of self.

A Personal Investment

When it comes to changing your life, it is very important to have an understanding that self-improvement is the wisest and best investment you'll ever make. Why? The reason is because that every single category of your life will either succeed or fail based on one simple principle. That principle is whether or not you are in a state of personal power to achieve and accept success in those areas of your life.

Having a clear understanding that self-improvement is the greatest investment you'll ever make is imperative, because it is the anchor to all your success. Think about it. Your ability to create a life filled with richness will rely on your ability to have a very specific mindset and self-worth. What about relationships? Your ability to have a long-lasting and meaningful relationship will depend on your ability to have a substantial amount of self-respect and self-love. Neither of which can be accomplished without a very high level of self-mastery and a commitment to constant improvement. That means you must have a peak level of understanding of who you truly are. When you invest in yourself, you add value to a multitude of things all at once.

Let's look at what some of those things are. When you invest in yourself, first and foremost, you add value to the moment. Your life is comprised of moments, segments of time that can be potentially filled with richness. It is your level of self-mastery that determines how great your experiences can be from moment to moment.

The moments in our life truly create the quality that we extract from it. The more we have invested in ourselves and in our ability to love and be loved, as well as our ability to learn and contribute, the more greatness we can get out of and put into those moments. Imagine living your life in a way where you know you are continuously improving those special moments in your life. Now imagine what it would be like to increase the frequency of those great moments so that they happen more often. That is the power self-mastery can give you.

Second, investing in yourself allows you to shape your future as well. As much as living in the moment and adding value to it is important, the ability to foresee and shape your future the way you see fit is also equally important. This ability to constantly improve upon yourself and develop your self-mastery creates a rich and compelling future as well. Close your eyes for a moment and just envision what it would be like to know that you can see your future clearly and that you are moving toward it with certainty. Let that vision be a large part of your inspiration as we move on.

It is my belief that certainty in people creates great levels of confidence. When a person knows that their future is being shaped by their will and ability, it gives them great confidence and joy. It is the uncertainty of the economy, the job market, of relationships and all other aspects of their life that, when not under control, lead to great levels of stress and fear. However, how we feel and what we do about these external uncertainties is up to us. We can choose the meaning we would like to extract from these situations and turn the fear and stress that would potentially oppress us into power that can build us up and make us better.

Investing in yourself ultimately adds to your ability to contribute to other people. As you will read later, relationships are everything and all around you. Your ability to have fulfillment and happiness in this life relies not only on your ability to gain things in life, like joy, peace, and fulfillment, but also on helping others achieve them as well. The more things you can give, as well as the more quality you can give, the greater contribution and impact you have upon the world and all those in it.

You'll find that almost every single person that is not contributing in some way shape or form feels pain to a degree. That is because you can only get so much satisfaction from adding only to your own life. However, when you can add quality to the lives of others, then you reach a whole new level of joy.

Think about how much you will be able to increase the quality of other people's lives when you yourself have a high level of self-mastery. You will be an inspiration and a testament to others that may be struggling. You will be able to help them out of their rut because you were able to do the same for yourself.

I would challenge you, as you and I move forward together, to do so with a mindset of improvement. Realize that the time you invest in yourself is the best use of your time and will return to you thousands of times over. The more you are willing to put in yourself the more of your life you will be able to live.

My Story

As I sit here in Santa Barbara, California, with the sun on my face, the scent of flowers and the sea flowing through my nose, I think about how grateful I am to be here. I think about how thankful I am that I can live my life on my own terms. I feel excited and fulfilled knowing that when I am not enjoying my own personal time that I am helping others live their lives to the fullest. The combination of all these things together incites an overwhelming amount of joy in my soul, yet at the same time, I feel intensely happy for no reason at all. Through my life coaching business, I am able to help people get from where they are in life to where they want to be. My time and money is leveraged in a way where I enjoy the benefits of being financially independent while also being able to do what I want, when I want, where I want, with whom I want, and as much as I want. However, it was not always this way. In fact, it used to be quite the opposite. I would like to share with you my story so that you can better understand the man behind the words. I want to bear my past to you, not just so that you can get to know me a little better but hopefully so that I can illustrate for you a picture of my own personal revolution.

I was born in a small hospital in the heart of Vermont on September 23, 1982. As my mother looked down overjoyed at her first son, she smiled adoringly. My father on the other hand was nowhere to be found. He had left my mother after finding out she was going to have his child. She was not prepared at that time to be a single mother, just as I don't think any single mother ever is.

We moved to a small island off the coast of Maine called Peak's Island. We lived there for a few years in a small house that had a small bridge. I can still somehow clearly remember playing with my construction worker toy and dump truck on the little bridge. This is where I was also introduced to my first love, the sea. I would play in the icy waters of the North Atlantic without hesitation. My lips would be as purple as a hydrangea in summer and yet I loved it like no other.

Shortly after, my mother and father decided they wanted to give things a second chance. So we packed everything into a U-haul and left for Florida where my father lived. I still remember the car ride to be much longer than I wanted. My father was a sailboat captain and taught sailing. He was not around much but when he was, he did his best to spend time with me.

Not long after, my mom had my younger brother Chris. He was a great addition to my life. I played with him, protected him, and at the right moments, which always turned out to be the wrong moments, I got into trouble with him. Since my father was not around all that much, I was my mother's "helper" and was beginning to take on roles that were the seeds of growing up too fast.

My half-sister Kim, my father's daughter, lived near us but not with us. I didn't see her much but she was very good to my brother and me whenever she was around. She would take us to the beach on nice days. And when it rained, she took us to the mall so we could play in the arcade. Even with as little as I saw her, I cared a lot about her and was always excited to see her.

After that, my half-brother Pan moved in with us. He was my father's son from a previous marriage. Pan had a rough childhood, which resulted in the formation of a problem child. My father was unsure about how to discipline him and he would not listen to a word my mother said. This created friction between my parents. They would fight about how children should be raised, who was right and who was wrong. The differences in opinion between my mother and father when it came to my half brother were simply a metaphor for the grand differences they had between themselves.

My mother felt disrespected and unsafe, so in a bold decision to do what she thought was right, she snuck a farewell letter into my father's duffel bag that he used for work and, while he was away at sea, she packed up my brother and I and left. I can still remember the sound of closing zippers in conjunction with massive confusion as we packed up and drove away, back up to Vermont.

Since my mother had not finished college, the job options were limited when we got back there. Her brother had committed suicide when I was a year old. The stress of the working world had pushed him over the edge and my mother swore to never have a job that could do that to her. Her financial resources were scarce and for the first year that we lived back in Vermont, our housing consisted of an old converted school bus. The days of fun in the sun were over. The crippling winter cold cut through that bus like a hot knife through butter. The snow would pile up so high that there were days that we simply couldn't open the door to get out.

My mother's best friend Kathy owned a daycare and since my mother had to work three jobs just to get by, I spent the majority of my time at the daycare. My good fortune was that Kathy had a son named Aaron who was my age. Most of the kids at the daycare were younger than us so, naturally, he and I became great pals. We would have grand adventures in the woods around the house and at night when we were not allowed to go outside, video games kept us entertained. From a kid's perspective, it was the perfect combination of physical and mental exercise.

I started second grade around the time we moved out of the bus and into a small apartment in town. As a result of all the moving around, I had to start school late, which meant I was a year older than all the other kids in my class. By this time, I felt more like a father figure to my brother anything else. I did not have many friends in school and because Aaron was slightly older, he was a few grades above me. I was beginning to juggle the responsibility of taking care of my brother and the pain and frustration I felt about my life, which I tried my best not to let my brother see.

I felt like I had the weight of the world on my shoulders. I was upset that I could not do more for my mother and I secretly wished she would do more for herself. At this point in my life, I had developed some strong feels of abandonment. My father had left my mother, my mother had left my father, and I felt to a large degree like they had both left me.

I didn't want to make friends because I didn't believe I deserved to have them. So I would run. Literally, as soon as it was time to go out to the playground I would run laps around the entire playground and would not stop until it was time to go back inside. This was my way of distancing myself from the rest of the kids and it worked very well.

Then in 1995, my brother and I went to Florida to visit my father for Christmas, which we did every year. However, this year was different. I remember the phone ringing and watching the color in my father's face fade. Kim had committed suicide and that was the first time in my life I had seen my father cry. As tears rolled down my father's and brother's cheeks, I just sat there like a statue. I remember packing the feeling down into the bottle that was already over flowing.

From there, things got worse. I felt like I had less and less control over my life. By age fourteen, I started working as a housekeeper to help support my family. All I can remember was laying awake at night thinking about how most fourteen-year-old boys played and had fun, while I worked and helped take care of a family. I would think to myself, "If I am taking care of them, who is taking care of me?" I was approaching an all time low.

My grades started to slip and I started to care less and less about things overall. I had been involved with martial arts earlier on but did not take it seriously. I turned back to it and used it as another escape. I would avoid making friends and, rather than running, all I did was practice martial arts. I would train so hard that I would literally bleed, sweat, and cry. The better I got the more it allowed me to separate myself from other people.

Martial arts, as consuming as it was, was not enough to quiet the demons in my head. Alcohol seemed like a good fit. Although I knew it was the "easy way out," at that point, I didn't care. And as I expected, alcohol numbed the pain but didn't make it go away. So I thought drugs might be a better solution, but I also knew deep down would not help. My challenge was that I still felt responsible to help and take care of my family and be a role model for my brother. So, I had to make sure none of my vices were outwardly visible to my family. Even though I was angry, confused, and uncertain of who I was, I still wanted to try and be somewhat of a father figure.

I knew if my brother found out about the bad things I was involved with, there was a good chance he might follow in my footsteps and wind up like Kim. I wasn't going to let that happen. But I was still in pain, so the drug of choice was NyQuil. Sleep was the best solution I found to make everything go away. When I slept, I was at peace and the demons and harsh feelings seemed like they were millions of miles away.

I reached a point where my feelings of ambivalence got so bad that my soul screamed out. I needed to feel something again and unfortunately, I was not interested in things like sports or dating. The rush I was after was the rush of the dark side. I started studying things like lock-picking, bomb making, and thievery. Soon I was going out on "missions," where I would do anything from breaking and entering, forgery and theft, to counterfeiting.

The police couldn't touch me. I was always one-step ahead. Whether I would blatantly lie to them, misdirect them, or hide from them all together, they had nothing on me. The rush was in full effect.

Then one day, a few of the people I was involved with got

into some serious trouble with the authorities. Luckily, I could not be connected to anything, and just before I downed my sleepy time cocktail that night, I thought to myself, "What if I had gotten arrested?" My family was fragile enough as it was and I didn't know for sure what an incident like that would do to them but I knew it would be something very, very bad.

Suddenly I felt the worst I had ever felt before. It dawned on me that I was betraying my family and myself. And at the same time, I felt like I had no choice because the options I chose seemed like the only ones I had. In that moment I thought to myself that it might just be better to end it all over going on and messing up my own life and the lives of the ones I loved.

My heart started racing and a million thoughts crossed my mind at the same time. What would happen to my family if I were gone? Would it really be better? What would happen if I kept my life going in the direction it was headed? Was there a way out? None of it made sense. I had no idea who I was or why I was here.

Then the loud madness rumbling through my head was broken by the sound of an instant message on my computer. It was from Aaron saying that he had just gotten into a huge fight with his parents and he wanted to come to my house. His life had caused him to cross over to the dark side as well. So I told him to come over. When he got there, I didn't mention anything about what was on my mind. I just listened to him tell me about the fight he had with his parents.

Later, after I told him bits and pieces about how I was feeling, we both agreed that we needed to completely change our lives. Ironically enough, we had purchased some Tony Robbins material that we had yet to listen to. We realized there was no better time to try something new than right then and there. So there we sat in my driveway listening to Tony tell his story and we started to get excited Tony went on to tell Oprah Winfrey's story and the combination of those two stories, his and hers, was a turning point in how I viewed my own life. The immense amount of pain and struggles they both endured made me feel like my problems paled in comparison.

After that, I went crazy (in a good way). I read hundreds of self-improvement books, listened to countless hours of audio tapes, and did whatever else I could to try and expose myself to this new life changing information. There was a catch though. Just because I was privy to all this new information, it didn't mean it had become a part of me. For a short time, I became disillusioned about self-help all together. Yet, I couldn't help but remember the stories of Tony and Oprah and kept coming back to the conclusion that it must work somehow. I took the last of the money I had to my name and went to Staples and bought five over-sized white boards, locked myself in my room and wrote down everything I knew about self-improvement.

I realized I knew a million different things but I didn't *own* any of the ideas. Slowly but surely, I broke down all the information into what turned into a handful of either beliefs or tools. Then I decided to find a way to make that handful of assets part of my identity. I didn't leave my room for three days. My revolution had begun.

After a few solid weeks of immersion into the world of self-help, everything changed. After that literally every part of who I was changed. I dropped all of my old beliefs about who I was and who I was not. I transformed all of my negative habits into powerful rituals. I started to dress differently, act differently, move and breathe differently. I finally had a sense of identity and having certainty about who I was made my confidence skyrocket. My grades turned around, I started making friends, and I realized that happiness was an inside job. I was responsible for my destiny.

Naturally, everyone wanted to know what had happened to me. My friends, co-workers, and classmates all wanted to know how I had metamorphosed. They all thought I had had some type of religious experience. When I told them that it was all due to hard work and determination, they were inspired and asked me how they could handle challenges in their own lives. At that point, the second big part of my revolution began. You see, I had never really been motivated to help other people other than my family. And I hadn't learned about self-help so I could change other people's lives. I did it so I could save my own.

My intense white board experience helped me create some very powerful yet easy to follow tools and systems. I shared these ideas with other people and to my amazement, they would come back to me the next day, week, or month and tell me about the huge impact that I had helped them make in their lives. They would share these outstanding results with me and I was absolutely blown away.

After that, my purpose hit me like a sack of hammers. I was destined to help other people change their lives for the better. I experienced a passion and energy like never before. So much so, that I wanted to get out of school as soon as possible and start helping people, which is exactly what I did. I completed two years worth of schoolwork in one year and graduated a year early from high school.

Post graduation, I decided college was not going to work for me. Deep down I knew that I had this entrepreneurial spirit and, other than my first job at fourteen, I had been fired or quit every job I'd ever had. I took that as a sign. I knew that I needed a bigger pond - the entire population of Vermont at that time was about 620,000 people and the town I lived in had just over 2000 – I needed to be in a big city.

The closet and biggest city that caught my eye was none other than New York. So in a rash yet bold move, while I was at one of my jobs, I decided to walk out in the middle of my shift, drive myself to the airport, and move to NYC. I had ten dollars in my pocket and no friends or family there. I didn't even know where I was going to stay when I got there.

I parked my car at the airport and didn't look back. When I got there, the culture shock was humbling and I remember being in Times Square watching the people mill about around me. More people at one time than I had ever seen in my whole life. Skyscrapers and taxicabs were as foreign to me as aliens from Mars. As scared as I was, I was at the same time filled with this invigorating feeling, that Sinatra spirit, that if I could make it here I could make it anywhere.

I struggled while I was there. I juggled between working jobs I didn't want, while also helping people get the most out of life. The ironic part was that as I was hustling hard for money, I was also giving people a priceless service for free. Therapy, consulting, and counseling did not fit the bill. I didn't know how to turn what I was doing into a business. Life coaching at that time was so rare that is was nowhere on my radar. The struggle slipped beyond my control after I got a phone call from a friend whose apartment I had been renting. He had moved out to live with his girlfriend and I had moved in. Up until that call, it was working out perfectly. He told me that they had broken up and that I had to move out. With no money and nowhere to go, I remember a cold chill running down my spine. I frantically called everyone I knew in the city to see if I could stay with him or her. Nothing panned out and, at that moment in time, a roof over my head was simply not in the cards.

For the first time in my life I was really actually homeless. I slept on the subway that night and fell asleep bound and determined to find a way out of the mess into which I had gotten myself. In the morning, I resolved that going home was not an option. I had been fighting to move forward the whole time I was there and was not about to give up yet. I needed money in the worst way, but I promised myself that I would not cross back over to the dark side. I racked my brain to think of creative ways to make money.

The sack of hammers suddenly made its way back to smack me again and this time it smelled like cash. I thought to myself, "Why not do what I already do with people, just charge money for it?" At this point, I had never even heard of life coaching or anything like it. I went to the library and sat down at one of the computers. They limited your time on each computer so I needed to come up with something fast. I remember a popular classified website I had told Aaron about once, so I quickly put together a small ad offering my life changing services and posted it. I was 22-years-old.

I realized that if someone called me I was going to have to have my act together. I sat down in Central Park with a notepad and I wrote down some the things I thought I'd need to know or say if someone called about my ad. I received no calls the first day. The next day, it happened. I got a call from a man who worked on Wall Street and he needed someone to help him get his life back on track. I quickly told him I was the man for the job. I asked him to meet me at the Starbucks on 291 Broadway at 2:00 p.m.

As soon as he met me he said, "You gotta be kidding me! You're just a kid!" and proceeded to turn around to leave. I quickly blurted out that I would buy him a coffee and all he had to do was listen to me. Thankfully, he agreed. He crossed his arms in disbelief and sat down. I knew I had one and only one shot to make an impact on this guy and his body language was speaking loud and clear. So, I unloaded everything I had on him and slowly I watched as his body language began to shift. I could tell he was becoming engaged. After 30 minutes, I told him that if he wanted to leave, he could but before I could finish my sentence, he cocked back and snatched a pen out of the server's apron, started taking notes on a napkin and said, "You kiddin' me? This is great! Go on!"

After the session, he was ecstatic and said, "Okay, kid. I'm in. How much?" The one part I had forgotten to figure out in the park was how much I was going to charge. I saw the chink in my own armor but knew I couldn't let him see it. It was clear that I could not stall for thinking time here, so I just blurted out the first thing that came to mind, "I charge a hundred." I still felt like a schmuck because I didn't define

what that meant; was that a hundred a month? An hour?
So I just waited to see what he'd say.
"A hundred a session huh? Yea, well, this is worth it. Okay,
kid, Let's go." He grabbed me by the arm, took me outside
to the ATM, withdrew four hundred dollars and shoved it
into my hands. "Here ya' go, kid. I'll see ya' next week at
the same time. Thanks, life coach!" And that was it. He
turned around and walked away.

The phrase "life coach" - that was it! I was a life coach. It
suddenly made so much sense. And yet, I felt like I had just
robbed someone. Never had I ever made money doing what I
loved. It almost didn't feel right. There I was with four
hundred big ones in my hand and all I did was something at
which I had become good. My whole view of how money
was made and how the world worked was instantly turned on
its head. I had heard about entrepreneurs being paid to do
what they loved. But it was all just a story to me. It wasn't
real until that moment. But from that moment on it became
so very clear.

I decided after that, that NYC was not the right city for me. I
loved the hustle and motivation that the city ignites in a
person. But the grind and cold winters were out of line with
who I really was and what I wanted. My whole outlook
changed again and money by itself didn't matter anymore. I
turned down two jobs that paid really well shortly after the
four sessions were up with my first client. That allowed me
to move back to Vermont so I could focus on building my
life coaching business. After a few years, though I
remembered that nice weather was part of what I wanted in
my life. Don't get me wrong Vermont has nice summers, but
the winters are brutal. I wanted the sun and the surf back in
my life.

Once my business could support me, I made another rash,
yet bold trip. This time I decided to travel out to Santa
Barbara, California, again, never having been there, not
knowing anyone, and having no family that lived there.

It was one of the best decisions I had ever made. Santa
Barbara has the perfect climate, just the right amount of
people, and the beach. I could not ask for anything more.
And at 28-years-old, I sit with the sun on my face and the
scent of flowers and the sea flowing filling my nose. I think
about how grateful I am and what an adventure it has been to
get here.

This is the condensed version of my story and I hope that
someday I will be able to share the entire thing with you, but
more importantly, I hope to hear your story of personal
revolution in exchange. My sincere wish is that you achieve
the life you truly deserve. If you are ready to take the first
step in your personal transformation, then please turn the
page and let's begin.

PART I

<u>Clarity</u>

Over the last 13 years, I have made it my personal mission to find out what makes people successful and happy. I have been absolutely fascinated by the great power that we all have inside of us and how we can use it to win the war within. Through all of my personal external and internal battles, trials, and tribulations, I have come up with what I call the three keys to personal liberation. Those three keys are Clarity, Congruity of Self, and Tools.

I have found that the largest struggles in most people's lives boil down to clarity about who they are and why they are here, their inner conflict, and their struggle to have the proper tools necessary to build the life they deserve. These three categories are the essential keys to all success, be it personal or professional.

Over the years I've become what I call a "why guy." I became amazed at why some people feel large amounts of pain and others experience great amounts of joy. But more than that, I wanted to know what it took to take someone who experienced pain and lived life below their potential, and turn them around so they too could enjoy extreme amounts of personal power, joy and peace. I saw people who were unfulfilled and living in pain. Yet, these same people were all hiding below their greatness and, living far below their potential.

It's been the focus of my mania to understand why. Why do people do this and, why do people have potentially unlimited power yet continue to live in fear and self-doubt? It is my hope that as you go through this book you too will find some of the answers and solutions to how you can live a more fulfilled and successful life.

There is no doubt that currently, times are difficult. There are more options than ever, yet with those options comes more uncertainty. Coincidentally, there is also at this time, less guidance than ever before in history. The quality of people's lives is slipping out of their hands. Their relationships, their finances, and their personal lives are all taking a toll. The reason this book was written was so that you can regain that power. It's to help you, as an individual, to stand up and tap into the unlimited power that is within you. Whatever the current state of the world may be, it is imperative that you know that, as long as you are willing to take responsibility and have power, you can shape your destiny as you see fit.

The ability to create your reality relies on your ability to not only understand, but to master the three keys to personal power. So my friend, it is my personal challenge to you to make a decision right now. And when I say decision, I mean a 100% resolution. Make the decision that today is going to be the start of a new life. There is a war that wages on within each and every one of us and only you have the power to take control and bring peace to what is currently chaos.

The first key to personal liberation is clarity. The reason that clarity is so important is that it is your guide. Clarity is your map that shows you how to get from where you are to where you want to be. Unfortunately, most people have a very poor idea of where they're going in life. Most people definitely do not like where they are and are uncertain of where to go next. The best they can do is say that they do not want to be where they are.

Here's the challenge, you and many others like you are living far below your potential. You have this unlimited power within you, yet you either have never lived up to that power or you are afraid to admit that it is within you. On a daily basis you go around living your life as if you're a five, when in reality, hiding just beneath the surface, you're a total ten.

Due to your past, your beliefs, and other outside influences, you have gotten away from who you truly are. I can promise you that if you are feeling great levels of pain and frustration in your life, those harsh emotions are not the hallmarks of who you are. When you live below who you are meant to be, you feel a certain level of pain because the greatness on the inside wants out. It knows you are much bigger and better than what you're demonstrating.

Think about it, we get into jobs, we get into relationships, and we get into lifestyles that are not complementary to who we *really* are. We look in the mirror and we don't know the person looking back at us, so what do we do? We distract ourselves, we numb ourselves, and we even blind ourselves from the truth of what's really going on. We do this so we do not have to deal with the pain of not knowing who we are.

Not only that, but one day we wake up and are unhappy and we don't know why. We feel like, for the most part, that we are doing everything right, yet for some reason, we just don't feel right. Let me tell you, when you do exactly what you think is going to make you happy, or at the very least, help you get through life and it does the opposite, it actually ends up making you feel miserable, it can make you feel totally uncertain about your life. This is for one of two reasons. Number one is that you have not answered the questions, "Who am I?" and "What is my purpose?" You may even know the answers to these questions, yet for some reason, you are afraid to live and embrace them.

You have a need to grow, to expand, and to become more than who you currently are. At times, that need may feel foreign to you. The road ahead may be uncertain and your destination may be unclear. Yet, it is the understanding, the nurturing, and the embracing of this idea - that you absolutely must know who you are and why you are here - to have the power to transform your life and shape your destiny. It is an acceptance and commitment to this pursuit of clarity that will allow you to step into and live your purpose.

As your coach, here's a personal challenge from me to you. I want you to make a decision that today is the day for you to rise up. Today is the day that I want you to put your foot down. Today is the day that I want you to make a *wholehearted commitment*. Today is the day to let go of your past. Now is the time to become the "you" you've always wanted to be.

This moment right now is the time to take full responsibility for your life. You truly do shape your reality and create your destiny. Life is your canvas and it is yours to fill with all the magnificent colors you desire. You deserve a life that is much more than ordinary; you deserve a life that is extraordinary. Take a deep breath and envision the dawn of a new life on the horizon.

Take Action!

Get crystal clear about where you are right now in your life.

Get crystal clear about where you want to be in your life.

Get crystal clear about what it is going to take to get there.

Remember, life moves forward with or without you.
Knowing where you are, where you want to be, and the route you are going to take in order to get there will give you a strong desire to take charge of your life.

Put this book down and do it now!

Identity

There are two essential questions that you must ask yourself in order to begin on your personal path of revolution correctly. These two questions have loomed over mankind since the very beginning of time. They will continue to be questions that mankind will ask until the very end of time. As simple as these two questions are, they seem to be the ones that give people the biggest challenge in life.

The first question, as I'm sure you have already asked yourself at least once in your lifetime is:

Who am I?

People are naturally born with immense curiosity. As children, we are curious about life in general; we explore and try new things. As a means to quench this thirst for curiosity, even from a very young age, many of us asked ourselves the question, "Who am I?" Due to of all the curiosity and questions that we as people can have, it is the answer to that question that is of the most importance.

The question is who are *you*? Your ability to answer this question in a deep and meaningful way will allow you to set forth on your journey of self-growth and transformation. Remember you are not your career; you are much more than that. As a society, we tend to define ourselves by what we do and however important and meaningful your career may or may not be, who you are is still more than your title at work. Who you are is not defined by what you do. If anything, who you are should define what you do.

You are not your past either. In your search to gain clarity, it is important to be aware of the past but to keep your focus and attention on the present and future. That is where you have control; that is where you can create. Do you live in your past? Know that just because you may have lived a certain way for most of your life, that does not mean you have to continue to do so. It is time to let go of your past and embrace all of the glory that awaits you. Unfortunately, many people define themselves by their past. Even worse than that, some people will define themselves by the past lived by their parents and grandparents. A person can go their entire life living below their potential, while never knowing who they truly are, simply because they feel like their destiny is linked to their biography. This is where some serious renaissance thinking comes into play. These initial stages of your personal revolution take the most rebellious thinking.

Your qualities, talents, and characteristics make up who you are. It is the beliefs you hold and the standards you set for yourself that define you. It is easy to let your outer environment shape you. If you are not willing to take control and responsibility, then the constraints of society certainly will. It is your duty to become aware of this and do your best to avoid living a false reality.

What are the current forces that are shaping your reality? What are the sources that are influencing who you are? Is it the news, the media, fashion? It doesn't matter; no one has better intentions for you and your life than you do. Furthermore, no one should have more power or influence over your life than you. The news wants to control you, the media wants your money, and the fashion world wants to do both, while also turning you into a walking billboard. Not cool. And if you're not willing to break free and live life on your terms, then all the man deserves everything he gets from you.

To some degree, whether you like it or not, you've been programmed. And if it's not the media, news, or fashion industry programming you, it's your family, friends, classmates and/or coworkers and they have all had a good amount of time to influence you. By accident or intention, they have influenced you. This is a very important fact to be aware of because it can help you wake up and begin to make some distinctions between who you are and who you really want to be.

This brings us to one of the greatest stumbling blocks in self-improvement. For some reason, people have a very hard time thinking that they can improve or become someone new. They believe that the way they currently are is *who* they are and that they are powerless to change that. They believe that they are unable to become any better than who they are at this time. Often, people will give up before they even try, simply because they don't see how they can change. They think the way they are is the way they have to continue to be.

The secret of discovering your true identity lies not in creating or building a new self, rather, the secret is uncovering who you really are. At your very core, you are nothing but energy and the rest is all titles and details. By getting clear on who you truly are, you strip away all that is impure and all you are left with is a raw vision of your true self. That means any personality trait or quality that you want to develop is within you now. The challenge lies in finding a way to access these talents and abilities.

Take Action!

As of this moment, write out exactly who you are. As you move through this chapter, your definition of who you are will change. However, in order to get to where you want to go you must know where you currently stand.

Who are you right now?

What are your current:

- Morals?

- Values?

- Standards?

- Expectations?

If you are not impressed with what you have written, don't beat yourself up. This is about becoming clear about who you are now, so that you have a solid reference in regards to where you want to go. Write what you want your new traits to be like and get excited about how you are going to live up to them as we move forward.

Write out in as much detail as possible who you are at this very moment.

Put this book down and take action now!

Danger! Ego at Work

Your ego is your one of your greatest foes in this revolution. Your ego covers up all that is real and pure. It clouds your mind and causes your intentions to be skewed. Your ego is much more than just an inflated sense of pride. Your ego is one of the main reasons you pursue things that are unattainable. It is the reason you feel let down if you ever do catch up to those things. Your ego can be identified by some of the following needs:

- The need to feel superior

- The need for attention

- The need to be right

- The need to win

- The need for recognition

- The need to impress others

- The need to avoid being wrong

- The need for status

- The need to amass possessions

These are all functions of the ego. Look at this list and see if any of these relate to needs that you have. The ego is created when there is a weak knowledge of self, as a defense mechanism to hide you from the feelings of inadequacy. Let's go down the list and look at the core of each of these needs.

The need to feel superior: This need often comes with a desire for power and control over other people. It is a reflection of the lack of personal power and self-love a person has. This need to prove that you are better than someone else secretly means you are afraid that people will judge you negatively if they were to know that you're not aware of who you are. Generally, a person who has this need will brag and even lash out at other people. They would rather develop a reputation as a powerful jerk than be known as a weak nobody.

The need for attention: The need for attention often comes from a general uncertainty about true self. Someone with this need is most of the time afraid to be alone because of his or her low levels of self-love. They seek the love and affection of others to try and make up for their personal lack thereof. This person would rather fool themselves and get attention from other people than have to face the fact that they do not know who they are and do not love themselves.

The need to be right: This is a twofold need. The person who has this need may be related to the person who seeks power over others. Being right all the time is their way of proving to others that they are better, smarter, and more of an authority. The second side to this coin comes from a deeper need to overcompensate for having a dim sense of identity. Therefore, this person will use facts, statistics, and trivia as a mask of personality.

The need to win: This is a typical type-A personality. Very often, those who have a need to win also have a need to prove themselves to whomever they are up against. They desire to show they are the more powerful person. Two things happen when they do this. First, they often cause the other person to feel bad about their loss, thus increasing the ego. Second, it is also their way of hiding from defeat, which is a metaphor for being a loser. Deep inside this person is often not content with who they are and can even feel like a loser. So in order to hide those feelings they do their absolute best to show the world otherwise.

The need for recognition: This has to do with a need for value. Very often, a person who seeks recognition, be it through credentials, praise, or promotion has an inability to add personal value, or self-love to himself or herself. This is similar to the need for attention. The plaques, diplomas, and awards are all external demonstrations of value. If you ask this type of person who they are, they will attach their work title or the equivalent to their name. This type of person will generally name drop, as well, to try and be recognized by who they know, in hopes of being important by association.

The need to impress others: This need is almost exactly like the need for recognition. The difference is that this person may not necessarily want or need plaques or awards. However, they tend to be a show off. This type of person needs to be in the spotlight. They must be seen as the life of the party, out of their need to have others give them credit for whatever act they put on.

The need to avoid being wrong: The ego hates criticism. The definition of criticism to the ego is something that is harmful and that exposes the true version of the self that is trying to be hidden. This type will avoid blame at all costs. Nothing is ever their fault even if they are truly responsible for it. To them admitting fault is no different than admitting their darkest weakness.

The need for status: This need is similar to the need to impress others. Often people will strive for some type of glamorous status as a way to cover up their insecurity. Having a big name becomes the large illusion they get to hide behind. While people come to know them by their big name or reputation, they often, despite great external success, can be the same people who get involved with drugs and alcohol. Many celebrities are an example of this.

As you can see, many of these needs are related. And all of them, at their core, come from a lack of clarity about who a person believes they really are, what their purpose is, and an overall lack of self-love. You will also notice that the only person these egocentric needs fool is everyone but the one

person who matters. Do you have any of those needs?
Take a minute and think about the current state of your own
ego.

Before you move on, I want to encourage you to question
your motives. What are the things you want in life? But
more importantly *why* you do you want them? Are your
motives centered on your ego or do they come primarily
from a place of mastery? The needs of mastery are:

- The need for contribution

- The need for personal significance

- The need for self-love

- The need for connection

- The need to create

- The need for growth

- The need for certainty

Being driven by these types of motives will give you a great
source of power. By living from these motives, you will find
that your desire to prove things to other people goes away,
your ability to take responsibly increases, and your desire for
power transforms into a healthy one. You will become no
longer afraid to let people see who you really are, yet you do
not try to show it off. As you begin to understand who you
really are, you will see your egocentric needs fade away.

To give you even more clarity, I have put together what I
feel are the 14 traits of true champions. You will notice that
along the extra mile, there are many different types of
people, different background, personalities, etcetera, yet all
champions share at least some of the following traits. I
would encourage you to study this next area closely and

begin to figure out how you can personally apply these traits to your identity.

Take Action!

Your Ego is one of the biggest obstacles in regards to unleashing your ultimate-self. You must dissolve your ego if you are able to move forward and fulfill your destiny.

Which specific egocentric needs are holding you back?

How can you let go of your ego and transition your mentality into one that is mastery centered?

What would your life be like if you could live without the burden of your ego?

Put this book down and take action now!

The 14 Traits of Champions

As you move forward in your personal revolution, you will transition from being the victim in your life's story to the champion. As exciting as it is to be a champion, there are also many challenges the champion must face. No matter what type of champion you are, to achieve that status, you must develop and exercise the 14 traits that all true champions have. There is no doubt that you can be successful and prosperous without some of these traits; however, unless they are *all* in place, there will always be something in your life that is missing. Pay close attention in this chapter and do your best to master the 14 traits of champions.

Hunger: The beginning of every great and worthwhile endeavor requires you to be totally hungry for the goal or result that you require. The level of aspiration you have is a direct correlation to how probable it is that you will reach the pinnacle of your personal and professional success. Before any great achievement was realized, there was an immense level of desire. Think about some of your own achievements in life. Shortly after you came up with your great intention, you were filled with an amazing hunger to make those dreams a reality. Think about how hungry you currently are to change your life. If you have answered the call to become your ultimate-self in true fashion, you should feel an intense level of hunger at this very moment. Wallow in this feeling and make it as familiar as an old friend because it will surely be one of your greatest companions in your revolution.

Honesty: Honesty is one trait that is not negotiable in any way. In order for you to come to terms with who you truly are and why you are here, you must be able to be completely honest with yourself. You have to be honest in regards to how you treat yourself and others. You must make a commitment to be honest no matter what. It is far better to be brutally honest and face any personal or social reactions that may be negative, than to live your life outside of your integrity. Imagine how powerful you would feel if you were totally certain that all of your interactions with mankind were completely honest. It may be easy to dodge reality at times by rationalizing lying to others or ourselves but this is not about doing what is easy. This is about doing what's right.

Religion: I am not talking about religion in a sense of Christianity or Buddhism. Religion, in this sense of a champion trait, comes down to a daily ritual that is tied directly into your sense of purpose and identity. All of the greatest champions are highly religious and have daily practices that allow them to achieve such stellar results. To a true champion, these daily rituals are in no way debatable and are executed with the highest level of passion and concentration. What type of daily rituals can you begin to adopt to maximize your potential? How can you tie these daily rituals into your integrity so that they become something that you are not willing to go one day without? Remember a champion does not practice their daily religion as a way to satisfy their ego or to become more popular in the public eye; they do it for themselves. The bright side is that hard work and diligence are often rewarded socially. Let this be merely a bonus result from the already amazing benefits of your daily religion.

Modesty: As you become bigger and better, there will be more and more opportunities for you to feel bigger and better compared to other people. With that being said there will be many opportunities for you to make other people feel small and weak. You must be aware that your decision to revolutionize your life is no small order. By choosing to embrace and live up to your potential, you simultaneously take on one of the greatest fears known to mankind and that is the idea that you have unlimited power. Because many people are not ready to embrace this power yet, you must do your best to inspire them and not tear them down. As a consequence of being a champion of your own story, you also by default become a champion for other people. Knowing this, you must always make a great effort to practice humility. Remember that no task, no matter how unglorified, tedious, or difficult, is below you. Treat all people as equals, give others credit where credit is due, and always make good on your promises.

Accountability: A champion's personal level of accountability will allow them to achieve massive success. First and foremost, they are accountable to themselves then to other people. The opinion they value the greatest is their own because they know their dreams, goals, and aspirations are the most important to them. Personal accountability is the foundation of discipline and it is one of the ingredients that will help ensure your success during the hard times. There will definitely be times when you will have an opportunity to slack off. There will be days where you could skip your religious practices and there will be moments when you can lie to a person and they will never find out. There will certainly be days where you don't feel like doing anything at all and will want to stay in bed all day. If no one would ever find out if you were to be lax in any or all of these areas, that means the only thing that will hold you to them and keep you in line is your personal accountability. Your personal accountability is directly connected to your integrity and moral code. Ultimately, the respect and love a champion has for himself or herself is not worth sacrificing at any time.

Knowledge: In an ever-changing world, the champion knows that they must constantly fulfill their need for knowledge. It is important to be clear that knowledge does not just mean trivia, but more specifically, knowledge relates to intelligence and wisdom. As much as the champion knows that there are certain trades and timeless habits that one must have in order to constantly improve, they also know that everything in existence changes and because that is true, they too shift and adapt like the seasons. The more knowledge they can acquire about themselves and the world, the more mastery and peace they will find. As a champion grows, so too does their curiosity and therefore the pursuit of knowledge is a must. The better a person can understand themselves on the whole, the more certain they can be about who they are. Likewise, the better a person can understand and relate to the world around them, the better they can get along with and communicate in that world.

Focus: A champion would be nowhere without focus. Focus is one of the primary factors that separates ordinary from extraordinary. Look at any real champion in any category of life, music, sports, art, business, etc. They were all able to produce phenomenal results only because they were able to focus on one specific thing. They took their passion and they narrowed it down into one discipline and this allowed them to become the very best at what they did. Just for the sake of contrast, let's look at the other side of the coin. What about the people who dillydally, multitask, and try a little bit of everything, but never fully commit to anything? Those people never become champions and live lives that are mediocre at best. Imagine how powerful you would feel if you chose one thing to focus on it until you had mastered it or achieved it. As you proceed in your personal revolution, you'll need the ability to focus more than ever.

Love: Throughout your journey, you will encounter many trials and injuries and your ability to move forward and not harbor bitterness or resentment relies on your capacity for love. The champion's decision in hard times is to get better rather than bitter. In moments of doubt and defeat, it is love that will bring you from your knees back up onto your feet. You must be sure to show love for yourself always by respecting your well-being, hygiene, and standing up for yourself when necessary. Love also becomes the ultimate charity and there is nothing more powerful that you could give another person than your love. As a champion, you must always love fully and openly, and show unlimited loving and kindness toward all others. There will be times when you are motivated by revenge or out of a desire to prove someone wrong; yet, neither of these influences will fulfill you in a way that is positive and powerful. Remember in the land of champions, love is king.

Action: Champions are notorious for the ability to take

action. You must think of your dreams and aspirations as gifts that are so precious that nothing can get in the way of their manifestation. Procrastination, hesitation, and deliberation have no place when it comes time for taking action. If you started to live more like a champion, how much action would you take? If you were committed to living like a champion, what would you do when procrastination, hesitation, and deliberation reared their ugly heads? Action in the mind of the champion also relates to diligence as it becomes a work ethic. Moreover, it becomes a belief and an overall approach to life. It is the classic spirit of a champion that will never give up. Imagine what kind of life you would have if you knew your success was ensured simply because you were so dedicated to your goal that you would never give up and would continue to try until you achieve it.

Teamwork: As much as we may believe a champion's success is purely due to their individual power, it is important to remember that every champion has at least one person in their corner. The boxer has their coach, the knight in shining armor has his kingdom and princess, the soccer star has their trainer and team, and the business mogul has his mentor. It is said that two heads are better than one and in the case of personal and professional improvement, no truer words have ever been spoken. The value of outside information, collaboration, and objective criticism are priceless to the aspiring champion. We do not often see the support system behind the champion when we observe them; however, it is always there behind the scenes playing its part in the champion's pursuit of greatness. As a champion, you must know that you can only become so successful on your own. You will find that the more positive people you connect with, the more support and power you will have.

Patience: Patience is one of the secrets to a champion's success and it is one of the traits that is most often overlooked. The way that champions are generally portrayed would lead us to believe that they have achieved all of their greatness overnight, when in reality nothing could be further from the truth. Some of the greatest champions of our time experienced failure. Albert Einstein failed elementary arithmetic. Michael Jordan did not make his high school basketball team. Colonel Sanders heard no over 1000 times before he heard his first yes, when proposing his business idea for fried chicken. They all demonstrated extreme levels of patience, which allowed them to achieve their goals inevitably. You must be patient in your dealings with others and always be willing to forgive and resolve conflict. The prosperous farmer must be patient with his crops, a good father must be patient with his son, and you must be patient with all of the endeavors that are close to your heart. If your aspirations are truly priceless, they will certainly be worth the wait.

Presence: Along with your ability to be patient you must also strengthen your ability to be present. The past and the future will always potentially divert your attention. Both the past and the future are important and you must remain aware, however, they are not where they champion spends the majority of their time. The champion knows that to get the most out of any given moment, they must live in that moment. No matter what stage a champion is at in their progression, whether they are imagining, planning, or executing, being present throughout that process is key. In regards to other people, you will be able to serve and understand them the best when you are present with them. You will be amazed at how connected you can be come to someone when you decide to be present in that moment with him or her. Countless people can chalk up their failure to being absent which is the exact opposite of being present. The minute you take your hands off of the wheel and look away is the same moment you invite disaster into your life. From a social, aspect if you are absent, you begin to lose touch with the very people you are dedicated to serving. Think about how you can begin to be more present today.

Gratitude: Gratitude is another one of the unsung traits that all champions possess. Just as a mighty oak tree once started out as a tiny nut, similarly the great champion started out as a much smaller version of himself or herself. As you continue to grow and expand, it is paramount that you remember from where you came. It is also important to be grateful for everything in your life, and when I say everything, I mean literally everything. Without having gratitude for the good things in your life, you would not be able to enjoy the quality and richness that life has to offer. And without the bad things in life, you would have no perspective and have no appreciation for the good. Like a piece of coal, a champion is conditioned under great pressure to become a diamond, and without the immense pressure, that priceless value would never be able to be attained. Gratitude is about being aware and celebrating your successes along the way. The more grateful you are, the more you open yourself up to allow for new things to enter your life for which you can be grateful. When you are grateful, you cannot be fearful, for when you are grateful you are wealthy. Always remember to be thankful to others who have helped you. Remind yourself each morning when you wake up and each night before you go to sleep of at least five things for which you are grateful. How can you become more aware of the things that you are grateful for and how can you then strengthen that feeling?

Tranquility: The very nature of a champion is to take on more than they are currently capable of tackling. Being a champion means expanding yourself to become someone bigger and better. Although this sometimes means that you can sacrifice your quality of life. By overworking yourself you begin to see your greatness slip away. Just like a machine that is overworked, it begins to break down and this is why it is important to keep tranquility in your life. Let's face it; there are people who are on the long hard road of success who still struggle to maintain peace in their life. This means the possibility for chaos and stress in the life of a champion is a huge threat. You must find your Zen and find your personal way of taking time out and bring peace into your life. Unfortunately, the world will not go out its way to make sure there is calm in your life. If anything, due to the very consumer nature of people, they will continue to ask more and more of you. It is your responsibility to say no when needed. The more you can bring tranquility into your life, the better you will be able to move forward in your pursuit of greatness.

Spend some time thinking about these 14 traits. It is ideal to build up these characteristics now so that you can use all their benefits along the early stages of your progression. Beginning to develop any one of these traits is by no means easy, especially if it's one in which you are weak. In fact, to create a solid foundation for these principles may be one your greatest challenges. But keep in mind that the commitment to a life of improvement and greatness requires a great deal of work. Think of these traits as bricks that will help you pave the way toward your destiny. Honor them and take care of them and they will do the same in return. Your dreams and your imagination act as a preview for the upcoming events in your life. You bring them to life by deciding on the reality you want to experience and using your expectation to make sure those dreams are fulfilled. These 14 traits of champions will allow you to fulfill your destiny.

I want you to take some time right now, not tomorrow, not the day after… right now. This is about taking action and making progress *now*. Think about who you really are and don't say something like "Joe." that's not who you are. That's just your name. Don't say something like, "I am an accountant." That's not who you are either. That's just what you do. You are so much more than the labels by which you have come to define yourself. Think about who you *really* are.

If there's one thing I know for certain, it is that if your morals, values, standards and expectations for your life are low, then naturally the results you produce in your life will mirror that. Think about it, if you feel disappointed in yourself, why is that? It is because you have low standards for yourself. It is because you have low expectations for who you should be. Yet, deep inside, you know you can do better.

Ultimately, you know you must do better.

When you don't expect very much from yourself, it is pretty difficult to achieve a whole lot, don't you think? Similarly, when you don't expect much from yourself, where do you think your ability to contribute to others falls? I can guarantee you it's not in a place where it's going to make much of a difference.

Take Action!

The 14 traits of champions are ingredients that each and every person who is in control of their fate possesses. As you move forward, keep these traits in mind and visit them often. Be sure to grow these parts of who you are, as they will help you become who you are meant to be.

How can you begin to blend each of these traits into your character?

How can you personally identify with these traits?

To what degree are you currently living these traits and how can you do so even more?

Put this book down and take action now!

Purpose

That second question is…"Why am I here? When you can answer that question, you create a powerful and compelling meaning for your life. Each person is here on this earth for a reason. The challenge is most people do not know what that reason is or they have a vague idea of that reason, yet they shy away from it. Having uncertainty in this area of your life creates great turmoil. This is one of the primary reasons why most people are unhappy and unfulfilled in their career and life overall.

When you can reach a very clear and meaningful understanding of what your purpose is, you will be unstoppable. You will be filled with a compelling and powerful determination and resolve. You will move through life with utter certainty and the highest level of expectation. It is having true purpose that will get you out of bed early in the morning and keep you up late at night.

I'm sure there are some examples in your own life that you can draw upon to give you hints as to what your purpose may be. Think about times in your own life where you had an intense desire, where you had a mission or a goal; something big was driving you. Think about what kind of power you had at that time. Even if you can't think of a time in your own life, think about someone you know or someone you met who is just filled with purpose. They understand why they are here and they know exactly who they are. These are the kind of people that are filled with passion and who live life to the maximum. If you can stand up and face this question of why you are here, you will unlock all of your potential. Don't you deserve that level of freedom and richness in your life? The synergy that is created by knowing who you are and what your purpose is becomes the ultimate combination for creating a life of meaning and significance.

Here are some questions that will help you uncover why you are here:

What are your strengths?

What are you passionate about?

What is your personal definition of contribution?

What are your talents and skills or abilities?

What are some of the things that make you feel the happiest and most fulfilled?

Put some thought into this. Your purpose is the driving force in your life. This is going to be your guiding light. If you can discover and unleash your purpose, you will instantly begin living your dream life. Living your purpose will add value to every area of your life and you will make advances in those areas that you never thought possible.

Let's look into some different personality types to shed some light on this subject of purpose. An important part of having total self-mastery is knowing your personality type. And at the core of all personality types, you will find that people are either introverted or extroverted. Knowing whether you are introverted or extroverted will help you focus on certain types of careers and lifestyles that are directly in line with who you are.

Introverted Personality: An introverted person is focused primarily inward. Introverts are very analytical and heavily process their thoughts, feelings, and their observations of the world internally. Often they are very intelligent and witty, yet are nervous in large social settings. Introverts tend to be more passive in their behavior yet equally passionate. Because of their internal dialog, they will think, to a large extent, about what they are going to say before they say it. Introverts generally are very private people and let very few people see the inner workings of their life. Within the introverted realm, there are four sub-types, which are:

- Visionaries

- Analysts

- Improvers

- Assimilators

Visionaries: Visionaries are the dreamers. They have the ability to take in all of their internal analysis and create a compelling vision of the future from it. Visionaries often have a large drive to change the world. They have such an expanded view that they can easily see the areas of the world that need improvement and create powerful solutions to accompany them. Visionaries are often very insightful and intuitive. They have immense imaginations that help them think creatively. Also, they have a massive capacity for possibility thinking. To the Visionary, it is not a matter of "if" but "how," Visionaries value ideas and always seek out ways to innovate. Ideal careers for Visionaries could be:

- Artist

- Writer

- Architect

- Director

- Designer

- Marketing Specialist

- Inventor

Are you a Visionary? Do you have expansive daydreams about making the world a better place? Do you have a vivid imagination? If so, then some of the above career fields may be for you. Bringing your visions to life is a great way to express yourself and make an impact on the rest of the world.

Analysts: Analysts are the great problem solvers of the world. They have the ability to look at the challenges of the world in a way that is open and full of potential. The difference between an Analyst and a Visionary is that the Analyst is much more logic oriented. Their main focus is a combination of finding solutions while remaining practical. An Analyst will keep the majority of their thinking process to themselves until they are ready to put their plan into action. Analysts have a very systematic approach to thinking and problem solving. Potential careers for this type are:

- Engineer

- Auto Repair

- Craftsman

- Financial Planner

- Software Developer

- Data Analyst

- Beta Tester

Are you an Analyst? Do you constantly seek out and find logical solutions to the challenges in your life? Do you have a systematic approach to your thinking? Are you a very organized person? If so, you may be an Analyst and one of the above careers may be a good fit for you.

Improvers: Improvers are the great helpers in the world. Their strong personal desire to help others better themselves comes from their personal need to make the world a better place. Their approach is much more personal and individual. They are not concerned about changing the world at large, they would much rather change one person's world instead. And Improvers will show outstanding levels of empathy, understanding, and care for the people in their life, both personally and professionally. They feel most happy when they see others succeeding. Their one flaw is that they have a tendency to put themselves last, due to their intense drive to help others. Potential careers for this type are:

- Nurse

- Human Resources

- Youth Counselor

- Personal Trainer

- Interior Designer

- Doctor

- Life Coach

Are you an Improver? Do you find yourself constantly wanting to help others? Are you the type of person that would "give the shirt off your back" to friends and strangers alike? As an Improver, your work is some of the most needed and important in the world. If this makes sense to you than some of the above careers may be for you.

Assimilators: Assimilators are the great learners of the world. They are always in search of new information. They have a natural ability to bring people together to create a team that can get a job done that would not have been achievable otherwise. They are resourceful and depend greatly on their past experience to bring value to their life or work project. They tend to be professionals or specialists in their field. They often seek out new and innovative information related to their specific topic of interest. Likewise, they tend to disregard information that has little or nothing to do with what they are working on or passionate about. Assimilators are best fit for careers such as:

- Project Management

- Underwriter

- Consultant

- Business adviser

- Accountant

- Auditor

- Research & Development

Do you love to learn? Are you always looking for cutting edge information? Do you have a natural ability to construct and or follow set procedures? Are you good at planning and organizing? If so, some of the above careers may be for you.

Knowing if you are an introvert can drastically increase your chances of unlocking your purpose in life. By understanding your tendencies, you do two things at the same time. You gain a clear and direct vision of what overall direction you should go in life, as well as being able to qualify whether a certain career is a good fit for you or not. So many people get tied into jobs they absolutely hate simply because they are an introvert trying to work in an extroverted career. Had they taken the time to gain some clarity about who they are and what their purpose is, they could have avoided all the pain and frustration all together and instead would be able to live their passion and be excited to get up and go to work in the morning. What a concept!

Extroverted Personality: If the introverted personality type does not fit you, then that's ok. If you are not an introvert, then the chances are you are an extrovert. The extrovert is outgoing and thrives by being around people. An extrovert is happiest when they are in groups. Extroverts are generally outgoing and friendly people but do not necessarily have to be. Extroverts love social interaction and are the most successful when they are talking and collaborating with others. Talking is an extroverts strong point; they would much rather talk about ideas with someone than sit alone and think about them. There are four sub-types of the extroverted personality, which are:

- Reactors

- Adventurers

- Accelerators

- Contributors

Reactors: Reactors are the action takers. They have the ability to rapidly asses a situation and create powerful solutions. They can think on their toes, interpret information, and create products or services based on their rapid assessments. They have a natural talent to observe a challenge and see the big picture, which allows them to find new and exciting ways to meet their personal and professional needs. Reactors tend to be impulsive and often kick into action without hesitation. They have a tendency to "do" more than "talk." Some careers that fit with Reactors are:

- Fireman

- Club Promoter

- Military

- Lifeguard

- Emergency Response Technician

- Policeman

- Security

Do you thrive in the heat of the moment? Do you find yourself bored if you are not taking action? Do you prefer being around and working with people? If so, then you may be a Reactor and some of the above careers could be a good fit for you.

Adventurers: These are the great explorers. The Adventurer is always on the go looking for the next great endeavor. This type is drawn to the unknown. They thrive on finding solutions and uncertainty. If it is routine and practical, they don't want anything to do with it. Adventurers use their imagination to seek out and find new worlds. An Adventurer relies on their intuition and ingenuity to help them anticipate and create their future reality. Ideal careers of Adventurers are:

- Treasure Hunter

- Inventor

- Actor

- Entrepreneur

- News Reporter

- Photojournalist

- Entertainer

Do you live for adventure? Are you constantly wondering what is just around the horizon? Do you naturally gravitate towards situations that are uncertain? If so, then you may be an adventurer and some of the above careers could be an ideal fit for you.

Accelerators: These are the great innovators of the world. They have a natural ability to see how things can be improved and immediately find appropriate solutions to make them better. An accelerator can instantly spot flaws in a plan, system, or person and spontaneously give feedback that is powerful and positive. They have a natural need to improve things. They are very analytical and can think both in a detailed and open-minded way. Accelerators feel the most fulfilled when they are making something or someone better. They are also very good at delegating and organizing people to reach their objectives. Potential careers for this type are:

- Managers

- Officers

- Consultants

- Administrators

- Systems Analysts

- Information Technology

- Business Owner

Do you have a desire to work with a team? Do you have a natural talent for communication? Are you always finding ways to improve things? If so, then you may be an accelerator and some of the above careers may be an ideal fit for you.

Contributors: Contributors are the givers of the world. Their source of inspiration lies in their deep desire to help others. They are similar to Improvers in this way. The difference is that they often like to be a part of the contribution.

Contributors have a deep desire to connect with others personally and professionally. The Contributor loves to collaborate with others and organize events and functions. Contributors deeply enjoy seeing their community thrive and equally enjoy being part of the process. Some careers that are ideal for Contributors are:

- Non Profit Workers

- Volunteering

- Teacher

- Counselor

- Therapist

- Public Speaker

- Fitness Trainer

Do you have a large desire to contribute to other people? Do you love helping and working with other people? Do you enjoy teaching? If so, then you may be a Contributor and some of the above careers could be ideal for you.

Before you move on, take some time and think about whether you are introverted or extroverted. Think about your current career and past careers you have had. Are they similar? What are the chances that you are unhappy with your current or past jobs because they did not match your personality? What type of career do you fantasize about? These are all important questions to ask considering they are all directly related to your identity and purpose.

Take Action!

You must know your purpose! Knowing who you are, your personality and what path in life best fits you are absolute musts if you are going to live the life you deserve.

What have you learned about yourself so far?

What areas of your life currently do not match up with your true self?

What is your purpose?

Put this book down and think about these questions now!

Put this book down and take action now!

Your Personal Mission Statement

Successful people and companies alike both have one thing in common. They understand the importance of a mission statement. As mission statement is a plan of action that ties in the values and overall goals for both individuals and businesses. Now is the time to create your personal mission statement. Since you now have clarity about who you are and why you are here, you can use that knowledge to help you create a strong and powerful vision for your life. Having a personal mission statement gives you a constant reminder of how you expect to live your life. It will help you approach each day with passion and determination.

The thing about a personal mission statement, like all tools in life, is that it is your consistent and skillful use of that tool that makes it powerful. A personal mission statement is no different. If it is not backed with enthusiasm, commitment, energy, and determination, then your personal mission statement will be useless.

A personal mission statement is generally a short four-sentence statement that clearly and distinctly states who you are and what your purpose in life is. A personal mission statement is really a mirror of who you are on the inside and lets you know where you're going in life.

A large part of why people feel pain in their life is because they have a lack of direction. It is a clear sense of purpose and direction in life that makes us feel like we're living rather than just existing. It makes sense to, people aren't stupid. They know that life is moving forward regardless of whether they do or not. People want to know that their life has meaning they want to know that what they're doing is making an impact. By knowing your passion and living your purpose, a great amount of joy and fulfillment that can be obtained each and every single day.

In the corporate world, the company with a strong mission statement will have employees that are fully devoted to the expansion of that company, often because the mission statement strikes a chord with their own personal ethics. If a company has a strong mission statement, morale, motivation, and teamwork will flow effortlessly in the work place. On the other hand, companies that lack a powerful mission statement have little to offer their employees on a visceral level. At the end of the day, money and benefits will not compel a person to give their all, at least not for very long.

I would like to share with you my personal mission statement as an example.

"My purpose is to express my intense desire to give back. To embrace my strong vision and to fulfill my burning desire to help others become more than who they are. I will do my best each and every day to be honest, compassionate, and willing to learn from my mistakes, so that my life and the lives of others can continuously get better and better."

Here are some tips to help you with your personal mission statement. Remember, you want to keep your personal mission statement, clear and concise. The personal mission statement is about quality not quantity, so keep it simple and brief four to five lines is best. It should flow and sound appealing to you.

Your mission statement should touch upon that on which you want to focus and who you want to become as a person. Think about the behaviors and qualities that would have a significant positive impact on every category of your life. Remember to keep your mission statement positive. Rather than saying what you don't want in life remember to remember to say what you do want.

Include some type of morals, values, standards and expectations. Make your personal mission statement something that you can live daily, no matter where you are or what you're doing in your life. Be sure to make your statement consistent with all areas of your life. The key here is to make your personal mission statement relate and apply to your entire life. Remember this is not a list of goals. Your mission statement should not include things like a house or a car. It should be focused on internal attributes like excellence, attitude, and greatness.

A personal mission statement should be emotional. It should be packed with passion and it should be inspiring. You want your mission statement to be something that really grabs and empowers you. This is going to be one of the tools you use to change your life. That means it should pack as big a punch as possible.

Recite your personal mission statement upon rising in the morning and before going to bed at night. Be sure to do this out loud. You want to have your personal mission statement memorized so that throughout the day it resonates within you. The more comfortable you become with it, the more it becomes a part of who you are.

You might feel somewhat awkward about saying this aloud but I'm telling you verbalizing your personal mission statement makes it a hundred times more powerful. It shouldn't be something you're ashamed or embarrassed about. You should be excited to say your personal mission statement out loud. This is your declaration of personal freedom and power. Get into this!

It's time for you to make your personal mission statement. Put down this book and either get out a piece of paper or open a Word document; whatever you have to do to get this thing going. A powerful mission statement alone can reshape your life. Don't put this off, and don't take this lightly. You owe it to yourself to not only do this right now but to actually live this.

Take Action!

Having a personal mission statement is one of the greatest keys to having a clear vision for why you are here and where you are going. Write out your personal mission statement to the best of your ability.

Why is a personal mission statement important to you? How can you use your personal mission statement to get the best out of life? Get clear about your life! Having clarity about your identity and purpose are two of the largest pieces of the puzzle. Before you move on, make sure you can specifically answer the following questions with confidence.

Who are you?

Where are you in your life?

Where do you want to be?

What will it take to get there?

Why are you here?

Are you introverted or extroverted?

What are some ideal careers that would fit you?

Does your current life and career path fit you now that you have more clarity about your life?

What is your personal mission statement?

Put this book down and take action now!

PART II

<u>Inner Peace</u>

As you will learn in the following chapter, in order to reach the highest levels of your personal potential you must have maximum level of self-love. However, to do that you must get rid of all the current negative garbage that is keeping you from your greatness. If you've ever held yourself back or sabotaged yourself, then you know what I am talking about.

What I have found is that one of the biggest challenges that most people face in their personal and professional success is due to a dueling reality or inner conflict. If you look around the world, you can see conflict and war everywhere. We have a war on drugs, a war on crime and a war on terror, what most people don't realize is that they are also at war with themselves.

Dueling realities can exist in multiple categories within your life. For example, some people want to be wealthy yet they have a belief that they do not deserve to be rich. Other people want to be married and have a fairy tale relationship but they do not believe that they are worthy of such a high quality experience.

It is this type of inner war that creates negative feelings towards oneself and the world. No matter in what area of your life you would like to improve, you must make sure you are truly congruent all the way to your core. When you have inner peace, everything inside you is moving in the right direction. What you want and what you actually get become one and the same. The art of inner congruity can only be reached by first eliminating the negative from your life. From there you will be able to be filled with self-love.

One of the best and most powerful tools that you will use in order to create a congruent self is a formula that derived from the process of manifestation. I call it BTFAR, it stands for:

- Beliefs

- Thoughts

- Feelings

- Action

- Results

This formula is going to be a tool that you can use in your self-improvement to become aware of any negative programming you have in place that is holding you back. You can starting using it today and continue using it forever. No matter what level of personal mastery you ever get to, this tool will always greatly serve you. If you master this one tool, you will have massive control and power over yourself and your results in life.

I'm going to break down each part of this formula so that you can understand its importance and use. You will be able to see how it works and you can learn how to implement it directly into your life. The better you understand a tool and how to use it, the better it's going to work for you. Think about any tool or formula you already use in your life proficiently. The reason you are so skilled with this tool is because you know it inside and out.

We begin with beliefs. Beliefs are the master key to everything in life. Your beliefs are the very things that are shaping your life on a daily basis. Your beliefs are exactly what got you to where you are today. Beliefs influence every single part of your life. They influence what you think, they influence how you feel, they influence what you do, and ultimately they are responsible for the results you achieve.

Beliefs: As simple as they are, beliefs are the most powerful out of all the other components of this formula.

Why do people succeed on a consistent basis?

Why do some people fail on a consistent basis?

What is the difference between these two types of people?

The difference primarily is their beliefs. Like Henry Ford once said, "The man who believes he can, and the man who believes he cannot, are both right." When it comes to your own life, a very thorough examination of your personal beliefs is in order. If you are not currently getting the kind of results that you want out of your life then there must be some type of belief that is holding you back. The great thing you need to know is that no matter what type of beliefs you have or where they came from, or even how long you've had them, **beliefs can be changed.**

Look within yourself and if you find any beliefs that are negative, or that are holding you back, now is the time to change them. Now some people may feel like, as bad as their beliefs are, and as much as their beliefs may keep them from getting what they want in life, that they cannot change them because their beliefs make up who they are.

Nothing could be further from the truth. Your current beliefs and results are *not* who you are. Who you are right now and the results you are getting are simply a reflection of who you were at one time. The past does not have to equal the future. In your case, if your beliefs are keeping you from getting what you want in life, then **your past must not be your future.**

If you are not living your life at a total ten, then I can almost guarantee you that who you are now is not who you are truly meant to be. You're just hiding behind a number. Some days it's five, some days it's two. No matter what the number is, it is less than who you really are. Just because you're used to these old beliefs, just because you're comfortable with these old beliefs, simply because they have shaped you and made you who you are today, does not mean for one second that they need to continue to keep you from the glory you deserve.

There are two ways to begin to change your beliefs. The first way is to think about the negative beliefs you have and think about what the polar opposite of that belief is. For example, if you have a belief that you are no good. Then the polar opposite of that belief is that you are great.

By simply knowing what the polar opposite of your current belief is, you can begin to access a new and more powerful belief. Now the second way to change your beliefs is to think about the negative beliefs that you currently have. Then think about the belief that you would rather have in place of it. The polar opposite of the belief that you currently have does not always fit best.

You want your new belief to be something around which you can wrap your head. Your new belief may be uncomfortable, but you need to be able to believe in the new belief. It's very easy to think of new beliefs you need to have. And it's very easy to say, "I am great." However, if you can't get yourself to believe it on a very emotional level, then you'll just be lying to yourself. Your mental chatter may change but ultimately your life will not.

Therefore, it's not necessarily the new belief itself that's important. i.e. "I am great." Rather, you being able to totally buy into and convince yourself that this new belief is true is what's key. You need to be able to think about what your new belief is and believe it without a shadow of a doubt. It must become concrete and real to you - more so than anything else.

If someone were to ask you what your beliefs are, you should be able to tell them. Not only what they are, but do it in a way that is convincing, compelling and certain. There should be no hesitation or uncertainty about your beliefs whatsoever.

Once you have chosen what you want, your new beliefs to be and you have completely reinforced them, now it's time to exercise that belief. Even though it is positive and compelling, it is still new and foreign to you. You don't have that much experience with this new belief yet. It is like a dormant muscle that needs to get stronger and it can only get stronger by exercise.

That means the next part of changing your beliefs is finding a way to exercise them, to make them stronger. It's like anything else in life; in the beginning you will certainly have to get used to all this. Although it's just as they say, practice makes perfect.

What I want you to do is to write out all the current beliefs you have about yourself. If you find beliefs that are negative or that you would like to change, then take the time to figure out or create the new belief, either by understanding its polar opposite or by figuring out what new belief makes the most amount of sense to you.

Once you've done that, figure out a way that you can exercise this new belief. The beliefs you have right now are so strong is simply because you have practiced them so much. Remember, this whole self-mastery thing is about creating a new you. It is about taking action, it is about getting out of your head and into your feet and literally doing the things that we're talking about right now.

Put this book down right now and do this. When you come back, you're going to feel refreshed and excited that you have a new set of beliefs that will inspire and compel you, rather than old stuff to intimidate and hold you back.

Okay, welcome back. Doesn't it feel good to have some new and empowering beliefs laid out in front of you? I know it does. They may feel awkward and uncomfortable at first, but I promise you they will make such a huge difference in helping you shape your life.

Thoughts: Thoughts are the second in command when it comes to your ability to create a rich and exciting life. It is your thoughts that open up the possibility for greatness or shut down any chance of living your purpose. The challenge is on a day-to-day basis most people's thoughts just run rampant through their mind. There is no screening or censoring.

You have got to know that every single day you are being bombarded with information. Now granted, sometimes that information is good. But, often times that information can be very bad or at least unhelpful to you.

If there is no way for you to screen or filter what goes through your mind, then suddenly you are impacted by whatever you hear or see. Your very emotional state from moment to moment is a gamble. Some days are good, some days are bad, and a large part of that is because of what you are consistently thinking.

I want to stress that it is what you are **constantly** thinking about that makes the difference in your life. We can think positive thoughts every now and then but that's kind of like brushing your teeth every now and then. It's good, but it's definitely not going to have a big impact as far as your personal hygiene is concerned. Think about it, if you were in an intense loving relationship, which I hope you are, would you want your partner to love you every now and then? Or would you want them to love you each and every moment of every day without fail?

Unfortunately, people tend to think more negative thoughts than positive, yet still wonder why they're unhappy. There are two things that are important here. The first is the ability to filter the information that is constantly coming at you. Second is the ability to direct your thoughts with intention. One of the best ways to filter information is to choose its meaning. I don't expect you to lock yourself up at home and never again come out to be exposed to any news or other information. What I do expect you to be able to do is choose the meaning of the information that comes your way. If it's not positive, then you can make it positive and it you can't do that, then you can choose to ignore it. Your perspective is everything. "Is that information a good thing or a bad thing?" "Is this the end or the beginning?" "Does this really concern me?"

These are the type of questions you need to be asking yourself, in regards to the constant stream of information that comes your way. Also, your ability to choose on what you're going to focus makes a huge difference. Not to mention that, just because a piece of information comes your way, it does not mean that you **have to** entertain it for any prolonged amount of time. Remember, your greatest gift is the power of choice and when it comes to directing your thoughts that comes down to choice as well. Believe me, if you are not directing your thoughts, they will not direct themselves. Your brain is programmed to respond. If it does not have certain criteria, or specific guidelines of how to function, then it becomes a total mess.

There are people that lose precious hours of sleep, simply because they can't turn their mind off at night. There are so many thoughts and ideas running through their minds that they just can't get into a peaceful state to fall asleep.

The number one factor that comes into play for both of these areas is awareness. Your inability to be aware that your thoughts can and will hurt you if you don't take control of it will prove to be a problem. You must realize that sometimes your thoughts are not your own. You must develop an awareness that you don't have to think about anything that you don't want to think about.

Your mind is like a garden, and a garden has no bias. Whatever you plant in that garden and help to grow will flourish. The garden does not care whether the fruits of your labor will ultimately poison you or help you to become healthy and strong. That is the very reason many people are unhappy yet they don't know why. It is because they focus on and give attention to these ideas and thoughts that slowly poison them.

What you need to know is that it works the other way as well. If you want your life to be filled with richness and joy the only way you can manifest that is by thinking thoughts that are positive and powerful.

You can change your thoughts the same way you change your beliefs. First, think about what your current thoughts are. Not the ones that you think every now and then, but the ones that you think on a daily basis. Then figure out the polar opposite of that thought. Or come to your own conclusion of what you want the new and more empowering thoughts to be.

The exciting part about thoughts is that they are easier to change than beliefs. That is because if you have positive and powerful beliefs, they greatly influence your thoughts. Think about it, if you have beliefs that are negative, what type of thoughts do you think you're going to have?

If you have negative beliefs, do you think it is easier to be influenced by outside negative information? **You better believe it.** Just because you have new beliefs that are positive and powerful, it does not mean that your thoughts are going to change in an instant. Your way of thinking is such a chronic habit that it will take a conscious and deliberate effort to change your thoughts.

Once you have the new thoughts in place, then it's time to practice. It is going to take some effort because in the beginning, your thoughts will cross back-and-forth from negative to positive. They will go from, "No I can't," to, "Yes I can." Just know that as long as you are persistent and as long as you continue to work at this, it will take less and less effort and positive thoughts will flow freely through your mind.

Let's recap: thoughts are the second in command to all results in life. It is your most prevalent thoughts that make you who you are. You are constantly being bombarded with information that is good and bad and it is your choice to decide what the meaning of that information is and how long you're going to focus on it.

Your mind is like a garden. It has no bias. By directing your thoughts and filtering the information that comes to you, you can choose what type of experience you are going to have from day to day.

Ok, here we go. Put down this book and write out what your thoughts are. Write out what you want the new thoughts to be and begin to practice them. Remember, I don't want you to merely just know this stuff. I want you to practice it and to live it. Seize this moment right now and think of it as an opportunity. An opportunity to shift your thoughts for the better. Do it now!

Feelings: Feeling are directly influenced by your beliefs and thoughts. Think about the majority of things you do on a daily basis. There are some things you have to do no matter what but most of the things you do, you do because you want to. So it is safe to say that is the reason you do the things you do is because you **feel** like it.

Let's face it people generally just don't do things they don't feel like doing. In theory, there is nothing wrong with that. Often times there are many things in people's lives that they **do** want to do and yet they simply don't do these things because they just don't feel like it. The great thing about this formula is that the further you go down the chain, the easier it becomes to reshape how it all feels. Look at it like this, if you believe that you are no good and you have thoughts that are negative, then how do you think you're going to **feel?** Empowered? Excited? Enthusiastic? Definitely not, because you have to understand whatever you put into the machine is what you get out. If you have negative beliefs and negative thoughts, than your feelings are going to be negative. That's just how it is.

The bright side is that it works the same way with positive beliefs and thoughts as well. How you feel from moment to moment is most likely just a representation of what you're thinking at that time about what you are doing. Think about when you have a bad day. There is some type of initial thought that prompts that crappy feeling and it creates a snowballs effect for the rest of the day. Think about a day that was just mediocre but then you got some great news that transformed your day from good to great. Your entire life changed in that moment due to what you were thinking.

That does not mean that you have to have good news come your way to change your state of mind. I know for a fact that at any given moment there are plenty of things that you can think about and for which you can be grateful. Yet all the potential joy that those things could bring you is over looked and missed out on because you do not focus on them. By conditioning yourself to think thoughts that are positive, you increase the quality of how you feel. This will allow you to be more congruent when it comes to doing the things you want to do. It also allows you to have a constant state of that "good news" feeling.

What this is about is responsibility. You are responsible for all the results in your life. Good **and** bad. It is time to stop pointing the finger and it is time to stop blaming others. Most of all, it is time to stop blaming yourself. If your results are the product of somebody else then you don't have the power to change them, your life is not your own. However, when you take 100% responsibility for your life, then you are free. That means if you are not happy with the way something is going you can change it. If there's something you want to get done, but you just don't feel like it, you can do something about it. Or if you're having a day where you're just feeling crappy, you can change it for the better by directing your thoughts into something more positive. To give you more insight into feelings and emotions, it is important to understand the emotional guidance system.

The Emotional Navigation System

I spoke earlier about how fear is simply an emotion. It is an emotion that we get to choose how to interpret. Due to that fact, we get to choose the meaning and the outcome of that emotion. The following will teach you about how all emotions have a purpose and can be used to better your life. Pay close attention here because this is very important considering we all feel and face massive amounts of emotions each day.

Although that principle relates to much more than fear, it relates to all of your emotions. A large part of what will add to a person's inner conflict is the misinterpretation of their emotions. When you are in conflict with your emotions and what they mean, it becomes very difficult to achieve long-lasting positive results in your life.

On the other hand, when you have the ability to understand, control, and successfully interpret your emotions, then you gain great power, and that power allows you to create and shape your life as you see fit. Your emotions can either own you, were you can own them.

People have a tendency to ignore their emotions. Or when they feel their emotions, they have a tendency not to take the time to decide what that emotion is trying to tell them. That will lead to a great amount of discomfort and pain. Your emotions are there for a reason and it's in your best interest to learn how to listen to them.

There are hundreds and hundreds of human emotions. The ironic part is that they can all be broken down into one of two categories. Every emotion you feel on a daily basis can ultimately be categorized as either positive or negative. Also, each emotion that you feel is a result of something that you are doing, that you have done, or that you are going to do.

Think of your emotions as a guidance system. They are there to help you stay on track through your journey of life. The

more you can understand your emotions and work with them the more joy
and ease you will experience along your way. They are without a doubt something to celebrate and be grateful for, as hard as that may be to believe at times.

However, because people tend to have a great misunderstanding of what their emotions are and why they're there, all too often people give entirely too much power to their emotions. Now this is understandable because, in the moment, emotions carry a lot of powerful charge. Ultimately, what ends up happening is that people become a slave to their emotions, rather than having mastery over them.

In addition, people tend to be picky about their emotions. We all like and welcome emotions that make us feel good. Yet we do whatever we can to avoid emotions that make us feel bad. In order to live life to your full potential, it is necessary to become unbiased towards your emotions.

Now does that mean that you should welcome and enjoy emotions that make you feel bad? Of course not, but what that does mean is that you should give them the same respect and certainly try not to avoid them. The real question is not how can you avoid them? Rather, how can you learn from them? How can you use them to help make your life and the life of others better?

It is important to start by listening to your emotions. Many times, we become directly impacted before we get a chance to decipher what the meaning of a given emotion is. Along with that when we fail to listen to our emotions we also fail to receive any of the potential guidance that they have to offer. What if you are really feeling great and things are going your way and you were to stop and examine your emotions and their cause? Then you would gain some insight into what it was that was contributing or allowing you to feel good in that moment. Once you understood those aspects of what was allowing you were contributing to your ability to feel good in that moment then you would be able to duplicate those things and therefore feel that way in the future. You could also learn from those aspects and use them to make your next experience even better.

Now, let's say you are having a day that really made you feel like total crap. Those days specifically are the ones that you want to avoid everything and crawl under the covers. Be that as it may, those are the days that if you can face those emotions and figure out what they're trying to tell you about how you're feeling and how you got to this state, then you would be able to use that information to allow yourself to avoid that feeling in the future.

What's even more powerful is that if you can understand what those negative feelings are trying to tell you and what causes them, then not only can you avoid feeling like that in the future but you can use that information to start making slight changes in your beliefs, thoughts, and behavior. Those changes will allow you to feel more joyful and positive emotions in the future and they will eventually replace the negative ones.

Just imagine all the days that you've ever had in your life where you felt like total crap. A large number of those days could have been days that you felt good or great. That is, if you had listened to what your emotions were trying to tell you and what was causing them. We all know that life is much shorter than we think it is and I believe you deserve to enjoy as many great days as you possibly can.

Truly, your emotions are really just the voice of your inner self. More than that, they are the voice of your ultimate-self. Therefore, if you are feeling something negative, that is your ultimate-self telling you that either something that you have done, that you are doing, or that you were about to do is out of alignment with what will truly make you happy. That means your emotions are signaling you in that moment to change your course somehow.

Likewise, if you are feeling great, that is your ultimate-self telling you that what you have done, what you are doing, or what you are about to do is in alignment with what is going to make you and others happy. In that case, it is important to keep in mind that those emotions are telling you that you should continue doing more of whatever you're doing. Be it the way that you are thinking, something you believe, or actions that you are taking, that is your opportunity to find out how you can increase the power and the frequency of those things.

The goal here is to learn from your emotions and to use them to your advantage. If you notice, people who have a tendency to avoid their emotions often find themselves in dismay because they continue to relive the avoided emotions. That is because we cannot learn from an emotion if we avoid it. Why is it people avoid their emotions?

The answer is fairly simple. Each and every person has unlimited power within them. As we covered earlier, each person has the potential to live their life at a ten. We are much stronger, bigger, loving, and more powerful than we think. When a person is living out of alignment with all the potential power that they have, their emotions send them messages telling them that something is wrong.

However, people tend to avoid these messages. The reason for that is because when you listen to these negative messages and what they are telling you, you're faced with the fact that ultimately you are solely responsible for your life. That means that you can no longer point the finger and blame anyone or anything else for the condition of your life.

That is a very scary feeling, to know that all of your excuses and all of your scapegoats are truly invalid. All of the reasons you have for why you cannot succeed truly hold no relevance. We come to the conclusion that our life and our world are entirely in our control. To a very large degree, we are the cause of the pain and unhappiness in our life. That is a fact that no one would like to admit.

You want to talk about avoiding the world and crawling under the covers? Try realizing that the days you wake up feeling like total crap are caused by nothing and no one else but you. Along with that, if people do not understand or have the ability to do something different about the life they have created for themselves, then that can sway a person into even deeper despair.

I believe that people at times are more afraid to live their ultimate-self than they are to live far below it. Due to our conditioning, we are led to believe that all of the power is outside of us. We are led to believe that fate shapes our destiny. Rarely are we shown that we have godlike power within us. Rarely are we taught that we are the great architects of our fate.

As cold and full of disbelief as that might make some people it is at the same time equally refreshing and invigorating. That means that our destiny is ours to choose. That means that in reality there is no one standing in our way; only the imaginary barriers, rules, and excuses that we have created for ourselves.

Emotions are a way of letting us know how far or close we are to that power. They are a reference for us to use, in order to give us clarity in our pursuit of happiness. This sooner you can begin to listen to and understand your emotions, the sooner you will be able to unleash even more of your excellence.

Actions: Your actions are what you literally **do** from day to day. It's time to start examining your actions. Chances are, if your beliefs, thoughts and feelings are negative, then your actions are going to be . . .have you guessed it? Yup. Negative. Just like everything before it, if you have new and empowering beliefs, thoughts, and feelings, of course your actions are going to be more positive. It's not enough just to rely on that though. It's going to take a conscious effort to change your actions.

Changing your actions can be tough. That is because your actions are not only linked to your beliefs, thoughts, and feelings. They are also tied into your physiology. Because this is such a huge area to tackle, we are going to focus solely on the Rituals not Habits chapter. For now what I would like you to do is to become aware of your current actions. What is the quality of action you take on a daily basis? I want you to think about how your beliefs, thoughts, and feelings have been influencing your actions.

If you can begin to become aware of your actions and why you behave the way you do, then it will be much easier for you to reshape your bad habits into powerful rituals when you get to that chapter. I'd like to encourage you to think about how important having the ability to take action will be in the future. Ideas, plans, hopes and aspirations all get washed up on the boulevard of broken dreams if you cannot take action.

Results: Results are the last part of this formula and they are the most appealing for everyone in this day and age. Technology has become a double-edged sword. It's all about instant everything at this point. Anything from movies, pictures, information, and even electronic conversations – they all can happen instantly. There is a negative side to all this though and that is that no one is willing to wait for anything anymore. The overall patience level of mankind has dropped to about the time is takes to send a text message.

What's worse is that because of the instant nature of nearly everything in our world, humanity holds the belief that we can have anything we want whenever we want it. And because of that conditioning, people believe that their results in improving themselves can follow suit. This is exactly why people go on crash diets, jump head first into get rich quick schemes, and browse dating websites where all you have to do is point and click on a picture. And can you guess what happens when people do that? The diet fails, the get rich quick scheme doesn't work, and the hot blonde you thought you were getting together with ends up looking like King Kong in a mini skirt...not cool. It is exactly that type of mindset that will kill your progress in self-improvement.

There is not a single masterpiece has been created instantly. Outstanding people are no different. They became who they are through hard work over time. They did not download a "How to be Awesome" eBook, read it and wake up the next day cooler than the Fonz.

If you are to revolutionize your life, you must make a distinction between what you can have instantly and what you cannot. Take some time to think about your results mindset. Remember that earning your results is a large component of what you will help you integrate them into your identity. Easy come, easy go.

Your results are the proof. Your results are the evidence. Your results are the fruit of your labor. They let you know that the effort you are putting into a given area is working. Your results are simply just the sum of your beliefs, thoughts, feelings, and actions for better or for worse. The results you produce are just an outer reflection of what's going on inside.
As you continue to move down this BTFAR formula, things will continue to get easier and easier. The more you work on and develop your beliefs, thoughts, feelings, and actions the more you will see the quality of your results change. Your new positive and empowering results will become automatic.

Just imagine, your happiness, fulfillment, and joy are practically all on autopilot. They aren't something that you have to try so hard for. They become something that just flows and your life becomes like a beautiful piece of music. Keep in mind this is AFTER you have put in the work to build up and condition yourself to get to this state. You can have instant results, just not at first.

Remember that your results are simply the external manifestation of your internal world. I want to make a special note here and say that many people that are unhappy with their results in life try to change their results very strictly. You have to keep in mind that your results really are just the **fruits** of your labor.

Wanting to change your results without changing your beliefs, thoughts, feelings are actions is like seeing rotten apples on an apple tree and focusing all of your time and effort on only trying to change the rotten apple. The reason that apple is rotten is because there's something going on with the food, soil, and the roots of that tree. The only way for that apple to ever change is to change the things the things that really matter, which are the food, the soil, and the roots.

You will become disempowered and disenchanted with yourself and self-improvement in general, if you purely try to change your results without changing your beliefs. As much as it's the results you're after, don't fall into the trap of trying to change those alone. Remember that this formula is set up the way that it is for a reason and that beliefs are at the very top because they are the core that influences every other section of your life.

Don't worry! I am not trying to tell you that it will take weeks or months to see results. In fact, there is a great chance you have already noticed some new results simply from the work we have already done. You have put a lot of time into making yourself the way you are now, the good news is that it will not take the same amount of time to become your ultimate-self. The biggest reason for this is that it is much easier to be your genuine self than it is to be the phony version you have been in the past.

Take Action!

Take out a sheet of paper or something to write on and I want you to write BTFAR in vertical order, like this:

B

T

F

A

R

Start with your beliefs about yourself; list them out as clearly as possible.

Are your beliefs primarily positive or negative?

What new beliefs do you need to have in order to live the life you deserve?

Next, write out your thoughts.

What kind of thoughts do you have on a regular basis?

What are some new thoughts you can think in order to support your new beliefs?

Then write out your feelings.

What types of feelings do you encounter on a daily basis?

Do you primarily listen to or avoid these emotions?

How can you listen more to your emotions?

What is it that your emotions are trying to tell you?

How can you improve myself by learning from your emotions?

If you are someone who generally does not listen to your emotions, or if you are someone who avoids them altogether, then I want to challenge you to take some time to think about those questions you just read in detail. Write out all the emotions that you feel on a daily basis. Try to categorize them into positive or negative categories. Once you've done that then try to come up with some very powerful answers to the above questions. Do this now!

What feelings do you have that you need to change?

Now write out your actions.

How much action do you take?

What can you do to start taking more action?

And finally, write down your results.

What type of results do you produce on a daily basis?

Make sure the new beliefs, thoughts, feelings, and actions are going to produce the results you deserve.

Put this book down and take action now!

D.A.P.L.

At times, you have certain elements that may be working against you in your pursuit of happiness. The better you can understand, isolate, and replace those negative elements, the fewer barriers you have to get in your way towards achievement. The understanding of your personal DAPL is paramount to ensuring your success. Let's get started!

DAPL that stands for:

- Demons

- Assumptions

- Perceptions

- Limiting beliefs

Demons: Each and every one of us has demons. They are the little voice inside your head that tells you that you're not good enough. They are the little voice that tells you you're not smart enough. They are that negative voice inside your mind that makes you think you are less than what you really are. These demons are responsible for holding back and sabotaging your results and happiness in life. They lower your confidence, drain your motivation, and make you doubt your own beliefs.

Generally, there are two types of demons. The first type of demon is created out of necessity. Here is a dialog with one of my clients to illustrate this first type of demon.

Shannon: Hi Mary, from your email it looks like you want to talk about why you do not have the kind of friends you want. Is that right?

Mary: Yes, I have realized that all my friends are more like acquaintances. I don't have any deep and meaningful friendships.

Shannon: Ok, why do you think you don't have the type of friends that you want?

Mary: Well, I would say it is because I am too busy. But I know that is not completely true.

Shannon: Have you had good friends in the past or has it always been this way?

Mary: It has been this way ever since high school.

Shannon: So before high school, you had close friends?

Mary: Yes

Shannon: That leads me to believe that at some point something changed. When you entered high school, do you remember adopting any new beliefs?

Mary: Actually yes, when I got into high school I realized that I had to take my classes and such much more seriously if I ever wanted to have the career I wanted.

Shannon: So you wanted to do extremely well in school. What happened as a result of that?

Mary: I started to believe that I had to work harder than everyone else and that I did not deserve to have friends until I had reached all my goals.

Shannon: Interesting, I am guessing you got outstanding grades while also developing a great ability to keep yourself from making friends.

Mary: Absolutely, it continued on like that through college. As a matter a fact, in college it got worse. I was so focused on school that my need for friends almost disappeared completely.

Shannon: And after you graduated what happened?

Mary: I graduated magna cum-laude and ended up landing my dream job shortly after.

Shannon: It sounds to me like you created a demon. This demon was created out of necessity to ensure that you could reach your goals. The challenge is it also kept you from having friends throughout that process.

Mary: I agree. So what do I do?

Shannon: Well you created a demon that tells you that you do not deserve to have friends because you are on a mission. I believe that you reached your goals and no longer need to hold on that belief. What do you think?

Mary: I think your right and looking back, I could have made time for friends, it's just that I was so scared that I would sabotage myself.

Shannon: Great, so if the old belief told you that you did not deserve to have friends. What would the new one need to be in order to have friends?

Mary: That I deserve to have friends.

Shannon: Yes, and do you believe that?

Mary: Yes, I honestly do. But, what about the old demon, should I worry about it?

Shannon: No, in fact I want to shift your feelings toward that demon so that you can let go of it properly. The fact is that even though you could have done things differently, the demon you created allowed you to produce outstanding results and ultimately achieve your dream job. So, at this time I would encourage you to be grateful for that, thank that demon for doing such a great job, and allow yourself to let it go, knowing that it has served its purpose and is no longer needed.

Mary: Wow. That makes so much sense. In a way, I needed it then, but do not need it at all now. I can just let it go. Thank you!

Shannon: You're welcome, Mary. Great work!

That is an example of how demons can be created out of necessity. That is also why people tend to hold onto their demons, because in some way they feel like they still serve them, when in reality they don't. The second aspect of demons comes from outside influences like your parents, classmates, siblings, coworkers, etc.

Anytime there is a constant message that comes from one or multiple sources it can create a demon. For example, when you were younger, if your parents told you that you weren't good enough, if your classmates picked on you, if your siblings gave you a hard time, or if you had failures in your early life, all of that negative information can create a powerful demon that tells you that you are not good enough.

In this case, the demon is not created out of necessity the demon is associated with a belief that you are not good enough. The first step in dealing with and dissipating these types of demons is an understanding that the past does not equal the future. Many times people base who they are on who they have been. You are not your past.

Remember this is about self-mastery; it is about completely revolutionizing your life in a way that allows for the maximum amount of happiness and fulfillment. Your past does not have to hold you back from being who you truly are and unleashing yourself upon the world. This goes back to changing your beliefs. If you have a belief that you're not good enough, then it's time to get rid of that old belief and replace it with a much more positive and powerful one.

I want you to write out some of your demons. Write them down and examine them. Try to understand which ones were created out of necessity and which ones simply came out of negative influence.

Once you establish which demons are which, you can go through and attach the proper meaning to each one. Was this demon created out of necessity? If so, then you can thank it for doing a good job in helping you do whatever it was created to do. Then you can let go of it and move forward, knowing that the demon no longer serves you. Therefore, it is no longer necessary.

Now take a look and see which demons come from negative influence. Once you know which demons those are you can write out the new belief that replaces it, some ways that you can really start to believe it, and methods of how you can practice it. The more you can identify, understand, isolate, and detach yourself from these demons, the more power you have to become the person you are meant to be.

Assumptions. Assumptions are conclusions that we draw based on little or no information. Assumptions are dangerous because they can keep us from the truth. When you assume something, you limit any other potential reality that could be possible for you or someone else. Assumptions are based on the idea that because one thing was true in the past it will be true now. When you assume something you generally let your initial perception of a person, place, or thing be the deciding factor in that moment.

Making assumptions is dangerous for two reasons. One, things always change assuming they will stay the same just because they have not changed yet sets you up for failure and disappointment.

Two, assuming is dangerous because when you assume, you take away the possibility that something could be better than what you currently believe it to be. For example, people who have problems with relationships tend to have a negative assumption about relationships that works against them. That could be something to the effect of: you think because the relationships you've had in the past didn't work out, that it means that any relationships in the future will also fail. Or, when it comes to finances, people might say, "I'm not willing to invest my money because I tried that once and it didn't work out and I'm not go through that again."

In both of those cases, the assumption that something bad is going to happen keeps those people from receiving the benefits of things like a loving relationship or a profitable investment. To get over assuming, there are a couple of factors involved. The first factor in overcoming assumptions is having an open mind and being open to new possibilities. When you have an open mind about something, you are less prone to make a hasty decision about what something means.

When you are open to new possibilities, you allow yourself to discover what the truth is. Now you are using your intelligence and facts, rather than past information and beliefs that you may have. The second factor in overcoming assumptions is curiosity. The only way for you to know if a relationship is going to work out is to find out for yourself. The only way to know if the investment your making is going to be worthwhile or not, is to give it your best shot and see it through. Allow your inherent curiosity to lead you forward.

It's that curiosity that will get you over the initial stage of doubt. It will allow you to actually explore the things in which you're interested.

When you make an assumption, you pass judgment on someone or something, but that assumption is not based on facts. In that case, you've lost the race before you have even started. You owe it to yourself and to other people to take the time and really come to a healthy conclusion about things. Think about some of the things in your own life. What are some of the things you have assumptions about, that you pass pre-judgments on? Think about how these assumptions and pre-judgments are potentially holding you back. Here is a dialog with one of my clients to illustrate assumptions:

Shannon: So, Roger, it says from your email that you are unhappy with the number of friends you have and would like to work on making more.

Roger: Yes, that's right.

Shannon: Why would you say you do not have as many friends as you would like?

Roger: Well, I believe it is because it is hard to find people that are on my level. You see, as an entrepreneur I learned that I have to surround myself with like-minded people. So, I only try to befriend people who are as intelligent and wealthy as I am.

Shannon: And how is that working out for you?

Roger: Not very well. (laughing).

Shannon: The real question is why isn't that working out well for you?

Roger: Well I guess I assume most people just don't have much to offer me in sense of friendship. I tried a few times in the past to make friends with people and I was just disappointed.

Shannon: You assume, huh? You assume just because someone does not have the same amount of wealth or intelligence as you that they cannot add value to your life as a friend? And because you tried a FEW TIMES in the past to make friends and it didn't work out, now you believe that is how is has to be forever? How realistic is that?

Roger: Well, I suppose that just because a person is not exactly the same as me doesn't mean that they cannot be a good friend. Before I became successful, I was certainly a good friend and didn't have the money or know-how that I have now.

Shannon: Why do you want friends anyway?

Roger: Well, I'd like more people that I can learn from, share experiences, and have fun with.

Shannon: So, what are the chances of meeting someone that you can learn from, share experiences, and have fun with even thought they aren't necessarily the same as you?

Roger: Now that I think about it, they are pretty good! I very well could meet someone that has a lot to offer. And as a matter a fact, I really enjoy teaching people about entrepreneurship, which would add a completely new layer of value to the relationship for me and for them.

Shannon: It sounds to me like the assumption you had no longer holds any water. Do you believe you can get out and make some new friends at this point?

Roger: Absolutely! This is going to be great!

Shannon: Great work, Roger. I would like to congratulate you on opening your mind up to something new and reaching a new and more powerful mindset. Well done!

I'm happy to say that I meet with this man once a year in New York City. Each time I see him he has new friends. They are friends that he learns from, shares experiences with, and has fun. He also gets to add value to these people's lives by sharing his knowledge of business with them. What I want to challenge you to do is think about your own assumptions. Think about all the different categories of your life that you have assumptions about and think about all the glorious and wonderful things from which they could be keeping you. Don't you deserve to get in on those things? Don't you deserve that new level of happiness? Think about all the other people with whom you could be contributing. Don't they deserve a version of you that is without assumptions as well?

Start to think about what your assumptions are and how you can begin to have more of an open mind and more curiosity. I'm telling you right now that life is too short to close yourself off to all the possibilities that it can afford you. You owe it to yourself to find out and live up to that new reality. Not to assume, not to figure, but to really find out. There are potential worlds of happiness, fulfillment, and contribution on which you and others are missing out.

Perceptions: Many of the conclusions we draw about things in our life are due to our perceptions.

Is the glass half-empty or half-full?

Is this the beginning or the end?

Is a rainy day a bad thing? Or, does it mean that your car gets washed for free?

The way you feel about the world, and your personal and professional results, is based on how you see things; how you view the world. The first part of mastering your perceptions is an understanding about what kind of perceptions you have. Are they primarily positive or negative? This is another area where you want to crank up your own awareness. The more aware you can be about your perception the more you have the ability to change it and make it better.

Remember your perception defines your life, so make a conscience effort to be as aware of it as you can be. Imagine two people walking up to the same painting; they both see exactly the same thing. Yet their perception of that painting is what will cause both people to have two very different experiences potentially. I personally think that is fascinating.

Let me give you an example of this so you can see what I mean:

There was a woman who lived in Los Angeles and she
was on her way to work one day. She wasn't really paying
attention as she crossed the street and when she stepped
down off the sidewalk she was almost hit by a taxi. The taxi
literally came within inches of hitting her. There's no doubt
that if she had gotten hit by that taxi she would have been
killed or seriously injured.

As that taxi flew down the road, she became full of rage. She
was shaking her fist and cursing, asking God why he hated
her. She just couldn't believe that someone could do
something so inconsiderate. Her perception, at that moment,
shaped the rest of her day. She got to work and was upset.
Her co-workers didn't want to be around her. She was in a
bad mood and the quality of her work throughout the day
was poor. When she got home, she did not take the time to
ask her husband how his day was, all she wanted to talk
about is how that taxi cab driver was a total jerk and how she
was so mad. Her entire day was literally ruined due to her
perception in that moment with the taxicab.

On the exact same day on the other side of town, there was a
different woman who was on her way to work. She too was
not paying attention and she stepped down off the sidewalk
and was nearly run over by a cab. As the taxi continued
traveling down the road, she watched it and she thought to
herself "Oh my goodness!

I must be the luckiest woman on the planet!" She then
looked up into the sky, took a deep breath and said. "*Thank
you.*" This woman was so thankful just to be alive in that
moment. When she got to work, she was full of joy and
excitement that her coworkers swore she had won the
lottery. They were compelled and excited to be around her
that day. Her productivity that day was through the roof.
When her husband came home from work that night, the first
thing she did was hug him as hard as she could and looked
him directly in the eyes and told him how much she loved
him. She knew that had things gone differently, she would
have never seen him again. She went to sleep and all she

could think about that night was the many, many things she had in her life to be grateful for, her life being one of them.

Just think about that for a moment, how two identical situations turned out completely different, all due to a difference in perception. What that could mean for your own life? Think about how much more potential richness you could get in on and share with other people if you simply shifted your perception. Remember, at any moment you have a choice, no matter where you are on the road of life there are always potentially two ways to go.

The only true meaning anything has in life is the meaning that we give it. Just because you're in a potentially negative situation, or circumstance, does not mean that the outcome, or result of that situation, has to be negative. You can choose what you're going to focus on in that moment, so that no matter what ever happens in life you can come out of every experience with a positive outcome, even ones that most people would label as bad.

I would like to illustrate even further how the brain works in relation to your actions. As we have come to understand through the formula of BTFAR, our actions are simply the result of what we are believing, thinking, and feeling from moment to moment. When the senses are stimulated in a certain way, they ignite an emotion within us. This emotion is the result of either an internal stimulation, meaning something we are focusing on from the past, present, or future. Emotions can also be stimulated by external sources - things such as the news, the workplace, our friends and family. However, the danger here is that either one of these sources can be the cause of negative emotions. These negative emotions are draining, stressful, and very often can be depressing. What is also unfortunate is that we can be having a perfectly fine day and in an instance, one moment in time can completely ruin that day and turn it into a bad one.

I believe the quality of your day, and moreover your life, should not be left up to chance in this way. These rogue emotions do not deserve the power to designate the overall quality of your life. In order to revolutionize your life you must be up to the challenge of mastering your emotional state.

Limiting beliefs: Limiting beliefs are beliefs we have that hold us back from our true potential. Limiting beliefs are slightly different from demons and the difference is that demons tend to be more personal. Demons generally have an 'I' statement attached to them. "I'm not good enough." "I'm not smart enough." "I'm not attractive enough." Whereas, a limiting belief is simply a belief that you have which is negative but it is not necessarily personal. Limiting beliefs do not always start with an "I" statement although limiting beliefs and demons can be related.

Limiting beliefs are a result of your conditioning, your assumptions, and your perceptions. I'm sure that right now in your life there are certain things that you would like to do and one of the only reasons why you do not do these things is because you have limiting beliefs about why you can't do them.

Having a clear understanding of your limiting beliefs is very important when it comes to self-mastery. The better you can understand the things that hold you back the more you'll have the power to change them and overcome them, eventually replacing them with beliefs that will literally draw you to toward goals.

The best way to establish what you're limiting beliefs are is to think about some of the things that you want to do in life that you have not done and think about the reasons or excuses you have created for not doing them. You want to explore your limiting beliefs to the absolute core. Generally, you will end up at one of two destinations. Once you realize that by breaking down your assumptions and perceptions, by having an open mind while at the same time expanding your curiosity, you will come to find out that your limiting beliefs are not true and that they're not based on reality. This will make it much easier to overcome those limiting beliefs and it will also make it much easier to replace them with a more positive and powerful belief.

The real power here comes from your ability to question your limiting beliefs and follow them as deeply as they go, so that you can fully understand that they truly do not need to be there. When you analyze your limiting beliefs, you can also find yourself face-to-face with demons. Sometimes your demons hide in the form of limiting beliefs. Facing your ugly sides can be an intimidating task, but remember you created that ugly side and you therefore have the more to erase it and create one that is equally as beautiful.

There is a chance you may have adopted some of your limiting beliefs from society. If you notice there certainly are not a whole lot of rebels out there doing everything they can to change their lives and the lives of others. It can be difficult to let go of the cultural limiting beliefs because they tend to seem "normal." You may feel like by going against these norms you will be seen as weird, strange, out of line, or worse. However, by this point I would hope that the mediocrity of rest of the world has little or no bearing on you. As a revolutionist, it is up to you to disregard the opinions of those that "go with the flow." Keep this quote in mind as you move forward:

"Be who you are and say what you feel, because those who mind don't matter and those who matter don't mind." ~Dr. Seuss

Remember, the important part in all of this when it comes to your demons, assumptions, perceptions, and limiting beliefs is when you come to the conclusion that these things are holding you back and you no longer need them in your life. Keep in mind any and all of these things can be changed. And the truth is if you are going to live up to your greatest potential they MUST change. Fear neither the ugliness of yourself nor the words of the onlookers. Your work on this earth is far too important to be impeded by either of those.

Take Action!

Here's what I want you to do. Remember, this is going to take some courage because when you do this exercise it forces you to look within and it forces you to look at your weaknesses.

You must know the only way that you can ever improve and reach new levels of achievement in your life is to look at those weaknesses to face them head on and to work on getting rid of them and replacing them. Don't be afraid to question these things. Remember to be honest with yourself when you're doing this exercise. As you go down this list, be curious and ask some really powerful questions.

I want you to write DAPL in vertical order, like this:

D

A

P

L

What are your demons?

Where do they come from?

Do you need to hold on to them anymore?

What kind of assumptions do you have?

What is your perception like?

Do you generally have an open mind?

Are you willing to change your limiting beliefs?

You know what to do. Put down this book and do this

exercise, do this now!

Put this book down and take action now!

Self-Love

Once you have your negative beliefs and programming out of the way, now you are open to love yourself to the highest degree. Out of the infinitely vast Universe that is self-improvement, self-love is the binding element that brings everything together. Self-love is where the magic is created and without it, your efforts in improving your life and the life of others will be for nothing. Trying to make progress in the area of self-improvement without high levels of self-love is like trying to paddle a rowboat up a river with no oars. Yet having high levels of self-love does just the opposite when it comes to your self-improvement. When your levels of self-love are increased, you will find it easier and easier to grow and excel in your life.

Unfortunately, the challenge here is that self-love is not on the top of most people's to-do list. The real truth is that many people neglect themselves. The reasons why people neglect themselves are all different. Sometimes it's family, friends, classmates, coworkers, or even their own self-talk. For some reason a person's self-love in many cases tends to be left by the wayside. How true is this in your own life?

The ironic part is when there is a lack of self-love, a large number of the categories in a person's life will be out of alignment. When there is a lack of self-love, regardless of any and all efforts that are made in other directions be it finance, health, relationships, or career, unfortunately, people still wake up to find that despite their achievements in these other categories they still do not feel completely happy or fulfilled. No matter how much a person might gain, if there is a lack of self-love, no amount of external stimulation or possessions will ever be enough. Due to our conditioning, we are led to believe that happiness is found outside the source. Yet all the people to chase after it never catch up with it. Love is truly an inside job.

Before we continue, I want you to have a clear understanding of what self-love really is. Many people confuse self-love with narcissism. Narcissism is a personality disorder where people have a large need for admiration and an inflated sense of their own importance. People who are narcissistic often believe that they are superior to others, and generally have little regard for other people's feelings. Ultimately, the cockiness and hyper-confidence is due to a very low self-esteem, and this type of person is very susceptible to criticism. This is the opposite of self-love.

Next, is the belief that you do not deserve to be loved. Maybe someone somewhere told you that you were no good or maybe you had some negative experiences growing up. This type of strong negative message can easily lead people to draw conclusions about themselves that are flat out lies. Having a belief that you do not deserve love is to deny the greatest gift you can give yourself and others. So many results in multiple categories of a person's life can be affected by this horrible belief. Stop right now and think about if you hold this belief or anything close to it.

Remember, just because someone didn't have the capacity to love you does not mean that you are not worth being loved. You are worthy of love and deserve it from yourself and others. It can be hard to change this belief. In fact, this is may be one of the biggest challenges you will encounter. You will be happy to know that if you can transform this single part of yourself you will have 90% of the entire self-improvement game won.

Self-love on the other hand is the ability to fill yourself with kindness and compassion, along with a very deep and healthy understanding of who you are. More than that, self-love is the ability to honor your morals, values, standards, and expectations. It is a willingness to accept yourself for who you are and at the same time, remain committed to consistently improving yourself.

The core of self-love has to do with valuing yourself. This means valuing who you are right now and not waiting for others to give you credit or praise. Self-love means that you can look in the mirror and truly love the person staring back at you. Self-love is a realization that although you may not be perfect, you can still be perfectly happy with yourself.

Many of us are taught during childhood to put such things aside. We are taught that focusing on our self is selfish and that there are other people and causes to which we need to contribute. People gradually come to the conclusion that they have the ability to help others so they put their needs last. Some people are encouraged to be selfless because of their spiritual or religious influences.

There is no doubt that it is a very positive and powerful trait to be selfless. However, there is a challenge. When a person continuously gives to other people, and they themselves already have a low reservoir of self-love, then they start giving that which they do not have. It can cause great feelings of resentment and self-hate. As you can imagine, this can be extremely counterproductive for a person who feels like they are doing the right thing by giving to others, despite the fact that they are doing such nice things and since there is a low level of self-love, many people end up feeling unfulfilled by their selfless acts.

With that type of doubt comes insecurity and self-judgment. We all know that there is no worse critic or judge than ourselves. No one knows us better than us. Therefore, no one can cut us as deep as we can. If you are to achieve high levels of self-love and self-mastery, then all the abuse you put yourself through must stop. There must be a transition from abusing yourself to accepting, appreciating and nurturing yourself.

That means that your efforts in increasing your self-love in the end are nothing near selfish at all. In all honesty making drastic efforts in the area of self-love become self-less, because the more you can fill yourself up with love and appreciation for who you are, the more value you are going to be able to add to your life and the life of others. You will go from a state of giving that which you do not have, to giving something that which you have never been able to give before.

The more self-love you have, the more the quality of your life is going to increase. The more you understand your needs and who you are, the better you are going to be able to understand other people and their needs. Think about the kind of impact you would have on your friends and family if you truly accepted and loved yourself for who you are, and could turn around and do the same for them.

A very substantial and large part of self-love is gratitude. I find that in the end you can break people down into two categories. Those are people who are grateful for what they have, and those who are not. You'll find that people who are not grateful for what they currently have, will encounter unhappiness on many levels no matter what level they ever achieve.

Opposite of this, you will find that people that can be deeply grateful for what they already have and who they are *today* are some of the most happy and fulfilled people. You'll also find that people who are immensely grateful, often find themselves receiving new levels of abundance of all different forms. It goes to show that those that can be content with very little can go on to receive very much. Those who are not content with what they have and who they are will struggle to hold on to the little that they have.

When you are grateful, you are strong. When you are grateful to be who you are in spite of your imperfections, you are powerful. When you feel happy and lucky to be who you are, you're unstoppable. When you love and value yourself, your life becomes like a dream.

Let's not forget that self-love does not necessarily mean that you are totally content with who you are, and therefore you stop growing. In fact, it is just the opposite. The purpose of self-love is to accept yourself for who you are and then to ask yourself, "How can I become even better?" Keep in mind that one of your primary needs is to grow and to expand yourself continuously. Having a high level of self-love is necessary because it allows you to have the vehicle for your improvement and also gives you the best type of fuel along the way.

There is a misconception in the self-improvement world that you are perfect just the way you are. This is a very dangerous concept. This theory leads people to believe that they are perfect, and yet they continue on in their lives with negative beliefs, thoughts, feelings, actions and results. They move through their life feeling unsatisfied at their job, unfulfilled in their relationship, uncertain and unhappy about who they are. This is far from perfect, my friend.

The real power comes from the understanding that you are not perfect. Yet, with that understanding comes the fact that, be that true as it may, a person can always improve and become better than who they are. Just because you are not perfect does not mean that perfection is an idea on which you should give up. If anything, it should be something that inspires and compels you. True perfection is not a state it is a process. The ability to consistently woo and pursue a state of constant improvement is the true essence of perfection.

So forget about what other people have told you. As your companion and coach in this revolution, I am here to tell you that you are a beautiful person and that you are worthy of love. Regardless of how badly you or others have treated you in the past, you deserve love.

Use the following process to unleash your self-love:

- Identify

- Forgive

- Release

- Re-identify

- Embrace.

Identify: The first step in resolving your inner conflict is identifying the negative attributes you have that are contradicting the results you are trying to achieve. This again goes back to awareness. You have to be aware of the things that are holding you back in order to move forward. This comes down to is an examination of all the different aspects of who you are; that means your beliefs, your needs, your demons, you're limiting beliefs, and any and everything that is related to making you who you are.

An important thing to remember here is that not all the things that hold you back may be negative. They may just be contrasting wants or needs. For example, the want to be wealthy coupled with a want to relax and enjoy your free time, is not conducive to creating wealth unless you already have it. You will find yourself working hard some days, and doing nothing other days. Once you have created your wealth absolutely, you can enjoy your free time and relax. It doesn't work, the other way around, however. It is nearly impossible to build wealth if while in the beginning stages you are relaxed and leisurely.

Before you can fully love yourself, you must have a clean slate. You do not want dueling beliefs inside your mind fighting for dominance. I cannot stress how important it is to be congruent all the way through the process. What are some examples in your life where you can see evidence of a dueling reality?

This is about more than being aware of your BTFAR and DAPL. This is about seeing all the areas of your life that keep you from loving yourself to the max. They can be people, places, things, and habits. You must become aware of all the barriers that hold you back in order to be able to move forward with the most power.

Forgive: During this revolution, there will be no room for baggage, which is why you must be able to forgive yourself and others. All the emotional weight that comes from harboring resentment toward yourself and others I'm sure has already been enough of a detriment to you. It can be easy for you to feel anger, discouragement, and disappointment with yourself when you realize that at the end of the day you are responsible for being the way you are.

No one really wants to come to that conclusion. No one wants to realize that he or she and he or she alone is the reason that they are not getting what they want out of life. I'm telling you this because when you identify the source of what is creating your dueling reality, you also liberate yourself at the same time. You realize it's no longer your father, mother, or your boss that hold you back. And though you may be upset for not being where you wish you were now you finally are in a place where you can do something substantial about it. It is a matter of choice you can decide to be bitter, or better.

That is why you must forgive yourself. To forgive yourself for the unsatisfactory results that you have created. You have to be able to move forward, and in a completely clear and positive mindset. You can't do that, unless you have completely forgiven yourself for having those contrasting attributes. If you happen to have negative beliefs or acquired habits that come from other people, then it is time to forgive those people as well. Think about all the people you currently blame for your unhappiness. How's that working out for you? I know for a fact it isn't helping. Blaming others and holding resentment toward them will never allow you to unleash your love.

Also, you will be so distracted by determining whose "fault" it is that you will be unhappy. You won't be able to focus on how to make things better. In order to get some new results in your life you have to do something that you've never done before. Forgiving those who have hurt you can be a challenge, however, if you can do it. you open yourself up to immense greatness. That is why the forgiving side of this process is so important. It allows you to be more receptive to the bright future you have always deserved. Forgiveness is so powerful because it lets you move away from any shame or guilt that you have felt. It also lifts any negative feelings you might have towards yourself for other people. And it erases the hate that is imprinted on your heart and gives you a sense of lightness and freedom.

While hate may seem like the natural reaction toward someone who has caused you pain, that hate becomes a massive suit of armor which. It may keep you from getting hurt, but it simultaneously becomes a great burden. It weighs you down and restricts your ability to share and receive love, ultimately the suit of armor you don to protect yourself from harm becomes the stifling hell you wish so much to avoid. The injuries that one person has caused you are not worth missing out on the potential love of many others. Likewise, it is unfair to those deserving of your love to keep them from it due to an experience that has nothing to do with them.

Forgiveness is amazingly powerful it allows you to focus all your energy and time onto the things that you can help you move forward. Ultimately, it helps you move away from inner conflict and towards inner peace. Another important factor to remember is that in order to complete each step in this process of resolving your dueling reality, you must take each step in the proper order to be successful. None of the steps can be left out.

If you can't forgive, then you will not be able to get to the next step, which is release. Once you have forgiven yourself and others, then it becomes much easier to release all of the aspects of yourself that were contributing to your inner conflict. Before we move on answer the following questions:

Do you need to forgive yourself?

Do you need to forgive other people who have hurt you?

How can you begin to forgive right this moment?

Release: When it comes to the step of releasing, you may encounter some hesitation or some resistance. Even if you are making an effort to get rid of aspects of yourself that are holding you back, or contributing to your inner conflict, it may be difficult because those aspects are related to your comfort zone.

What happens when you do away with those aspects of yourself is that it can create a very high level of uncertainty and fear. As we know as long as you have the proper mindset and perception, then that uncertainty and fear do not have to be interpreted as a negative thing. If anything, they can be part of what pushes you forward.

The second aspect of releasing is faith. I'm not talking about faith in a religious sense, more so I am talking about a faith in yourself; a faith in that bigger better you that lies within. There is no doubt that even though you're going to be moving into a much brighter and healthier future, there's going to be some fear. However, if you can use your ability to interpret fear correctly and tap into your immense faith, then you can move through that time of transition with power and certainty. Faith makes a huge difference when it comes to your personal and professional transition because you're not always going to know what the next step is. There are going to be moments and situations where you are flying blind.

A strong faith gives you the ability to see the invisible and the power to do the impossible. The stronger your faith, the better your ability to create solutions where at one time there were only problems. A strong faith will enforce your ability to find or make a way, when at one time there was none.

How do you develop your faith? Well, many of the strategies and techniques that we have already talked about will help you build your faith. Knowing who you are, knowing your purpose, and understanding what your strengths are is a great start. All of those things will help you build a strong belief in yourself and it is that belief that creates a higher level of faith in who you are and what you can do. There is another side to faith that is equally as powerful and that is a faith in what I call the ultimate-self. That is the version of yourself I referred to in the beginning of the book. It is the one inside of you that is begging to get out. It is the bigger, better, and more powerful version of who you are. It is a faith in that great person within you. It is a faith ensuring that if you continue on this path of self-mastery, then slowly but surely, you will be unleashed and become your ultimate-self.

What about the people, places, or things that are affecting you in a negative way? What are those things? It is time to let those go. You must raise your standards for your own quality of life, the abusive and destructive people, places, or things in your life must be removed in order to re-identify and embrace new and more positive replacements.

It is one thing to be able to forgive someone, yourself included. It is another thing all together to be able to let go of the pain you have suffered as a result. You may have literal and emotional scars, however, I want to encourage you to let go of any negative associations they may have on you. You do not deserve to bear the pain of your past injuries one minute longer. Release the pain you have been holding onto. Let it go…

Having faith in yourself and opening up to the love your ultimate-self and others have to offer is why we are here. It is one of my greatest hopes for you during this whole journey. Imagine the pain you hold inside as chains. These chains keep you bound to the ground while your wings are urging you to take flight. See yourself dropping these chains and soaring high into the sky. The pain can no longer hold you down, you can be free from it all once and for all.

Re-identify: The first step in this process was to identify the areas and aspects of your life that are holding you back from becoming your ultimate-self. Therefore in this step, where we are re-identifying the areas and aspects of yourself that will be necessary to create inner peace, you must look into each category of your life and decide what is needed in order to create the life you deserve. Imagine looking at an unfinished puzzle and seeing the gaps. This is exactly what we are doing in this step.

For example, if one of the areas of your life that you want to improve is your relationships. Then it is important to know what it is specifically going to take to build up that area of your life. Do you need to be more trusting? Do you need to be more open? Do you need to be more committed? Now don't worry, at this time you are just going to be identifying these things. As far as how to actually put them in place and develop them, you will learn about that in the following chapters. I've got your back.

Once it is clear to you what those certain aspects are, then you can start building new beliefs and rituals around those them. That is when your life will start to become more congruent. Everything inside of you will begin working together. It is then that you will begin to see the greatest and most consistent results.

I want to stress the fact that it is also important to be as accurate as possible when you are re-identifying. The reason for that is because the more clear you can be when you are re-identifying the areas of your life that need improvement, the more helpful you will be to yourself when it comes time to strengthen those areas. Think about it, if you went to a personal trainer and said, "I want to get fit," they wouldn't know where to start. But if you said, "I want to lose 30 pounds," or, "I want to get toned," this would greatly help the trainer to know what direction and exercises they needed to do with you.

As an example, to build your relationships you must build your ability to commit. Then you want to clarify that, what it is personally going to mean for you to commit. What is it exactly that is going to have to happen for you to be able to raise your level of commitment? Once you know that then you can begin to focus all your energy and attention in that area.

Also, this is where you want to re-identify the new people, places, and things that are going to empower, inspire, and motivate you. Be sure to take the proper amount of time to nail down what those things are going to be. Imagine the difference between having a life filled with negativity all around and one where you were constantly surrounded with positive people, places, and things. How much would that increase the richness and quality of your life? More than a little, I promise you that. The re-identifying is also a very powerful step because it gives you something in which to invest all your newfound faith. It also is something that you can get excited about and to which you can look forward. You get to start with a clean slate. How many times have you or someone you know said, "I wish I could just get a fresh start."

You get to decide what your life is going to be like. If you've been living a life of inner conflict, then when you resolve that inner conflict the future becomes very bright. How does it feel to know exactly what is needed in order for you to become your ultimate-self?

Imagine yourself like Tarzan swinging through the jungle. Think about how difficult it would be to swing from vine to vine if you were not willing to let go of the current vine onto which you were holding. Likewise, if you could not see where the next vine was that you're going to grab onto why would you ever want to let go of the one that you have?

Like Tarzan, you must see your past vines as something you are willing to let go of in order to grab onto the next one. You realize that in order for you to move forward, you're going to have to let go and find a new vine. Also, if you can successfully see the new and better branch, you can let go of the old one with ease. It is then that your life becomes one continuous forward motion.

Embrace: The final step in resolving inner conflict is embrace. What that means is after you have identified, forgiven, released, and re-identified you must find a way to become totally enveloped in the building and daily practice of your ultimate-self. Immersion is the separating factor between people who succeed long term and people who do not. Take for example, someone who is fanatical about exercise, diet, or religion. The reason that that person can get so much out of any of those things is because they are totally sold out. Their results are so high because they have completely immersed themselves in those things and made doing those things part of who they are rather than just something in which the participate.

Think about anything in your life in which you are really immersed. Maybe it's training for some event or preparing for a test that you have to take. Whatever it is, think about a time in your life where you totally had to be immersed in something. Weren't the results you got in that situation much more substantial? Weren't the results also much more powerful than the results you would have normally gotten? I'd bet the farm they were.

A large part of why that is, is because when you really believe in something and you have a very deep and substantial purpose fore why you want to do that thing it becomes very easy to embrace it. When you embrace something, you focus yourself on it completely. That means you must find a way to become fanatical about your self-mastery. There is a huge difference between people who are interested in improving their life, and the people who are completely fanatical and embrace the improvement of their life. The difference is the first group gets inconsistent and poor results. The second group will achieve constant and remarkable results.

It is here that having a strong faith in yourself and a faith in the journey that you are embarking on is the most important.

Remember as I mentioned before, it is belief that will cause a person to become a doctor and save lives. Likewise, it is belief that will cause a person to join a radical group, and fly a plane into a building. Both these people achieve extreme results, because they wholeheartedly believe in their cause. They have a very powerful and clear understanding of who they are, and what their purpose is. Once they apply that sense of purpose to a specific cause than their results in that area become nearly immeasurable. Those are the people that end up changing the world for better or for worse.

Changing the world might not be one of your interests. But changing your life certainly is, and your life is your world. That is why you must embrace changing your life to the highest degree.

Before we move on, I want to give you a chance to soak everything up. I don't expect you to be able to have this area of your life 100% certain and clear. However, I do want you to at least start thinking about the steps of resolving inner conflict that I spoke about earlier. Allow yourself to be overtaken by the great power that is within you. Allow your inner magnificence and love to wash over you. Take some time right now to at least create an outline of each one of these steps so you can get an idea of what needs to be done in that area, and how you can start to approach it. These initial chapters are the most important of this entire book. You owe it to yourself to complete this exercise with the greatest amount of enthusiasm and self-respect.

In some way, shape or form, picking up this book was an act of self-love. My question to you is how can you continue that motion, how can you continue that trend of giving to yourself? I don't mean in a materialistic way but in a healthy nurturing way that allows you to grow and expand. My suggestion would be to take some time this very moment.

Think about your own personal level of self-love. Where is it? On a scale of one to ten, ten being the absolute highest and one being the absolute lowest. Try to rate yourself and find out where your level of self-love is. Begin to think about what you can do to increase your self-love. Start to think about how you can accept yourself more, and abuse and neglect yourself less.

Take Action!

You deserve all the happiness and joy that can possibly come your way. In order to be able to receive that you must increase your level of self-love to the maximum. Of course, I encourage you to take all of the exercises I recommend seriously, but out of all of them please do your best with this one, because I personally believe that you deserve it and you owe it to yourself to have that self-love as well.

Do you genuinely love yourself?

What do you need to do in order to love yourself to the highest degree?

Identify: what is holding you back from total self-love.

Forgive: Forgive yourself for any injuries you or anyone else has caused you.

Release: Release the pain you feel inside. Now that you have forgiven, it is time to let go of the past.

Re-identify: Zero in on the aspects of yourself that you love. Get as clear as possible about what those things are.

Embrace: Get fanatical about having a strong and healthy love for yourself!

Put this book down and take action now!

Self-Nurture

An understanding that more than anyone else you should be the one to love and accept yourself leads us to the principal of self-nurture. Because the fact remains that many of us did not or do not have picture perfect parents and do not have flawless spouses or friends. Sometimes we don't get the love we should from the people that are closet to us. However, that does not mean you should be without it, it simply means it has to come from you rather than them. In a way, you must be your own parent, in a way you must be your own best friend. This comes back to responsibility. Ultimately it is your responsibility to take care of yourself.

There are many ways that self-nurture ties into your life. Both your personal and professional life is affected by your levels of self-nurture. The quality of your life is in direct correlation to the quality of love and care you are able to provide for yourself on a daily basis. An easy way to understand where your personal level of self-nurture is at is to look at the current habits you have and determine how much pain you are allowing yourself to you experience on a daily basis.

For example if you do things like worry, stress, doubt, complain, or over eat chances are you feel some level of pain inside. The lack of self-nurture allows you to cross the line from joy to pain sometimes unknowingly. Without the awareness that a healthy level of self-nurture gives you can find yourself in state of pain and often times be unsure of how you got there. The line that determines good and bad, just enough and too much is not bold enough. This is understandable if there has never been any guidance in the past regarding these lines.

This is where you must create your own ideas about the rules in which you are going to live your life. There is so much influence from the outside world even without a strong parental presence. The news, social groups, and the media all seek to infiltrate your mind with information. Some of that information is good and some of it is bad. But the ultimate determining factor in all of it is you. It is up to you to define what is right and what is wrong, more than that it is up to you to adhere to the laws of self that you set in place so that you consistently stay within the boundaries of right and wrong.

The more you define and clarify these laws of self, the deeper and more convicted you become in what you believe. This is powerful because this allows you to be put into a potentially healthy or harmful situation and have a clear understanding of which is which. Therefore, you can clearly see the line and know exactly when you are crossing it. Along with this comes the ability of self-limiting. This is important because potentially every healthy situation can easily become an unhealthy one due to a lack of boundaries.

Let's take over eating, there is a distinct line between eating just enough and eating too much. If you have a clear understanding of yourself and what is just enough then it becomes easy to know what is too much. Your ability to commit to the standards and expectations you have set up for yourself will allow you to stay on the healthy side of the line and refuse to eat more than you should. The clearer the line is the sooner you can stop yourself from crossing it.

In what ways do you cross the line in your own life?

Where do you need to strengthen your boundaries?

What are the things you always say you are going to do but fall short on? Example:

"I should go to bed earlier."

"I should start exercising."

"I should start a business."

"I should eat a healthier diet."

Your desires, need for instant gratification, and over indulgence can very easily fill your life with pain and uncertainty. The funny part is that those who over indulge can never seem to get enough no matter how much they get. They always seem to want more. How true is that for you in your life? This sheds a bright light on this approach that so many of us take and shows us unmistakably that excess leads to distress. If nothing else this shows us that what the majority of us go after in excess are the wrong things.

On the other hand, things like joy, peace, and contribution are things that we can get involved with to even a small scale and still feel huge benefits. What is even better is that those are the kind of things you really can't go overboard with. I am fairly sure that no one ever complained because they had too much joy. This should help give you some perspective on where to designate your focus and from a self-nurturing standpoint. Isn't it ironic that for some reason the things people neglect are often the things they need the most, and the things they over-do are the things that are slowly but surely killing them.

If you can successfully self-nurture, then you will constantly be living your life in harmony. Along with that harmony, there is a great sense of personal power and pride. Just imagine how strong you would feel if you made healthy self-nurturing decisions every day. Think about how much confidence you'd be filled with if you had crystal clear laws in which to live your life and stuck to them each and every day.

As you can see, there are a few challenges here. The largest of these is the amount and quality of self-love you have and how well you take care of yourself. Imagine if you had peak levels of self-love and did specific things to take care of yourself each and every day. Do you think you would continue to indulge in the behavior for which you currently beat yourself up? Not a chance. What would happen to the quality of your life if you starting actually doing the things you said you "should" do?

Your criteria for happiness are another aspect of creating congruity within yourself. Most people struggle to be happy because they are unclear about how to be happy, or their criteria for what will make them happy constantly changes. This becomes a large stomping ground for inner conflict. Happiness is something that is projected out into the future and more often than not, it stays there, like a rainbow that is always out of reach. Having strict criteria for happiness along with projecting it into the future is a sure-fire way to make sure it becomes nearly impossible to obtain. When you love yourself to the highest degree, you allow yourself to be happy right here, right now. Self-love and happiness with your life go hand in hand and it is one of the biggest and most important forms of self-nurture to be able to give yourself the gift of happiness at all times.

Think about what your current criteria for happiness and ask yourself "Is my current criteria for happiness realistic?" And if it's not, how can you begin to make it more realistic? And secondly, what are you doing to make those things are reality? What can you begin doing that will allow you to start to meet some of that new and more realistic criteria?

The thing is, when your life does not stack up to the expectation of how you think it should be, you're going to be unhappy. Although the good news is, you are the one that determines your expectation for your life. You are the one that sets the criteria for what's going to make you happy. If those expectations and criteria are not being met, because they are unrealistic than the great thing is you have the power to change them.

Also, it is important to keep in mind. The more steps you put between you and what it will take to be happy, the longer and more difficult it's going to be get there. Your happiness can and should be instant rather than being ten feet away from you at all times, no matter how much progress you make.

Along with thinking about how you can make your criteria for happiness more realistic, think about how you can start to change what you're doing in that area. They say the definition of madness is doing the same thing over and over and expecting a different result. Therefore, along with your criteria for happiness it is also time to look at your approach to happiness.

That does not mean you should have no ambition or low expectations. What that means is you must have a successful combination of long-term goals and the ability to be happy from the first step rather than having to wait until you cross the finish line. It is also important to dig deep down into the essence of the things that you believe will make you happy. For example, if being financially free is one part of your criteria for being happy, think about why. What is it that you are going to get out of being financially free that you feel will make you happy?

Let's say that you want to be financially free ultimately because you want a feeling of freedom. In that case, I would challenge you to get creative and think about how you are already free. If you can do that, then you will be able to receive all the feelings and results of being financially free instantly. As I said, that doesn't mean you should give up on your pursuit of obtaining wealth, if that is what you desire. However if you can extract some of the heart of the matter, then you can fulfill that inner need you have immediately, which will give you the power and enthusiasm to move forward.

The truth is there should be no barrier between you and your happiness. People tend to feel like they need to earn their happiness. Or that they have to deserve it. People feel like they have to do or have a certain number of things in order to be happy.

The greatest example of true happiness is a newborn child. They know very little about the world yet they are filled with happiness. They can smile and laugh at just about anything. Their personal criteria for happiness are very limited. They don't need a reason to be happy, they just are. They don't feel like they need to accomplish certain things to be happy, they just are. They don't feel like they need anything to be happy, they just are.

As adults don't do that, do we? We come up with all these crazy rules that we that we must follow in order to make us happy. The thing about happiness is that it is not a science. X + Y + Z does not always equal H. More times than not, when we do the things that we think are going to make us happy we find out that they don't. Often times we will sacrifice all our happiness for extended periods of time in hopes that the grand pay off will be worth it. Guess what? It's not, no future happiness will ever be more than the happiness you can experience from moment to moment.

The whole time that we were chasing after those things, we were unhappy. Well, I'm telling you right now that you deserve to be happy in the future without a doubt. But you also deserve to be happy right now. Happiness is an art, not science. If it were a science, then everyone who thought a car, a house, and a fair amount of money would make them happy would be happy. And we know that's not true.

It's time to stop putting all your love and admiration into things that can't love and admire you back. That especially goes for things that cannot add value to your life right now. Here is an interesting fact: the average amount of time that someone wildly celebrates and is happy after achieving one of their major goals is less than 60 seconds. Can you imagine that? Imagine finally obtaining whatever you thought was going to make you wildly happy only to go crazy with joy for less than 60 seconds? That is definitely not what I am talking about

Take Action!

Loving your self is second to none. If you cannot love yourself, then you will never be able to unlock your full potential and have the type of impact on the world that you want.

How can you nurture yourself more?

In what ways can you nurture yourself better?

Do you have beliefs about caring for yourself that might hold you back?

How can you adopt and embrace a mindset that allows you to be number one in your life?

Find a way to make your barrier to happiness as absolutely low as possible. How realistic is your current criteria for happiness? Think about what you can start doing that is new and different that will allow you start to fulfill some of those new criteria. How can you shorten the distance between you and your happiness? Remember, you don't necessarily need anything to be happy. You deserve to be happy right now, just the way that you are. Also remember, the longer and more immense your criteria for happiness the further and more difficult it will be for you to achieve it. In the next chapter you will learn about how bring the fun back into your life.

Put this book down and take action now!

The F-Word

When I say the F-word, I'm not talking about the four-letter curse word that you were taught not to say growing up. I am talking about the three-letter noun, that when missing from a person's life despite the amount of possessions, money, status, friends or family, will leave a person feeling empty inside. You would imagine such a strong mental program, that we are all innately born with, that is the source of our happiness in our early years would never fade away. Unfortunately, this is not true, if you haven't figured it out by now, I'm talking about fun.

Think about how important fun used to be to you when you were a kid. As a matter of fact, I am willing to bet that, as a kid, fun was your primary objective. Back when you were young, you didn't care about dating, money, or success. All you wanted to do was have fun and I'm not talking about some fun, or a little bit of fun. Your whole day revolved around having fun. Do you remember how easy it was to be happy back then? The quality of your life at any given moment would skyrocket, you would be smiling, and genuinely happy simply because you are having fun.

As a kid, your biggest worries related to fun, didn't they? It was the classic who, what, when, where, and why? Who am I going to be playing with today? What fun and exciting thing are we going to do? When are we going to be able to do it? Where are we going to have fun? And why oh why do our parents ever make us stop? Somehow, without anyone teaching you at such a young age you already had one of the biggest secrets to success wrapped up. And the thing that absolutely blows me away is that somewhere along the line, you stopped having fun, or at least the quality and frequency of your fun dramatically decreased.

The really ironic part is that most people try to fill the void they have with something that will never do. This intrinsic need we have for fun never actually goes away, rather we turn a blind eye to it or we come up with new ideas or criteria for what fun is and how we should go about getting it. What's even worse is sometimes we will keep ourselves from having fun because we believe that it is not "mature" or "responsible." So what do we do instead? We focus on the nitty-gritty aspects of life that stress us out, worry us, and ultimately keep us living below are potential and away from our dreams. Why is it that we have a nearly flawless system for bringing fun and enjoyment into our life and at some point, we scrap the entire thing and try to re-create the wheel? Now it would be one thing if we all changed our criteria for what fun meant and how we went about it and it actually worked. If new rules for fun that we came up with actually brought laughter and joy into our lives than that would be fine, but if you look around it's pretty easy to see that it does just the opposite.

You see, one of the key ingredients to all success, personal or professional, is fun. Look at some of the most successful people of all time: Leonardo da Vinci, Thomas Edison, Pablo Picasso, Walt Disney, and Oprah Winfrey. All of these people decided to go after what they loved doing. And just by its very nature, when you do what you love you have a lot of fun. From inventing, to painting, to cartoons and contributions, all of the above names had large amounts of fun in their lives. Arguably, all of those people also made it easier for everyone else to have fun through their works. People get so caught up in their day-to-day lives that all they're doing is focusing on how to get by and they lose sight of what is really important.

This idea of fun for some people is totally inappropriate. Some of the questions or statements they say to themselves when considering the idea of adding more fun into their life are things like:

"I am older now and I need to be responsible."

"I am jaded by the real world and have lost my innocence."

"How can I have fun when I'm supposed to be mature?"

"I cannot have fun because I'm a professional."

"Even if I wanted to have fun, how would I do that now?"

"I've got things to do there's just not enough time."

"Playing and having fun is childish."

Here is my rebuttal to the above statements, as far as the need to be more responsible goes, I agree with that completely. However, I believe that as you get older you have a responsibility to make sure that you have more fun not less. You have to become intentional and go out of your way to make sure that you have fun because otherwise life will certainly get in the way. Age has no bearing on fun, just because you get older and gain knowledge does not mean for a minute that you should sacrifice having fun.

What's really interesting to me is if you observe older people, people who would be considered senior citizens, they for some reason come full circle and realize that now that they can't chase money, success, and the opposite sex the way they used to and all of a sudden, they reevaluate what is important in life. They begin to go back to their roots and just start having fun again.

If having fun is one of your primary goals when you are young, before you get too smart for your own good and begin sabotaging it, then having fun when you're older should be a primary goal. It's easy because now you realize with your golden wisdom that life truly is short and having fun and spreading joy is one of the most important parts of it. I would suggest learning from both those examples and have fun all the way through, rather than just the beginning and the end.

In the case of being jaded because of the nasty dark real world. I would challenge you to think about this, certainly when you are young bad things happen. You lose a toy.

Another kid is mean to you. You fall down and get hurt, or you're sick and you're stuck inside when everyone else gets to have fun. What did you do back then? Did you completely give up on having fun because the world was too harsh? No way. As soon as you were able, you got back out there and had fun. You weren't naive either you knew what things meant. If the kid was nasty to you on the playground, you understood that not everyone in life was going to play nice. And if you broke or lost of one of your toys, you understood that nothing lasts forever and that life is not all candy canes and lollipops. However, regardless of all the negative information that came your way, you remained focused on having fun and the smiles and happiness went on and on. I'm not sure why, but for some reason, at some point, people change their focus and they begin to focus on how bad the world is and the people that are in it. Do you know what we call these people? They're called skeptics, critics, cynics, nonbelievers, party poopers, pessimists, doubters, haters, and stupid heads.

If you feel like you fit the bill for any one of those, or have ever been called one (or more) of them, then I would like to challenge you to change your focus. Remember, just because the ugly things in life exist, it does not mean the beautiful things go way. Our reality is made up of where we hold the majority of our focus. I am not asking you to look outside when it's raining and tell yourself that there is no rain, I am asking you to see the rain and go dance in it.

Speaking of which, do you remember how much fun it was to jump in puddles when you were a kid? Whatever happened to that? The things that you used to do for fun didn't change, you did. All of those things can be fun again if you allow them to be.

What about this idea of not having fun because you're supposed to be mature. Who came up with that idea anyway?? What is hilarious about that statement is that the normally the people who tell you that you need to stop having fun and be mature are the same people who don't

have very much fun themselves, and their dreams,
potential and quality of life all suffer because of it. Is that
really the opinion of someone you want to listen to? I would
really hope not. If anything, you should see the results that
they get in their life or lack thereof. I would suggest you
should do the opposite of what they say. Again, I believe in
win-win, I believe that you can be mature and still have fun.
Just because you have responsibilities, duties, deadlines,
bills, and maybe even kids of your own doesn't mean you
should stop having fun. The idea has been spread around of
"one or the other" type of thinking. This type of thinking
would lead most people to believe that those who focus on
having fun are not responsible, and have an aversion to the
real world. That thinking would also lead people to believe
that people who focus on having fun are selfish, and have a
Peter Pan syndrome where they are unwilling to grow up.

Let's look at some of those beliefs a little more closely shall
we? The idea that people who are focused on having fun are
not responsible and have an aversion to the real world would
lead you to believe that people who did the opposite are one
hundred percent responsible and are greatly involved in and
contribute to the real world. Which we know is total lie.
There are many people who practically neglect having fun
altogether yet are not responsible whatsoever. Likewise,
these same people who have minimal amounts of fun often
are the people in society who contribute and participates the
least. This shows us is that just because you have fun or do
not have fun does not necessarily mean one thing or the
other. And speaking of the real world, it seems to be filled
with people that are absolute professionals at this "one or the
other" type of thinking. So I would ask you, is that really the
kind of world you want to be a part of anyway?

What about this belief that people who have fun are selfish?
I know plenty of people that don't necessarily have a ton of
fun but are totally selfish. Conversely, I know people who
revolve their life around fun and they are some of the most
giving and selfless people I have ever met. I believe that
what happens is that people start to confuse being childish

with having fun. Which is understandable because the age at which you have the most fun is when you're a child, so it is only logical that fun and being childish becomes somewhat blurred in peoples minds. But, as we just discovered, traits that we might think are childish like being selfish are not behaviors that are strictly for children. We see it in adults all the time. Unfortunately, due to this blurred definition of what fun is, as we get older we begin to a catch words like:

Irresponsible

Selfish

Foolish

Unsophisticated

Not serious

Feather Headed

Un-Profound

Senseless

Impractical

These are all words that people in the "real world" associate with fun. Pretty sad, don't you think? What about some of the words that people use to define fun who see it as a necessity to life. Let's look at some of those words:

Happy

Amusing

Entertaining

Joyful

Merry

Pleasant

Silly

Cheer

Delight

Exciting

Enjoyment

Priceless

I want you to study the last list of words intently and think
about how important it is to have those things in your life.
And if right now you're saying or feeling like those things
are not as prevalent in your life is you'd like them to be, I
would like you to get curious about what your life would be
like if all of those words were words you could use to
describe your daily life. That'd be pretty cool, wouldn't it?

Let's look at the people who believe they can't have fun
because they are professionals. Well, I admire your wish to
look serious and have other people take you seriously,
however that is no excuse to sacrifice your fun. This is
another area where we can apply the win-win thinking. I
believe that you can both be a professional and have fun.
Remember the famous people I listed who went after their
dreams and had fun, while all of them were or are very
professional at the same time? You may say that it is
important to be professional so that you can be a valuable
worker. Well guess what. In this day and age, that most
valuable employees and business owners are people who are
creative and innovative.

Let's look at another list:

Bill Gates – Mircosoft

Sergey Brin & Larry Page – Google

Steve Jobs – Apple

Pierre Omidyar – Ebay

Jerry Yang & David Filo – Yahoo

What do all of these people have in common other than
having multi-billion-dollar companies? To create these
companies and to become so valuable they all had to be
immensely creative and innovative. And I will put BBQ
sauce on my hat and eat it if they didn't have fun in the
process. That is because being creative and innovative is
synonymous with having fun to them. So, while you are
frantic about trying to be as professional those guys are,
hanging out doing whatever they want, it hardly seems fair,
does it? But it is fair. That's the beauty of the whole thing.
As a matter of fact, there is a new software company called
Atlassian and they have done something very interesting.

They started off by creating what they call FedEx days
where they give their employees 24 hours during the
workweek to work on anything they want and the only rule
is that it cannot be work-related. What happens is they get to
use all of their cool software and hardware on things that are
purely fun and interesting to them. The next day everyone
gets together to share their ideas and what they've come up
with. It is called FedEx day because everyone must deliver
something overnight. Similarly Google implements an 80/20
principle, where 20% of an employee's time may be focused
on anything they want throughout the day. And it comes as
no surprise that over half of Google's new products that
come to market are created during the 20% time. The highest
level so far that I've seen of this creativity nourishing work
system is a system called ROWE. ROWE stands for Results
Only Work Environment. In a ROWE there is no such thing

as an employee schedule; schedules don't even exist. An
employee does not have to show up to the office at a certain
time, or show up at all. The one and only rule in a ROWE is
that the employee's work gets done each week. Where they
work, how they work, and when they work is completely up
to them.

Across the board, companies who utilize this strategy see
employee productivity and creativity increase phenomenally.
All of these big companies seem to get that having fun is
crucial to expanding and growing. This shows us that the
need or desire to be "professional" is becoming a thing of the
past and the need for employees to be more creative and
innovative has become the hot new commodity.

Now the big picture is really starting to unfold. Not only is
fun important strictly from a personal level to increase your
enjoyment and happiness in life, but as you can see being
creative and having fun also has massive career benefits as
well. What a concept!

Hopefully you can see the real importance fun can have on a
person's life. Whether in life or business there are always
going to be problems the challenge is that the majority of
these problems are more like puzzles. They do not have
clear-cut answers or solutions. The linear right-brained
thinking often just doesn't work when it comes to challenges
that require out of the box type thinking. This idea of win-
win that I have been mentioning is proof of that. Logical
thinking would lead us to believe that a given path or
solution must be this or that, never this **and** that.

The core principle that lies behind many of the problems we
face individually and culturally have solutions that can only
be arrived at by pushing the boundaries of what we believe is
possible. One of the greatest examples I can give you of this
is a puzzle created in 1944 by a man named Karl Dunker.
The name of the puzzle is *The Candle Problem*. The object
of *The Candle Problem* is to attach the candle to the wall so
that the candle does not drip wax onto the table and you may

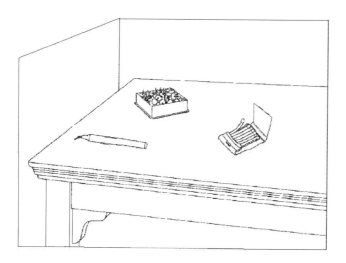

only use the object on the table, the candle, a box of tacks, and a book of matches. As seen here:

The solution to this problem can only be found by using creative thinking. During psychological testing, people who approached this problem with logical linear thinking found it very difficult or impossible to find a solution. On the other hand, more creative outside the box thinkers generally solved this problem with relative ease. Can you solve this problem? Take a moment and try it out.

If you were able to solve this problem, congratulations! If you couldn't solve it all that means is your creative thinking brain needs some exercise and that's ok. That's why we're here. The solution to this puzzle can be seen below.

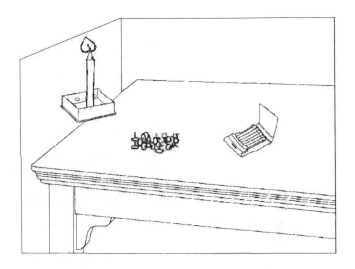

One of the main obstacles of not only this challenge but many of the problems we face in life has to do with overcoming what we call functional fixedness. Functional fixedness is a cognitive bias that limits us to using an object only in the way it has traditionally been used. Duncker defines functional fixedness as a, "Mental block against using an object in a new way that is required to solve a problem." Experiments in paradigm shifts show us that people who are given familiar objects to solve unfamiliar tasks often are unable to overcome their bias and ultimately are unable to solve the given task.

Let's now look at the other side of the coin. When five-year-old children were given the same experiments to test their functional fixedness, it was found that they had none. Children age five and below had no functional fixedness whatsoever. Any given object could be used to solve any given task. Think about it, when you were a kid didn't you use your imagination more? Of course you did, that old blanket or towel could become a super hero cape one minute, or the wall to an awesome fort the next. A pencil could be anything from a rocket ship to a submarine. The possibilities were endless.

Back then, the sky wasn't even a limit. A football helmet turned instantly into a space helmet and suddenly visiting other galaxies was a breeze. Literally, anything was possible back then because there were no rules and no limits. Having fun was simple then because adventure was always right around the corner.

I would hope by now you can see all of the traditional excuses that people have to avoid having fun are honestly not very valid at all. Likewise, I hope you are starting to see the personal and professional benefits of having fun. When you get right down to it having fun should not be an option, having fun should be an absolute must in your life. Let's now look into some of the ways that you can start having more fun. I believe there are a few key elements to reigniting the fun in your life.

1. You must change your beliefs about having fun and why it is important. How can you begin to have fun again? What is it going to take to get back to a mindset where fun as a priority? Once you have oriented your mind towards having fun, it will become very easy to make playtime possible.

2. Once you are committed to and love the idea of having fun again it's time to figure out exactly how you're going to have fun. Unfortunately, the same ways you used play as a kid probably aren't going to work anymore. The playground, a sandbox, and a swing set, sadly are just not built for adults. But that's okay because there are plenty of other ways to have fun. Here is a list of ideas that will help get you started.

Art - make it, go see it, or both

Music -play it, make it, listen to it or all of the above

Hiking

Go to a park

Go camping

Go to the movies

Read a book

Have a dinner party

Take a bath

Go for a drive

Complete a puzzle

Write a poem, play, or story

Go to an aquarium

Go to a garden and smell the roses

Lie down and watch the clouds drift by

Rearrange your room or house

Buy some new clothes

Play a sport

Go for a walk

Cook or bake something for someone

Go to the beach

Go on an adventure

Find somewhere new to explore

I would like you take a look at this list and see if anything on the list that excites you. If you have done some of these things in the past and enjoyed them, how can you get started doing them again? You will be amazed to see what happens to your quality of life when you get back to having fun. Don't you miss having fun? Don't you miss the feelings of laughter and being carefree? Make the decision now that you are going to be more like a kid again.

In order to have more fun and be more like a kid you're going to need to rediscover some of the qualities that are necessary to have unlimited amounts of fun. Those qualities are:

Imagination

Curiosity

Spontaneity

Adventure

Imagination: Your imagination is what makes everything possible. There is an old motto that says, "I'll believe it when I see it." Now some people may view this adage as negative or pessimistic. Wayne Dyer even has a modified version that says, "I'll see it when I believe it." However, I think that when looked at with a specific perspective, it is actually quite fitting. You see, anything that a person can see in their mind, and believe in their heart, can be achieved through their work. All of the greatest milestones, discoveries, and achievements of man all started out as a simple image in their mind. Without the power of imagination, none of these great successes would have ever been possible. Now you're starting to see that imagination just isn't for kids huh? I truly believe the power of your imagination makes all the difference. Not only to come up with grand ideas, but also to creatively find ways to make those ideas a reality. Think about your imagination, how much do you use it on a daily basis? How strong would you say that your powers of imagination are? Here is a quick exercise to test your imaginative skills.

Imagine a red balloon. Now imagine the color of the balloon changing to yellow. Imagine the yellow balloon changing into a glass bottle. Imagine the air around the glass bottle turning to sand and the bottle falling to the ground. Imagine a glass bottle turning into a ship and sailing through the sea of sand. Zoom in on this picture and look at the wheel of the ship. Zoom out until you can barely see a ship at all. Go back into a normal view. Now view the ship and sea of sand from 360° and rotate the image in your mind. Look at the back of the ship and see it moving away from you. Pan to the left until you can see the front of the ship moving towards you. From this view do a flyover from the front to the back of the ship. As you look around you notice that you the ship in a bottle and the sea of sand are all inside of a red and yellow balloon.

This exercise helps test your ability to change the relationship and context in which things happen. It forces you to use the side of your brain that is creative so that what you would normally consider impossible becomes possible. Being able to view an object in a three dimensional space from multiple angles exercises your spatial intelligence, which is one of the key areas of your brain related to problem solving.

What did you struggle with during that exercise?

What parts of that exercise came easily to you?

This will begin to give you an idea of the current fitness level of your imagination. Make a habit to use your imagination at least 30 minutes every day. That does not mean that you have to take 30 minutes out of your day to sit down and focus on training your imagination. Although just as food for thought, think about what would happen if you did. Luckily your imagination can be trained very easily you can use your imagination while you're commuting to work, while you are doing chores, while you are at work, when you're in the shower, when you are cooking, and etc. At any moment, you can use your imagination.

There are plenty of opportunities for you to use your imagination throughout the day and as long as you're aware and intentional, you that can take advantage of them. Not only that, but using your imagination by itself can be fun, which means there are plenty of great chances for you to have fun throughout the day.

Curiosity: If there is one characteristic that makes kids as fun and enthusiastic as they are it is curiosity. When a person is curious, they are hopeful about what can happen and what they can do. Curiosity propels you towards the unknown in a way that is exciting and uncertain. A man named Abraham Maslow created what is called a Hierarchy of Needs. He goes on to explain that one of the greatest human needs that we have, is the need to know. I certainly agree with this idea because of what I know about human potential. If a person has limitless potential, then certainly they will always be curious about what the next step is. Think about one of the most annoying traits of two-year-olds, that stage where they get to where all they do is ask, "Why?" As annoying as it may be to parents, it clearly illustrates this human need to know. And as soon as a person stops being curious that is the exact moment they stop learning and growing.

Now it's time to evaluate your personal curiosity. From day to day how curious are you? And when a sense of curiosity strikes you how much do you indulge in it? Sadly, because of most people's focus is on being "responsible" and living in the "real world," when an urge to be curious mounts up it is often subdued and ignored. The habit of kicking your curiosity to the curb has got to go. If you are going to have any chance at having massive amounts of fun, curiosity is going to be a key factor. The great news is because curiosity is hardwired into your genetics is not a skill that you need to develop. It is simply a characteristic that you need to nourish and encourage.

How can you start to be more curious right now?

In what areas of your life can you apply more curiosity?

How can you get more interested and excited about the things in your life?

How can you learn more about a current subject you enjoy?

How can you become a happy-go-lucky detective?

Think about some of the greatest achievements in your life. Prior to accomplishing them, can you remember how curious you were about them? Wasn't that curiosity a large part of the driving force that moved you toward those great successes? Curiosity is what helps keep your life interesting. Everything from your personal life, your social life, relationships, friends and family can all benefit from you being more curious. We see examples of the opposite all the time; people who have lost their passion for life, who at one time were completely compelled. Their personal lives, professional lives and relationships are on the verge of ruin because everything has become routine and boring. Due to the zombie like nature of day-to-day life people rarely break out of the norm and indulge in their curiosity.

Spontaneity: The more curious you are the more spontaneous you tend to be. Being spontaneous is a huge factor when it comes to having fun because having fun should not always be planned. Don't get me wrong I certainly believe that with everyone's busy schedules these days, going out of your way to schedule time to have fun is important, otherwise it may never get done. But the element of surprise and spontaneity is immensely valuable. Being spontaneous shakes up your world and spices things up and if one of the major complaints is that life is too boring and predictable, then without a doubt some spontaneity is needed.

What's great about being spontaneous is that it is like fuel for the soul. Let's go back and look at the behavior of children. They are completely spontaneous, one moment they can be eating breakfast at the table and the next they're up and dancing around. No one told them to do that, they had not planned to do that in advance, they just had an urge to dance so they got up and did it. Let's look at that ability from a success standpoint. One of the biggest factors that keeps most people from their success is simply the fact that they stand in their own way. They have an idea for a goal, or a business, or an invention and this idea would greatly help themselves and the rest of mankind. Yet they begin to allow the inner trappings of their mind to sabotage all of their momentum. That is probably why only two percent of the population truly lives life on their terms. Kids do practically the opposite, if they have an idea or if they is something they want to do, they do not hesitate, they do not think twice, and they do not put any limitations on themselves. They just go for it.

What would your life be like if you had that kind of mentality where you could just think and do it? Are you starting to see the value of being spontaneous? Being spontaneous is similar to curiosity in that it is not necessarily a skill you need to develop, however it may feel that way if your powers of spontaneity are at an all-time low. Flexing your spontaneity muscle is easier than you may think it is really a combination of two things.

Indulging in your curiosity.

And embracing your urges.

What that means is if something catches your attention or you become curious about something, then by all means, you need to go check it out. If you see something that is interesting to you, go look at it and examine it further. If you walk by a store and you are curious about what is inside, go in and take a look. If you are wondering what somebody is thinking, ask them. All of these little side adventures begin to add unexpected juice to your life. This is fun and enjoyable. You weren't planning on it but it is only possible when you indulge in your curiosity.

Then there your urges, embracing your urges has a tendency to be looked down upon because it is commonly thought that giving in to your urges means that you are doing something bad. Of course, I recommend being personally responsible and using your moral compass but at the same time, but I do not believe that you should neglect your urges all together. It is simply a matter of being aware of your urges and handling them intelligently. So, for example, if you have the urge to get up and dance while you're at the breakfast table, or get up and go for a walk, those are urges that if given in to would make your life better.

This is not about giving into urges that will decrease the quality of your life like overeating, oversleeping, or drinking too much. I am talking about giving in to the fun silly urges you have or sometimes even the grand adventurous ones.

Adventure: Speaking of adventure how many of those have you had lately? Be honest with yourself, how many adventures do you have on a weekly basis? If the number floating around in your head right now is less than seven, then it's time to ramp it up. The big bone of contention with adventure is that everyone thinks the word adventure is synonymous with some type of epic event, in some exotic location, that is filled to the brim with mystery, intrigue, and high stakes.

That's a very strict criteria for adventure wouldn't you say? If that definition is the only way that you could experience adventure, then the only people that could have adventures would be James Bond and Blackbeard (the pirate). It is time to redefine your definition of adventure and expanded it so that adventure is possible every day. Surely children do not need all of the crazy ingredients of adventure that we as adults place on it. Luckily, if you begin to apply your abilities of imagination, curiosity, and spontaneity than fulfilling your need for adventure will be a snap.

If you started exercising your imagination, curiosity, and spontaneity, you would automatically begin to have more adventures. And adventure by definition is an engagement that is exciting and bold. By that definition, a lot of things could be considered adventurous. At any given time no matter where you are, you are capable of doing something exciting and bold. Remember that the next time you are in your home, at the mall, grocery store, at work, or anywhere else. Without a doubt, adventures will not fall into your lap and since this is true, you must not only be open to them but you must also live in a state of expectation. While living like Blackbeard the pirate may not fit into how you want to live your life, the hunger to seek out and find adventure is certainly a noteworthy trait.

Fun does not have to be something that disappears from your life once you reach a certain age. Having fun on a regular basis does not mean that you are a delinquent or irresponsible. Having more fun in your life will increase the quality of every area in your life. Having fun when you're older is not difficult or hard to do. Professionally, having more fun will help you become more creative and innovative in your career which inherently means that you will become more valuable as an employee. Yet after all the sound and logical points, my hope for you is to get back to a place in life where you want to have more fun simply for the sake of having fun.

Take Action!

Fun is the juice of life! Find a way to incorporate fun into your life each and every day.

What are your beliefs about fun?

How can fun become a priority to you?

What can you do today that would be fun?

How can you start to exercise your imagination, curiosity, spontaneity, and adventurous side?

Put this book down and take action now!

Personal Patterns of Excellence

We are all different. We all have different beliefs, morals, standards, and expectations. What might motivate one person may do nothing for someone else. What may excite one person may be absolutely boring to someone else. I have created what I call Personal Patterns of Excellence. As you move forward on your journey of self-mastery is important for you to know what your Personal Patterns of Excellence are.

Chances are you have already been exposed to some different types of self-help material. And surely, with this book you are being exposed to even more. However, what is important for you to know is that not all of the information is going to work for you. That is why as you learn and begin to implement some of these tools, you must be honest with yourself. You have to ask yourself, "Is this something that's really going to work for me?"

It is no different from a career or a relationship. There are some careers out there that would be perfect for you and there are also careers that absolutely could not and would not ever be a fit for you. Likewise, there are people out there who are potentially your soul mate with which you could have a deep and meaningful connection with effortlessly. And there are also people out there who, no matter how hard you try, will absolutely drive you crazy. The real basis of Personal Patterns of Excellence is simply a very deep and strong understanding of how you personally operate and then taking advantage of that information so you can maximize your daily performance. You must make some important differentiations here. Undoubtedly, for you to be able to tap into your peak potential, to revolutionize yourself, you must change. However, there are parts of who you are at your core that will never change and are a large part of what you need in order to succeed.

As you go along, be aware of the things you are trying to change about yourself. Decide whether they are parts of your false-self that you can truly get rid of. Or, are you trying to change parts of who you are deep down inside? Because if you're trying to change the fundamental aspects of who you are, then that is no different than trying to change your very DNA... It's not possible.

Another large component of Personal Patterns of Excellence is doing what you know. So many people *know* the things that get them in trouble. But very few people actually use that information to keep them out of trouble. Examples could be: staying out too late, eating the wrong kinds of food, taking on more work than you can handle, choosing to reward yourself before a task is complete, or anything else that you know is going to make you feel some type of pain or discomfort but not doing anything about it.

On the other hand, you have people who use the information to their advantage. They *do* what they know. If they know that staying out too late is going to throw them off their game and potentially ruin their day the next day, then guess what. They don't go out or if they do, they're smart about it and they make sure to get home at a reasonable hour. If they are out at a restaurant with a bunch of friends and everyone is eating the atomic chicken wings with extra nuclear hot sauce and they have acid reflux or get bad indigestion from food like that, guess what. They order something else!

Personal Patterns of Excellence really has two parts. The first is doing what you know, and the second is knowing what to do. For example, when going to workout, you would need to know that you are going to go to the gym, actually go, and know exactly what you are going to do when you get there. The part that makes it personal is you have to know exactly what exercises are going to work for you. What works for some people may not work for you. This is about knowing how you get the best results and putting that information to use.

What I would like to challenge you to do is to look at your life. Look at all the different categories of your life and think about where there are aspects that you can really tap into your Personal Patterns of Excellence. Think about your career. What do you know about yourself that you could apply to your job that would make your overall experience at your career better? What about your home life? What are some things that you absolutely know for a fact that will increase the quality of your home life? It is time to take these things you know about yourself and become more aware of them, and then use that awareness to put these things you know into action.

There might be parts of your life that you examine and find you don't have many or even any Personal Patterns of Excellence. Don't let that scare you or discourage. That simply means you have the opportunity now to create some. You have a chance to try some new things that will build up your character and increase your personal power. You can begin to do this by looking at some of the results that you are getting in different areas and focusing on the areas where you are getting results that are below your expectations. From there begin looking at everything that leads up to that end result so you can begin to understand why it is not the way you want it to be.

For example if you get to work and you have low energy, you're groggy, and unmotivated in general, then think about everything you did beginning with when you woke up that led up to that moment. If you hit the snooze button eight or nine times, got out of bed at the last minute, were unorganized getting your things together, rushed through breakfast or didn't eat one at all, and made it out the door thinking to yourself that you are probably going to be late. When you add all of those factors together, it is pretty obvious that you would arrive at work with low energy, feeling groggy, and unmotivated.

Often times the solution to helping you find your Personal Patterns of Excellence can be as simple as doing the opposite of what you are currently doing to get a new result. Your new approach might be something to the effect of packing your things the night before so they are ready for you when you walk out the door, waking up earlier and doing some type of exercise, eating a full and healthy breakfast, and leaving the house knowing you have ample time to make it to work. Whatever the areas of your life are that you are currently unsatisfied with, start to think about what type of opposite actions you can start taking to produce new and more powerful results. Sometimes it's more complicated than just doing the opposite to get a new result. In that case, I would challenge you to get creative and ask yourself, "What can I do that is new that will produce a better result that I'm currently getting?" Remember, your brain is set up in a way to serve you as long as you ask it the correct type of questions. This is all about setting yourself up for victory, making it so that success flows in your life.

Double check and make sure your motivation for change comes from yourself and not other people or what you think you "should" do. Here is a story from one of my clients to show you what I mean.

An artist I worked with from Italy had this challenge. In his culture, it was natural for him to drink wine throughout the day and out of a regular straight glass. He would be doused with inspiration throughout the day and with his wine in one hand and his paintbrush in the other, he would create beautiful works of art. When he came to America, he was ashamed of his ritual because he saw the American culture did not have a similar lifestyle, so he stopped doing it. Can you guess what happened? His inspiration for painting plummeted. And he didn't want to invite people over to his house because he was embarrassed by the thought that they might think he was an alcoholic that drank wine out of a straight juice glass.

I explained to him that he had nothing to be ashamed of. His drinking had nothing to do with him trying to suppress any negative feelings or cope with some type of depression. He drank a moderate amount of wine throughout the day simply because that was part of the culture where he grew up. And after he concluded that being himself was actually a good thing, he started partaking in his Personal Pattern of Excellence again. When he did, an interesting thing happened. His friends would come over and see him drinking the wine and asked why he was drinking in the middle of the day. After he explained to them that it was part of who he was, they were inspired. His friends wanted to figure out what their Personal Patterns of Excellence were as well, because they saw the great results they produced for him. He came back to me the next week and explained how he was so glad that he had gotten back to being himself. From there forward, his friends didn't judge him. In fact, they were inspired by him.

Do you have rituals or habits of which you are ashamed? I would encourage you to think about why that is. Are they actually bad habits that are detrimental to your life? Or are they in fact Personal Patterns of Excellence? Just because they may be different or odd compared to what everyone else does, does not mean that they are bad. You must have the confidence to carry out your Personal Patterns of Excellence even if other people are around. Remember they are nothing to be ashamed of. If they make your life better and increase the quality of your life overall, then the fact is that is those are kinds of things you must embrace. Here is another story from one of my greatest clients.

To tap into his creativity, Tom used to walk around in circles. For some reason this really got his brain working and he would always come up with amazing ideas this way. So much so, that he ended up becoming very successful and buying a large home. This was a great personal victory for him because he had come from great poverty and had always wished to own a nice home. With all the excitement and space in his new home, he had plenty of space to walk in circles but for some reason he had forgotten about his powerful ritual. It was not long after that that his world started to fall apart. The quality of his work started to decline. He felt like he was losing his edge, and indeed he was. He came to me a total wreck. I was able to uncover his

Personal Pattern of Excellence by asking him what the difference was between when he was successful and when he wasn't. At first, he wasn't sure. It seemed like things should be better with the new home and all. I asked him to lay out the details of his creative process for me. And as he explained it, suddenly I heard him gasp and say, "The walking!" He realized he had stopped doing the one thing that was making the biggest difference in his overall performance. Immediately after our conversation, he went back to walking in circles and everything returned to normal. The quality of his work went back up and he regained his edge. He became so committed to his circle walking that he created a room in his house strictly for creative thinking and circle walking.

This story just goes to show you that sometimes it can be the strangest littlest things that can inspire our truest self to come out. This is why it is so important to be aware of them and how you can use them to your advantage. It is also important to embrace them, as well. There must be no shame around your Personal Patterns of Excellence.

This clearly demonstrates that knowing who you are and living it on a daily basis does not have to be something you are embarrassed about. Even if your ritual is different from most people it can still be a source of inspiration for them. And if nothing else, it allows you to tap into your greatness.

Take Action!

What are your Personal Patterns of Excellence?

What are the ideal conditions you need to succeed?

How can you become more aware of your Personal Patterns of Excellence and put them to use?

Do you have habits that tie into your Personal Patterns of Excellence that you are ashamed or embarrassed about? If so, how can you free yourself from the guilt and embrace these habits?

Put this book down and take action now!

The Art of Change

There is one thing that you must never forget and that is out of all the uncertainty in your life and in this world, there is one thing that always was, always is, and always will be. That one thing is change. Change is constantly happening all around us. Days change to night. Summer turns to winter. Young become old and hot becomes cold. As ironic as it is, change one of only things of which we can be certain.

If you observe nature and the planet Earth in general, you will see that change happens constantly all the time, all day every day. If we look beyond that, we can see that the moon, the sun, and the stars constantly change as well. If we look even further, we see the Milky Way, all the galaxies, and the entire Universe constantly changes.

Yet for some strange reason humans tend to be the only ones who want to resist change. People will put themselves in amazingly uncomfortable and unhappy situations simply so that they can avoid change. The idea of change for many people inflicts an utterly paralyzing state of fear. Why is it people are willing to put themselves through such torture?

Much of it has to do with a person's comfort zone. It also has to do with their inability to face themselves and to resolve their inner conflict. There is a state of fear that comes from one of two places. The first of those two places being a feeling of inadequacy, meaning that people have a great fear that they are not smart enough, good enough, or deserving enough for anything better than what they have. They don't believe they can achieve anything better.

The second category comes from a fear of one's own power, as I also mentioned earlier. This is what I call the "what if" fear. That means that a person is afraid of all the potential possibilities of their success and power. They end up reaching conclusions that make them believe that to achieve such things would, in the end, produce negative effects.

The funny part here is that the people who are least accepting of change seem to be the ones who are affected most negatively by it. When a person resists change, they resist the bigger and better self within. In addition, when a person resists change they fail to prepare and adapt to the world that is changing around them as well. This will create a large level of pain and discomfort.

When it comes to your personal and professional success, the ability to be flexible is absolutely crucial. Your personal level of flexibility will determine how much or little you are affected by change. It is flexibility that gives you the power to flow with change as it happens.

How does a person become more flexible?

Perception: Your perception of what change means defines how you feel about change and ultimately what you do or do not do about it. One of the biggest defining factors in the quality of your life is simply the perception that you have attached to it. It works no differently with change and how you perceive it.

Most people perceive change as a bad thing. And most people view change as the end of something rather than the beginning. Change becomes very similar to fear in this sense because for many people, change means the anticipation of pain. Therefore, change and fear become synonymous.

The great part is that change is very much like fear. However, it is not a bad thing. Change like fear, is simply an opportunity for us to get better in some way. Change is a way for us to take our personal or professional lives to the next level. The real question is not how you can avoid change. Rather, how can you embrace it? How can you shift your perception so that your personal definition of change is something that you are ready for and are excited by?

Again, this is an area of your life where it is very powerful to have an open mind. The more open-minded you are about change and what it means, the more open you can become to the potential possibilities that change brings. Being open-minded about change also accesses your possibility thinking. When you're possibility thinking is turned on you at can react to change completely differently.

The more flexible you are, the more you can have a positive perception of change. The more open-minded you can be about change, the more you are going to view change in a positive way. You'll find what happens when you do this is that all the sudden the problems that change once created now become solutions. You no longer view things as the end but rather the beginning. Rather than cursing and shaking your fist at God, wondering why he has chosen you to punish, you are grateful because your life has variety, and on top of that, the kind of variety that makes you a better person.

Anticipation: Being able to see what's coming is the next step in mastering change. The fact is that change can and will happen no matter what, and you should know that you have some choices about what you can do about it. For one, you can be like the majority of people and pretend change doesn't exist. You can hide from it and hope that you never have to face it. Then when change comes along you are completely afraid and unprepared for it, and will find yourself in an even worse state than you were to begin with.

Secondly, you can alter your perception of change. You can adjust your level of flexibility towards change. Then you also become more open-minded about change. If you were to do that, there is no doubt that it would be great. Although that means that change is still something that takes you by surprise.

However, your ability to anticipate change will put you way ahead of the curve. It is one thing to be ready for change, but it is something entirely different to be able to see it coming. The benefit here is that if you can see change coming, then you can begin to do what is necessary to prepare and shift so that when that change comes you are already in the optimal position.

As much as it is important to live in the moment, it is also very powerful to be able to see into the future. The more you practice the ability to anticipate change, the more you are going to be able to control the direction of your life and ultimately your destiny. What's even better is that if you build up your ability to anticipate change, often times you will see challenges or problems that lie ahead of you that you can avoid completely.

It comes down to a conscious effort to become aware of what's going on in your life. More than that, it is about taking responsibility for your life. If you have a very specific way that you want to live your life, then it is in your best interest to do everything you can to make sure that you stay on the path that you have created for yourself.

Trust me, there is going to be plenty of change and uncertainty in your life for which you will never be ready. That being the case, you owe it to yourself to master the art of change. The whole key here is asking yourself, "How much of my life is in my control?" Once you've answered that question, then the next question is how can I increase that?

Become Change: There is one final step in the art of change. It is the most difficult yet the most rewarding step of all. It is one thing to be open-minded and flexible about change. It's even better if you can add the ability to anticipate change to your life. Although to truly have the power to shape your destiny, to live life on your terms, and to master your fate, you must become change.

You must reach a stage where change is something that you not only anticipate but also you crave. You must become an agent of change. You must become so fanatical about the improvement and progress of your life in every category that you are constantly doing something about it. Complacency

to you must become like a prison. Stagnation in your
mind must equal damnation. As drastic as that is, you must
know that there is no way to achieve drastic results without a
drastic mindset to follow.

I want to challenge you to become like a hunter; to seek out
and find ways that you can change yourself and you can
change things around you. Integrate this idea into part of
your quest for life. Seek out and track down areas of your
life where you have been avoiding change. Then make a
conscious and deliberate effort to make a positive change in
that area.

In the end, there are really only two options. You can be
affected by a change. Alternatively, you can be responsible
for it. You'll find the people in this world that are the most
successful, don't wait for things to happen. They make
decisions, they create plans, and they make things happen.

In order to master the art of change, you must have the
strength to take control and own change. Make change just
as much a part of you as your own beating heart. Do this and
your fate will be completely in your hands.

Take Action!

Seize this moment to further your understanding of change. Make the decision that you are no longer going to be afraid of change but that you are going to embrace it. Make a decision that you are going to master change so that you can better control your life and in the end your destiny.

What are your beliefs about change?

How can you embrace change?

How can you see change as an opportunity?

How can you become a catalyst?

What new belief about change do you need to adopt?

From there, begin to think about how you can anticipate change. Ask yourself how you can learn from experiences, and use that knowledge in the future. Start to exercise your ability to become more aware. Become more aware of the things that have gone on in your life, that are currently happening and that you can foresee happening. This will train your insight and your ability to see into the future.

Lastly, start to think about how you can become an agent of change. Start to look into the areas of your life where you may avoid change. Ask yourself what you can immediately start doing to make a difference in that area. Remember that true power becomes yours when you become change.

Put this book down and take action now!

PART III

<u>Tools</u>

In order to build the life of your dreams is it necessary to have the right tools for the job. Clarity, and self-love, are the foundation. Once you have unleashed all your passion and enthusiasm, then it is time to master the actual systems that will help you make a reality out of all the greatness that is in your heart, mind, and soul. Imagine yourself as a block of marble. By establishing clarity about who you are and what your purpose is, you remove yourself from the quarry so that you may stand alone as an individual. By having self-love you remove the excess rock that covers up your ultimate-self. And the following tools will allow you to do the detailed work that will give you the ability to fully chip away at the remaining pieces of metaphorical rock that surround the masterpiece that is your true self.

One of the biggest similarities I see in the clients that I work with is that they all have a great capacity for improvement. However, one of the major things they lack is the actual set of tools to get the job done. Unfortunately building a dream life takes more than enthusiasm and good intentions. I have seen stress levels at all time highs simply because either a person is trying to fit a triangle peg into a square hole or they are trying to push a door that is meant to be pulled.

The real magic happens when you combine your passion and excitement with effective tools. This combination allows you to not only envision a better life but also gives you the means to make it a reality. They must work together as one. As the creator of your life, it is your responsibility to master both of these areas so that you can unlock all of your potential. We will begin with rituals.

I.P.I.D.D.
The destiny shaping decision

IPIDD stands for **I**ntentional **P**ersonal **I**mprovement **D**one **D**aily. It is a system that I created after studying the work of Dr. William Deming. Dr. Deming is best known for his work in Japan. After the Cold War Dr. Deming was sent to Japan to help rebuild the Japanese economy. While he was there, he taught Japanese businesses a philosophy that would eventually be come to known as Kaizen, which is Japanese for "improvement" or "change for the better." At that time, the Japanese economy was in such dire straits that they adopted Dr. Deming's philosophy wholeheartedly. And to this day, the Japanese economy has continued to implement Kaizen into their business practices.

After I saw what a huge difference this principle could make, I decided to modify it so that I can apply it to my life and the lives of the people with which I work. I would encourage you to take this principle as seriously as possible. The more you incorporate this philosophy into your life, the greater it will be.

The thing about personal improvement is that many people approach it with the wrong mindset, primarily because they have the idea of habits rather than rituals in their head. Their hope is that after 30 or 90 days that this new aspect of self-improvement that they've been focusing on will become automatic. And it is that mindset specifically that robs people of their potential and keeps them stuck.

People like the idea of habits because it alludes to the idea that their greatness is on autopilot and they don't have to work for their results. The reality is that anything great and worth achieving takes work. More importantly, anything that you truly want in life should be something that you are willing to work towards forever. Just as much as this is about shifting your mentality from one that revolves around habits and results you don't have to work for, IPIDD also comes down to shifting your definition about what work is and what it means.

For some reason or another, people attach negative feeling to the word "work." This proves challenging when it comes to changing your life because people naturally have a built-in desire to avoid things that are painful. Interestingly enough even if there is a multitude of positive logical reasons for a person to do something, that expectancy of pain that comes along with the work involved is enough to keep someone in their current state.

When you begin to live by the principle of IPIDD, your perspective on *work* begins to change. Once you begin to see *work* as a positive thing, that's when you can fully take advantage of IPIDD and the ritualistic mentality that comes with it.

Let's take a look at how you can use IPIDD to build new levels of self-discipline while drastically improving the quality of your life. Let me ask you this question, which is going to be better for you: working out one day a week or working out five days a week? Obviously, if you work out five days a week it is going to be better for you. Self-improvement is no different. To get the maximum benefit out of self-improvement, and ultimately uncover your ultimate-self, there has to be a serious time commitment. That's the only way it'll ever happen. There is no shortcut. There is no back door. There is no express lane to achieving serious results. You have to dedicate serious time.

Think about anything that you're currently good at. The reason that you're so good at it is not because you did it every now and then. It is because you committed a fair amount of time to that thing, be it a skill, hobby, or what have you. Think about the mindset you had to have in order to become really good at something. You knew the hard work that was involved and welcomed the challenge. We live in a day and age of instant gratification. We all want the magic bullet, secret pill, or potion. Well guess what? They don't exist. The truth is there is something to be said for reaching premium results through hard work, dedication, and perseverance. Also, you are more likely to hold onto and maintain your results if you know what hard work and effort you had put in to acquire them. Though you may live in a world where the general approach is "quick and easy," for the solutions you desire a bigger and better approach is needed.

Intentional: The first word in this concept is intentional. People tend to live their life on autopilot. They get into this day-to-day life where they're really just existing and not truly living. They have plenty of habits but very few, if any, real rituals. The majority of their life revolves around waking up, going to work, coming home, eating dinner and going to bed. There is no real intention. In order to shake yourself up from your zombie like existence you must become intentional about your life. That means being aware of what you want to change and improve in your life then taking the necessary steps to make sure that you move forward with your plan each and every day. Intention is the foundation of rituals.

There are two reasons that make being intentional so important. First, the level of happiness, enjoyment, and fulfillment that comes out of someone's life has a lot to do with the happiness enjoyment and fulfillment they are able to give as well as receive.

The only way you can get into a state where you can give and receive the most is by being intentional about the things you are feeling, thinking, and doing. There is so much potential richness in life that is unseen or overlooked when a person is living their life on autopilot.

However, when a person becomes aware of the things that they're doing, and also intentional about them as well, then they start to be much more receptive to the world around them. Second, the more intentional you are, the more control you have over the results in your life. When you're intentional, you make things happen. When you're intentional, you start to experience life in an entirely new way. What would your life be like if you were more intentional?

The more you can cherish your rituals, the more you're going to be able to participate in them on a regular basis. When you are intentional, you take responsibility into your own hands. By valuing yourself and the rituals, you have decided to make them a constant part of your life.

Intention alludes to the fact that you are going out of your way to make deliberate choices and actions. This also ties in with your purpose and sense of identity. If you have a purpose driven life you also have a need to be intentional because all the great aspirations and goals you have in life can truly be reached no other way. You will certainly not stumble upon your greatness. Intention is directly related to decision. The quality of the decisions you make on a daily basis shape the overall quality of your life. The more decisions you make that are congruent with your ultimate-self the easier it will be to uncover and live as that self.

Personal improvement: Now, you might think that's pretty straightforward although there's more to it than that. Personal improvement can actually be harmful if you have negative motives regarding it. Also, some people can believe that focusing on themselves is selfish, which is an idea we squashed earlier. Keep in mind, for you to be able to contribute and receive at the highest levels you have to be at your personal best. That means you have to take time out for you. With all of the demand stemming from the different people in your life, that is certainly understandable yet no reason to deny yourself the results you deserve. In reality, taking the time to work on and improve your self is really **selfless.** Personal improvement in regards to IPIDD comes down to a clear understanding of how committed you are to your personal excellence.
As you move forward, make sure that your intentions for personal improvement are **personal.** It is good to have other reasons of why you want to improve. An example of this

would be friends and family. Yet like the external motivating forces these should be supplemental to your desire to improve who you are.

Done: When I first came up with the idea for IPIDD I realized that the word "done" might not be as meaningful as the other words. I really wanted each word in IPIDD to stand for something substantial. I was a little bummed out in the beginning because I thought the word done just wasn't as powerful and meaningful as the other words. After some thought, I realize that it's just as important as the others are and here's why. The word done implies completion. It implies that you actually did something. You went from your head to your feet. You took action and got something done, what a concept!

That means you took an idea about something that you wanted to do and you made it a reality. It shows that you were committed and followed through on the thing you wanted to do. One of the biggest aspects of self-mastery is about **actually getting things done**. How many of us know people that are lazy? How many of us know people that are inconsistent? How many of us know people that are fearful of moving forward? How many of us at times are that person?

The truth is, we all are at times. The direct opposite of that stagnant state is action, plain and simple. How much would the quality of your life increase if you took constant action on the things you wanted to do? Do you think it be increased a little, or do you think it increased a lot? You had better believe it would increase a lot.

Action is the missing key that links everything together. If you only take two things away from this entire book I would truly hope that it was the ability to have certainty about who you are and why you are here and then take serious consistent, actions towards toward the fulfillment of your purpose.

In addition to getting things done also are able to enjoy the fruits of your labor. When you begin to set goals and achieve them, you build your personal power; your momentum for setting goals and achieving them grows. You build your confidence because you have this new power of coming up with ideas or things that you want to do, and then literally doing them. What's even better is that the more your confidence grows, the bigger and more intense the goals and ideas you will want to take on.

Think about the difference between someone who wants to do things and then procrastinates or is inconsistent. Compared to someone who wants to do things and takes consistent action, the difference between these people is night and day. Intellectually the two people may be exactly the same. Yet one of them chooses to finish the circle and actually live what they know. Either one of those realties could be yours. Although at this point in your life, I would hope you are sick of knowing everything and doing nothing.

You see intelligence is only as good as the results it helps you to produce. You could hold some of the most valuable and important information in the world and you may be considered a genius by your natural or acquired intelligence. Yet I believe true genius comes from the ability to do something useful and meaningful with what you know. Otherwise having all that intelligence becomes nothing but a storage bank for information. And I do not personally recommend going toe to toe with a computer. They are much better at storing data than you.

This means that IPIDD is about being intentional and having your personal motivations. It is also about getting things done. I mean, isn't that where the results lie? Let's face it you can be intentional until you're blue in the face. You can make your motives more personal than ever before, but if you are not literally taking action on the things you want and making them happen, then it's all a joke.

I would like to add here that there is a major difference

between productivity and being busy. When you are productive, you are creating results. When you are busy, often that means that you are doing a lot of work that doesn't really amount to anything. Make sure that when you are taking action that action that produces results.

Daily: The difference between people who succeed on a high level and people who don't is consistency. That is where the magic of rituals comes from. Just like the person who goes to the gym once a week compared to the person who goes to the gym five times a week, the difference between the two is consistency. Yes, IPIDD is about being intentional. Yes, it is about being personal, and yes, it is about action. But more than anything, it is about doing all of these those things daily.

It is not enough to be intentional once in awhile. It is not enough to be personal about your improvement, every now and then. It is not enough to take action when you feel like it or when the timing is right. It is about being so compelled and fanatical about your improvement and personal success, that literally every single day you do something big or small to move you forward in your life.

I believe it's not what we do occasionally, or when we feel like it that defines us. Rather what we do every single day, religiously without fail that makes us who we are. Whether you like it or not your rituals define you as a person. The real heroes are not people who did something one time, the real heroes are the people who are faced with challenges every single day who decide to rise up and take them on. These are the people that cannot be thrown off or distracted from their rituals. Are you one of them?

This is where the real power comes from, the ability to do something in some way shape or form every single day that can make you better. Imagine how much personal strength you would have if you could command yourself to do something positive and powerful each and every day; how much of a difference would that make in your life.

The true goal of IPIDD is to help make your life more structured and intentional. As you continue to raise your standards and expectations for yourself, you will need higher and higher levels of focus and rituals. Begin to think about the areas of your life you need to add rituals to. The more you can command and direct your life the more certain and rich it will be.

Imagine what your life would be like if, rather than having your mediocrity on autopilot, your personal achievement was practiced and ensured every day. How does that make you feel? How would that life be different relative to life you have now? How would that affect your family life, your personal life, and your professional life? Put this book down for a minute and really think about that.

This is IPIDD, I wanted to introduce you to this concept first, before we got any further into the tools in self-mastery, because if you can begin to use and apply this concept, then it is going to make everything else much, much easier.

Take Action!

Here's what I want you to do - I want you to write out
IPIDD on a piece of paper. Then get clear and certain about
what each level of IPIDD means to you. Write it like this:

I

P

I

D

D

How can you be more intentional?

How can you make your self-improvement more personal?

How can you take more action?

And, how can you create a structure or formula that will
allow you to practice all these things on a daily basis?

I'm dead serious about this, put this book down and take the
time to do this. **I want you to take action!** Do not pick this
book back up until you have developed a very strong and
clear idea of what your personal commitment to IPIDD is.

Put this book down and take action now!

Rituals Not Habits

What is the difference between a ritual and a habit? The biggest separating factor between the two is intention. A ritual is something that you consciously go out of your way to perform in a methodical fashion. Psychologically, the rituals a person has are very valuable to them and are congruent with their morals and sense of identity. Rituals often tend to be mentally, physically, or spiritually fulfilling.

Habits on the other hand are different. Habits are practically the opposite of rituals. A true habit is not something that is intentional but involuntary instead. There are many different types of habits; personal habits, cultural habits, and social habits. Habits can be good, they can be bad, and they can be neutral. There are even habits that you have, things you think say or do, that you perform on a regular basis and you may have no idea how or why you acquired them.

The second big difference between rituals and habits is perspective. As you begin to start to transform your beliefs, you begin to view the things you once saw as small and insignificant as things that are large and irreplaceable. Suddenly everything shifts and the little things become big. Things like working out or eating right are no longer things that you are willing to be lax about. They shift from things you "should" do to things that you "must" do. Like magic, all the toxic habits in your life will be things you naturally stray away from. And the positive rituals become things that you are automatically propelled towards. Imagine literally being pulled toward greatness.

My hope for you is that you begin to focus on and building your rituals. If you want to live a life where you feel totally free, then you need to be conscious and deliberate about the things that are important in your life. You will always be a creature of habit. That is just human nature. However, it is the quality of the rituals that you have that define the quality of your life.

Before we get into your negative habits and how you and turn them into positive rituals, I would like to share with you some insight and solutions that are related to shifting or putting a stop to negative habits all together. That way once we get to the point where you are listing and thinking about your current habits that you would like to change, you will have a very clear idea about how to do it and how to make them work, not just once and a while, but for the rest of your life.

That being said, there are two types of habits: response initiated habits and acquired habits. It is important for you to understand each and how they work in order to be able to put an end to them or to transform them into rituals.

Response initiated habits: This type of habit is created in response to a need that you have. For example, if a person is feeling stressed, their response is to do something that will change their state. That could be anything from smoking a cigarette, drinking alcohol, or watching TV. All of which provide a way for this person to meet the need they have to extinguish their stress. Habits have such an addictive nature because of their ability to produce certainty in the moment. The thought process is, "If I feel X and I do Y, then I will feel Z and it will make it better."

Although this logic looks good on paper, it can lead to negative habits that are often more detrimental than the initial feeling itself. Let's take smoking for example. A person may initially begin smoking as a way to cope with their stress, anxiety, or any multitude of other annoying emotions. So they smoke a cigarette and quickly these negative feelings begin to subside. Though that person may have dissolved their stress in that moment, cigarettes become more of a crutch than a solution. And after a while a person will begin to experience a whole new set of problems that come directly from the smoking itself; heart disease, emphysema, and cancer just to name a few. Not exactly a fair trade if you ask me.

There are three main forces that will keep someone
locked into a habit even if it is as bad for them. Those are:

- The chimp brain

- Certainty

- And the comfort zone

The Chimp Brain: Genetically humans and chimpanzees
are over 97% similar to one another. That means the only
genetic difference between you and the monkey at the zoo is
4%. Yet one of the biggest differences between chimps and
humans is that humans have been graced with forward
thinking. Forward thinking is the ability to think and act in
regards to consequences and benefits that will happen in the
future rather than in a moment. Chimpanzees are unable to
do this on a large scale. Most of their thoughts, actions and
results are based on the moment.

Unfortunately, just because people have the potential ability
to use forward thinking, it often does not mean that they will.
If you observe society and culture, on a whole you will see
that a lot of decisions and motives are based on what people
can do or get in the moment, often times with very little
regard to what might happen in the future consequently. One
of the greatest examples I can give you is, smoking…
surprise!

There are literally no positive long-term benefits to smoking
whatsoever. And if that's not bad enough, as I pointed out
there are a multitude of negative long-term effects of
smoking. On top of that, consumers aren't completely stupid.
The vast majority of them are well aware of the negative
effects from smoking. So why on earth do they continue to
smoke? The answer is the chimp brain.

Though a person may know logically the consequences of
their actions, the core operating system that they are running
on is connected to the chimp brain. The chimp brain is only

concerned with the moment. Moment oriented decisions lead to things like, over eating, drinking too much, and overreacting. This is what is also known as impulse of thinking. How many times have you heard the phrase, "It was an impulse buy!" You see, marketers are smart. They know that if they can speak directly to your chimp brain, that they can bypass your logic and get you to do something impulsive in that moment.

In order to get away from chimp brain decisions you must exercise your forward thinking ability. Along with your primal desire to purely think and act in the moment, you simultaneously have the ability to apply your forward thinking capability to that moment, so that you can make decisions that will make you happy, not only in the present, but in the future as well. How good would you feel if you knew that the majority of the decisions you made in the moment were not only going to benefit you at that specific time but also down the line as well?

Certainty: At our core, we must have certainty when it comes to specific aspects of our life. If we have a need that absolutely must be met, then by our nature we will find a specific way to meet that need. A.k.a., "If I feel X and I do Y than I will feel Z in order to make it better." Whatever Y is, it becomes embedded into your brain as the go-to option when the X feeling arises.

This is where the logic is thrown out the window. Take the person who sporadically eats "comfort food" because they feel bad about themselves. Although they may logically know all of the negative short and long-term consequences of eating impulsively, the immense certainty that they have will lead them to indulge in the negative behavior almost involuntarily. And what happens because of this? Almost instantly, after they have finished their eating spree, they feel guilty and begin to beat themselves up.

Response initiated habits can be the hardest ones to break because they are attached to such a high level of certainty. It is easy to tell a person that they should not partake in their negative habit. However, it is much more difficult in actuality because without that habit, a person loses their certainty about how they're going to resolve their negative feelings from moment to moment. That uncertainty creates such a great fear that the person is paralyzed, and even if they want to adopt a new behavior, they revert to the old negative one. Because this person does not have any experience with this new habit, they therefore do not have any certainty that it's going to work. And, especially in the moment, while they are contemplating a potentially different solution, all the while the feeling the stress and the anxiety is building and building.

Ultimately, we all have a need to be certain, however, as individuals we go about obtaining that certainty differently. Unleashing your ultimate-self comes down to finding more empowering ways to gain your certainty. You want the things that help you meet your need for certainty to be things that reinforce who you are and what your purpose is, rather than things that make you feel bad about what you've done and who you are.

The Comfort Zone: Disguised as something to keep you safe the so called "comfort zone" becomes the stealthy killer of all potential dreams and realities. The comfort zone may seem nice and friendly but make no mistake it is most likely one of the greatest pitfalls that your ultimate-self has been come across in a long time. Certainty and the comfort zone are partners in crime. They both work together to keep you from moving forward.

Why is the comfort zone so comfy? It is because of its amazing ability to make you feel certainty. When you have a habit that meets a certain need, you become comfortable with that habit. You know exactly what is going to happen and in certain circumstances, you may even know when. There are specific areas of a person's life with which they are just not willing to gamble. When you live inside your comfort zone, you can control everything that happens in your little world. You know when things are going to happen, where they are going to happen, and why they are going to happen. In theory, it's a pretty neat idea. Until we look behind the curtain.

The comfort zone will put a person into what is at its core an uncomfortable or unhappy situation to get a small amount of happiness. You see this being played out all over the world in all aspects of life. Generally people will go for the "sure thing" rather than what they imagine to be the "gamble." For example, the man that works a nine to five job, absolutely hates it and is obviously unhappy, stays, knowing that if he continues to work at that job he's going to get a paycheck every week. He will be able to pay the bills and continue to live the specific lifestyle that he has. He has created a comfort zone and as uncomfortable as it might be, he is at least happy with the idea that he's making enough money to cover his needs. When it comes to the idea of doing anything new, as much as he might know how to get a new job, sadly he will continue to do the same thing out of the certainty he gets from his current job, even if it causes him pain. Yet the thought of a new job or even the thought of quitting his current job creates a very high level of uncertainty in him, which paints a very vivid picture of unhappiness in his mind. Even if he knows from a logical standpoint that a new job could make his life better in a multitude of ways.

This is where the "What If" factor plays a role. What if he was to quit his current job and for some reason was only able to find a worse job? Or what if, worse than that, he couldn't find a new job at all? Then he'd be seriously unhappy. He would not be able to pay his bills. He'd get kicked out of his apartment. From there he thinks, "What if I end up on the streets hungry, broke, and destitute?" All of a sudden, his current situation compared to the illusion of what might happen is not so bad or at least more bearable. The curious part about all of this is that this man, and most people in general, base their lives and actions on what is going to make them happy in the moment and by what they believe will help them avoid pain in the future. However, we can obviously see this approach does not work and in reality, it ends up creating pain in both the moment and the future. What is even more ironic is that we avoid the things that we believe will be painful, that we are afraid of based on our imagination. We have no solid facts or evidence that these things will really be as bad as we think.

It is very unfair for people to hold themselves back from a very real and potentially positive future based on an imaginary idea that is also often very unrealistic. And so, we will take life as it is rather than how it could be. Now we come to the true core of what holds the man at the nine to five job and most people back from the things that they want to do in life. It's not a lack of desire and it's not the comfort zone. Ultimately it is fear. Even more than that, it's that it's not just fear itself because fear is simply an emotion. The ugly truth is that your comfort zone is really more like a cage. Breaking a habit or doing anything new takes an act of courage. Creating a new ritual takes a version of you that is willing to step outside your comfort zone. Here is where things get interesting. The simple thought of stepping outside of your comfort zone is enough to make most people so afraid they stay right where they are. Welcome to the fear of the unknown. You become stunted because your view of this new or better solution is something that says it "might" or "could" work and not as something that "will" or "must" work. Since you have not experienced this new positive replacement yet, there is no certainty and thus the low level of confidence that comes along with inexperience reverts you back to your old ways. More specifically, some of the main reasons a person will stay stuck are:

- The fear of failure

- The fear of success

- The limiting beliefs we have about the outside world

- The belief that we are not good enough

- We cannot or are unwilling to imagine a better life

- The resources we need are out of reach

- The avoidance of change

So, maybe now is a good time to delve into fear and what it really is.

Fear: Fear is generally perceived as something that will directly cause pain, or it at least gives people the anticipation of pain. It is the anticipation of pain on some level that keeps people from taking action. So how do we overcome fear? More than that, how do we change our association of what fear means to us so that fear does not have to be something that holds us back? How do we turn it into something that pushes us forward? There are two keys to changing your association with fear. First, is an understanding that fear is simply an emotion. And emotions are just electrical impulses, signals to our mind. Remember, the great thing about reality is that we get to choose what the meaning is. It is the same way with our emotions. Does the term "emotional guidance system" ring a bell?

For some reason or another, fear to most people means something bad is going to happen. That just happens to be what most people have decided that fear means to them, whether they know it or not. Is that what everybody believes about fear? Absolutely not. That means that fear does not have to mean one specific thing. Fear does not have to be defined as something negative.

The big difference between people who are successful on a large scale and people who are not comes down to their ability to interpret fear in a positive or negative way. Is fear something that mobilizes them rather than paralyzes? Think about your association to fear, is it something that creates a sense of avoidance or is fear something that creates a sense of curiosity and excitement?

Fear is an emotion and from a biochemical standpoint, fear is nothing but a signal interpreted by your brain. However, fear from a neurological standpoint does not necessarily have a definite meaning. This is why two people can experience fear and have two very different reactions and outcomes. Think of a stoplight in traffic. When person number one comes to a stop light and the light is yellow, that person interprets the yellow light as a sign to slow down and stop. The other person interprets that yellow light as a sign to speed up, so they do and they continue through the light. Fear works exactly the same way. It doesn't mean any particular thing you get to choose the meaning. The question is what is the meaning of fear to your ultimate-self? How can you start to adopt that same idea now? How can you begin to see your fear as a way to move forward rather than to stop?

Your ultimate-self understands that fear is a signal and that signals are important and you should pay attention. Just as it's important to pay attention to what the traffic light is doing while you're in driving. The color of that light determines what you're going to do if you don't pay attention to the color of that light you could be in some serious danger. Certain colors do have definite meanings. Green means go and there are no two ways about it. Likewise red means stop and that is definitely not up for interpretation. From an emotional standpoint when we are happy we are happy, and when we are sad we are sad. Although when we feel fear we can go one of two ways, and that is what makes it so potentially powerful for you.

Often times people want avoid things that make them afraid. That is because they don't want to think about the pain that could be involved. Successful people know better. Successful people know that fear is an emotion that's trying to tell them something so they listen to it.

The second aspect of changing your association to fear is to create a new and specific definition for what fear means. It's not enough just to know that something is open for interpretation. You have to make a serious decision about what you want fear to mean to you. "The light is telling me I can slow down or speed up." That information is useful but the meaning and action you interpret from that information is what makes the difference.

You must decide fear means that success is around the corner. Most people will stop short of their success, because they know they are on the verge of something big, but rather than thinking they are on the verge of a breakthrough, they believe that they are on the verge of something potentially painful so they stop. Have you ever done that?

Even if people don't have a fear of failure per se, they might have a fear of success. That is, they might believe that if they are successful, certain things that make them happy will go away. They have limiting beliefs about what success is. Maybe they believe that successful or wealthy people are bad. Or that maybe to reach higher levels of success they will need to step on other people.

This is another great example of the "what if" factor. People begin thinking about "what if."

"What if I become successful and my friends no longer like me?"

"What if I become successful and people want to use me?"

"What if I lose my spirituality because of my success?"

Unfortunately, all of these thoughts are based on imagination and not reality. I know this idea of fear, being a positive thing may be a tough pill to swallow but think about some of your greatest accomplishments. Didn't you feel fear? Yet didn't you decide that you were going to move forward anyway? And, because you did make that decision, you went on to achieve new and better results in some area of your life.

If you are on the verge of graduating, you may be afraid that fear is just telling you that you needed to prepare and have all of your studying and homework in order. If you are up for a promotion, you could be afraid that fear was telling you that you need to be on top your game and that you need to be a very likely candidate for that position. If you could not clearly demonstrate that you were a worthy person of the position, then you weren't going to get that promotion. If you did prepare yourself and you were ready, then you would get that promotion and that promotion would ideally mean you were living up to more of your potential. That promotion also would hopefully mean more contribution and a higher level of personal and professional success, therefore you are on the verge of a breakthrough whether you know it or not.

It's just a matter of being aware. That that is the case, choosing to look at the more positive sides of the fear. The more compelling and exciting parts. Of course, if you think you're going to fail and it is going to be painful, then you'll stop yourself from even taking the action in the first place. If you can think of fear in a way that allows you to see all the amazing sides of what is to come, then you will move into a new level of achievement and you can have practically unlimited success in any area of your life.

Fear can also be used as a learning experience. So many people are afraid to try something new, because they are afraid to fail. Yet at the same time, you'd be amazed at the amount of people absolutely love to learn. What if your failure could be a learning experience and not something that was painful? What if your failure moved you even closer to success? This puts a completely new spin on the fear of failure, doesn't it?

If you want to know what one of the absolute keys to personal and professional success is, it's continuous failure. The one stipulation that makes it success is that it is continuous failure from which you *learn*. Think about all the times you tried something and failed, learned from the experience and then went on to have success. Imagine if that process was part of your daily life.

When it comes to success that's the ultimate formula, try something and if it doesn't work, learn from it, change your approach and try again in a better and smarter way. And continue to do so until you get the result that you want. If you do not have a fear of failure, then it becomes much easier to be motivated. That's a fairly simple formula, however if you have a massive fear of failure due to the anticipation of high levels of pain because of that failure. Then success becomes as foreign to you as the moon. How powerful would you be if fear and failure actually helped you to be successful?

If you can go into a potential situation with the mindset of "I am feeling some fear right now and I realize that it is a signal telling me I need to be prepared." What that means is if you don't happen to achieve your goal on the first try, at least you will be able to learn something from the experience that will ultimately help you achieve that goal. By changing your mindset, you also change your expectations and set yourself up for victory. It will also aid you in not making that same mistake in the future, which is a large asset. Remember, the only thing that stands in your way is standing in your shoes. There are no real barriers and the things you are currently afraid of can't actually hurt you.

Think about how valuable it would be to learn from your mistakes rather than have to repeat them. Just the ability alone of not having to fall into the same pitfalls repeatedly is priceless. Also, as you move forward and apply this positive possibility thinking mentality, it will naturally build your confidence. Your ability to bounce back from a failure increases, as well as your ability to make quick and decisive choices. One of the biggest things that will take the wind out of a person's sails when they fail is how long they are out of the game. The longer you dwell on and beat yourself up about your failures the more time you waste trying to figure them out. The sooner you can bounce back and step up to the drawing board, the sooner you can figure out why you failed and use that information to help you succeed.

This is exciting because what that really means is that if you are willing to have an open mind, interpret fear as a signal that can help you prepare, and be ready to learn from your mistakes, then truly there is no such thing as failure. At the core of who you truly are is where this new mindset lies. I certainly do not believe that living a life of fear and lack is in accord with who you truly are. By understanding the idea that having a mentality that allows you to improve your life continuously and live up to your greatest self, you begin to find that motivation is a non-issue.

If that was your mindset for success, if that was your criteria for how you evaluate its success and failure, do you think your life would change? Do you believe that you would be constantly motivated to improve as an individual?

If you take on this new mindset about what fear really is, then not only will that create motivation for you, but it will also create some serious desire as well. When you're not so afraid of your fear, you become compelled by it. When you're excited about something, you're motivated and even attracted to it.

To supplement this mindset I would like to share a philosophy called "stretching" with you. The concept behind stretching is this statement, "If I can't, then I must, and if I must then I can." Stretching is about expanding who you are. It is about breaking down the walls that confine you as an individual. Stretching is the comfort zone killer. Look at the things people say they "cant" do – working out, commitment, healthy eating, or having fun. People tend to be so wrapped up in their lives that they miss out on the things in life that really matter.

All the things that you are currently saying I can't to are most likely things that you should be saying I must to. If you can't find time for exercise, chances are exercise is in fact something that you must be doing. The same goes for whatever else you currently aren't making time for. Deep down aren't those the things that would make your life better? You know they are.

Imagine what your life would be like if you started saying, "I must!" to the things to which you currently say, "I can't." What do you think would happen to the quality of your life? Whether you are saying "I can't" because you don't believe you have time or because there is fear involved, either way it's time to start experiencing all of the great results and benefits that you have been missing out on. The greatest lie you could ever tell yourself or someone else is that you can't do something.

Stretching is in many ways similar to IPIDD. It is an approach to life where you are constantly doing things to push your personal boundaries and achieve new levels of growth. Mediocrity is the very thing that keeps the amazing results you deserve slightly out of reach. And by stretching yourself, the things that once seemed unattainable then become inevitable.

Before you can get to work on stretching yourself, you need to be aware of the types of bad habits you have developed. Having a clear understanding of the different types of habits you have will allow you to take the necessary measures to put them to an end. Because bad habits can be so automatic, often times you may not even know you are doing something that is counterproductive to the results you want. If you can put yourself under a microscope and start to notice your bad habits, you will have the power to do something about them in the moment, and ideally change your psychology so that they disappear from your life.

Now let's look at acquired habits, what they are, and how you can become aware of them and get rid of them.

Acquired habits: Have you ever been around a friend of family member who says or does something that is exactly like their mother or father? That is an acquired habit, a habit that they have involuntarily learned by seeing or hearing a specific behavior over and over again.

Acquired habits have the potential to be very bad and here's why; they are automatic. There is no level of awareness around them what so ever. That means a person could have acquired a negative habit from their parents that they exercise on a daily basis and they are completely unaware. What makes this so bad is that awareness is the first step to change. In order for you to change any area of your life, you have to be aware that work needs to be done in that area. Imagine driving a car and not being aware of where you were going. One of countless potential catastrophes would surely unfold.

What makes acquired habits even worse is that sometimes, even though you are a good-hearted person and mean well for others, you can still greatly damage people who your habits by saying or doing things that will hurt them unintentionally. Especially if you develop your acquired habit at a very young age. You never get a chance to distinguish whether that habit is bad or good. And since it is repeated either in your household or in your environment, you accept it as it is.

Some acquired habits are harmless. For example; the father who only fills the lemonade pitcher 85% full, simply because his mother did it that way growing up. Curious one day about why he does this, he called his mother to find out why she did that, only to find out that the pitcher they had growing up had a crack near the handle and lemonade would leak out if it was filled past that point. The son, unaware of that fact, grows up to fill his pitcher to 85% even though it is not broken, simply out of the acquired habit he has developed. After seeing how silly it was to fill his unbroken pitcher to 85%, he had no problem dropping the habit.

There are other types of acquired habits however, that can have a serious negative impact on your life and the life of others. Things such as:

- Racism

- Violence

- Closed mindedness

- Poverty consciences

- Poor eating habits

- Cursing

- Lying

You may have acquired negative habits from friends of family members. And as easy as it is to be mad at them for "making" you that way. Remember your life is your responsibility. You may not have been able to control acquiring those habits, but rather than curse your past, you have an opportunity now to turn them around and shape tomorrow. It is always better to create the future, then to damn your biography.

The best way to become aware of your habits whether they are acquired or response initiated is to crank up your curiosity. Curiosity and awareness go hand in hand. The more curious you are about the habits you have, the better you can understand them and ultimately change them. You may be asking yourself, "But, Shannon, if they are habits that happen without thinking, how can I become aware of them?" Great question. The more curious you become about your thoughts, feelings, and actions, the better you can determine what type of habits they are, acquired or response initiated. Get curious and ask yourself, "Why am I doing this?" If you find yourself becoming aware of an acquired habit, then you can ask yourself, "Is this habit helping or hurting me?" At that point, you may be able to drop the habit

completely now that your brain realizes that is it not
necessary, similar to the man and the lemonade pitcher. Not
all habits can be dropped so easily, however the more aware
of them you become, the more you increase your ability to
change them.

Becoming aware of and changing response-initiated habits is
where the real courage comes in. When you have developed
a bad habit as a response to a certain feeling, when you trace
that habit back to the original feeling, you may not like what
you find. As an example, as a smoker, your desire to smoke
may come from a feeling of stress or anxiety, which is
caused by the hate for your job and a feeling of being
underappreciated. Ultimately, those feelings can be traced
back to the belief that you are not good enough or do not
deserve greatness.

Coming face to face with this fact is certainly not something
that is on the top of most people's to-do list. As you know, if
you can look at the biggest ugliest part of yourself and
decide to do something positive about it, then that is real
power. It can be tough to do this because it's not always easy
to conclude that the habits you have created were created as
a way to shut up the voice inside. The voice that is telling
you that you are insecure, or uncertain about who you are or
where you are going in life. Remember, this is your personal
revolution. There has never been a more important and grave
task.

Being conscience of your habits and what of type they are is
good. Although being aware by itself is not enough to
change them for the better permanently. You may become
aware that you have a bad habit of stepping on people's feet,
although unless you have tools that can help you stop, it will
be tough to change. The following tools will help you have
power over your bad habits once and for all. From there you
will have a fresh start on developing empowering rituals. For
now answer the following question and bring awareness to
the current habits you have.

Take Action!

What is the quality of your current habits?

How can you shake up your world so that the forces that have been contributing to your negative habits can be erased?

How can you adopt a mentality of rituals not habits?

What new rituals would you like to create in your life?

Put this book down and take action now!

Decisive Decision Making

One of the greatest rituals I could ever encourage you to create would be that of Decisive Decision Making. A large number of people have trouble making decisions as it is, and in this day and age with more choices than ever, option paralysis is at an all time high. What would your life be like if you could consistently make rapid and firm decisions? How liberating would it feel to be able to know with full confidence that you made the right decision? Pretty inspiring thought, isn't it? That is exactly what you are going to learn how to do in this section forward.

I believe one of the biggest reasons why people have such a tough time making decisions is not because they have too many options. People with two options or less can still have just as hard a time making decisions. Therefore, if the underlying challenge is not too many options, it must be something deeper. People thrive off of certainty, and when a person is presented with a choice to make it has the tendency to rob someone of their certainty. The age old thought, "Am I making the right decision?" creeps in. It is this thought, this black and white thinking that one is right and one is wrong, that freezes people in their tracks. The fear of making the wrong decision is often too much to bear and a person will many times go to lengths just to avoid having to make a decision, lest they make the wrong one.

Here is another place where we see the imagination hard at work. We have a tendency to imagine all the horrible things that would happen as a result of our bad decision. The ideas and images we create are so scary and involve such a high anticipation of pain, that it is no wonder why people like to avoid them. But there is a secret; a secret to making decisions that will turn your world on its head. There are no wrong decisions only good or better ones. At first glance, this idea might sound crazy and in some ways it is, but let's go a bit further down the rabbit hole and see what is really going on here.

First, the idea that a decision can be right or wrong is extremely limiting and misguiding. Think about a decision you once made that you thought at that time was "a good one," only to find out somewhere down the line that it was "a bad one." How about a decision that initially you thought was dumb, stupid, or bad, only to find out was one of the best decisions you have ever made. As you can see the idea of choices being right or wrong has some holes in it. There is no rhyme or reason to decisions, it would seem.

How can you ever know a decision is the right one? It's simple, you decide. You must make decisions about your decisions, if you will. You must get into the ritual of deciding that the decision you made is the right one and that is final. If that decision turns out to give you a result or destination you didn't intend to have, that's fine. Now you have new information and the ability to make a more refined decision from there and in the future. For example, you go to a restaurant you have never been to, look at the menu, and find two things you want but do not know which one to choose. Both choices sound great and you think to yourself, "Which one is better?" The truth is it's nearly impossible to know which one is going to be better, but if they both look good, chances are you are going to enjoy EITHER one.

On the chance that your food shows up and it is terrible, well guess what. You can send it back and get the other option! There is no rule that says once you make a decision that you have to stick with it. Plus, you have learned that the first choice is something on that menu you never have to get again. So not only do you end up with what you want, but you also end up with the ability to make a swift firm decision at that restaurant in the future. There are certainly times where you will not be able to "take it back." Sometimes you will have two or more decisions and when you choose, then that is final. These types of decisions are seemingly more scary than the first because they cut off all possibility of going back, however these decisions can often be even better for you overall if perceived the right way. Henry Ford once said, "Whether you believe you can or you can't, you're right." And, when it comes to your perception of the decisions you make, whether you believe they are the right or wrong, you're right.

You see, often times people doubt, second guess, or all together defeat themselves on the decisions they DO make. That means that even if a person makes a decision they could be happy with, because of all the doubt in their mind they turn a perfectly good choice into what seems to them to be the wrong one. This is where Decisive Decision Making comes in. By choosing one of the options you have and dedicating yourself to the idea that you have made the right choice, you eliminate all the doubt and worry that comes from second-guessing yourself. There are two keys to Decisive Decision Making and those are, deciding in advance and enjoying the moment.

Decide in Advance: with so much uncertainty in life, there is no reason to add more. We tend to struggle finding a balance between the things we have control over and the things we don't. Often we get the wires crossed and try to control people, places, or things that are completely out of our control. This only leads to frustration and a larger feeling of helplessness. On the other hand, far too often, we do not take control of the things that are within our control, so now we have two categories in our life that are totally out of order. Pretty nerve racking, huh? The good news is that the art of deciding in advance will allow you to take control of the things in your life in which you do have the ability to control, and also will give you the power to make decisions about what you are going to focus on in situations that are out of your control. The truth is there are many more decisions that you should be making in your life, and as scary as that may sound, the reality is the more decisions you make in a decisive and certain way, the more personal power you exercise and ultimately gain.

Right now, there are tons of things in your life about which you could be deciding in advance. A client of mine wanted to start taking dance classes. And as excited as she was to take the class, she had a lot of fear involved with getting started. Her imagination had gotten the better of her, she had rampant thoughts of people making fun of her, judging her, and ultimately thought she would be better off if she just didn't take the classes. After she had come to understand all of the negative images she had in her mind were all based on imagination and had nothing to do with reality, she started to feel better about it. What allowed her to really get excited about taking dance classes, however, was the idea that rather than it being this horrible negative experience, it *could* be something fun, exciting, and liberating. What a concept!? Shortly after, she began to understand that she could decide in advance that she was going to have a good time, no matter what. She went to her first class and ended up having one of the greatest nights of her life.

This story demonstrates how a person can go from a place of total fear and avoidance, to deciding in advance that it is going to be a great time. What do you think having that ability would do to your life?

Imagine experiencing some of the following scenarios on the list below and how you could decide in advance that you were going to have a high quality experience:

- Taking a walk

- A date

- Taking a class

- A business meeting

- A wedding

- An interview

As you can imagine, the list is potentially endless. The idea is that these are all things that normally people don't place any intention or decision on. They are involved with the above things with no idea about what type of experience they are going to have. Maybe it'll be great. Maybe it'll be horrible. It's all just a roll of the dice. If IPIDD has taught us anything, it is that in order to get the greatest results in life, we must have an equal level of intention and expectation in what we are doing. Deciding in advance comes down to the ability to use your powerful imagination in your favor, rather than letting it get the better of you. By creating an image that is positive and exciting, one where you see yourself having a blast, you naturally become compelled toward the idea rather than repelled by it. What are some of the things in you do in your life where you could start deciding in advance about? What would happen to the quality of your life if you started creating a ritual out of the idea that every experience you have, be it old or brand new, can be positive and fulfilling.

Enjoy the Moment: Imagine all the time that is wasted when you worry, stress, second-guess, doubt, question, deliberate, hesitate, back peddle, and regret your decisions. If you were to add up all that time, I can guarantee you that it would be time you wished instead that you had spent enjoying yourself, as opposed to torturing yourself. Time being your most valuable asset, you should be in the habit of not wasting your time as it is. And, it is important to point out that mental distractions such as worry and doubt are just as real as any other type.

Creating the life you truly deserve boils down to being able to enjoy each moment to its fullest. By intentionally deciding that you are going to choose one thing over another and determining in advance that your decision is going to be a good one, you free yourself from all potential negativity that normally robs people from enjoying their life. This means that decisive decision making comes down to deciding that you are going to value yourself and your time to the highest level. Therefore, you are going to expect that you are going to swiftly make decisions, enjoy them, and draw the line there. I can tell you out of my own experience that I have had absolutely priceless moments that I would not trade for anything, that were only attainable because I decided in advance that I was going to enjoy myself and that I was going to make a decision quickly and be 100% content with it. Had I not taken that approach, some of my most treasured moments would have been lost in the fog of uncertainty and doubt.

If you begin to implement this strategy into your life, you will start to experience life in an entirely new way. You will begin to have moments that are filled with richness in places and at times that you never thought possible. At one time where you would have feared making decisions, now you will look forward to making them. Not only that, but you will start to seek out and find new and exciting ways to make even more decisions. As you do, you will see your personal power grow and grow.

Enjoying the moment goes back to the idea of having fun. Each and every moment has so much fun locked up in it, and all you have to do to enjoy it is decide in a very assertive way that you are going to reach out and grab it. That means the next time there is something in your life you need to do or go to rather than dreading the event you can decide in advance that you are going to be present, and have fun. Which means you can get creative for how you can have that fun. You must be willing to take responsibility for the quality of your life in every situation. That way, no matter what happens, you can do no wrong. All of the decisions you make no matter what are the "right" ones.

Enjoying the moment also has to do with things that are out of your control of well. For example, you cannot control the speed of the driver in front of you. But you can decide in advance, BEFORE you fly off the handle and stress yourself out that you are going to enjoy that moment. Directly after that you can decisively decide that you are going to focus on something that empowers you. You can have fun here too, because what you decide to focus on in that moment could be anything. It could be the top five things you are grateful for in that moment, it could be you decide to put your favorite song on and sing along. It doesn't matter. All that matters is that you take control of your state and understand that even though you may not be able to control that slow driver ahead of you, you can still have a great time. This can be very liberating because all of the situations that used to make you upset can actually add value to your life. This is one of the highest forms of responsibility because this means that no person, place or thing can MAKE you upset. Only you have the ability to do that.

It is also important to remember that one of the best tools to use when making decisions is intuition. Some of the best decisions in history had nothing to do with facts or figures. They had to do with gut instincts. How much do you trust your gut? When all the noise of anxiety, doubt, and mistrust creeps in, they can easily drown out the natural sound of your intuition, which is too bad because that means a fair amount of the time, you have sound decision from the get go but you do not trust it. So do that; trust yourself more. Allow your ultimate self to guide you, because I can promise you, your bigger and better self knows better than you. When you listen to your intuition, you send your brain a direct message that says, "I trust you!" Imagine what kind of power you could unleash if this was the constant message you were sending your brain.

Making decisions that are decisive has to do with action. The more time that falls between you and a decision, the more you allow fears, logic, and doubt to creep in. This makes it far less probable that you are going to take action. Also, if you do make a decision with fear and hesitation it can be the formula for disaster. Think about anyone who performs at a peak level: musicians, athletes, business people, anyone. In order for them to produce the highest results, their mind has to be clear. And what happens if that is not the case? What if there is doubt or hesitation in them when they perform? They mess up. One wrong move due to fear or insecurity can lead to total calamity.

This is yet again, another area that the more you practice the better you get. The more you allow your intuition to guide you, the more and more it comes out, often in times and places that you aren't even intending it to. That is the magic of all of this, which is the more conscious you become about your efforts to do things like make decisive decisions, enjoy the moment, and decide in advance, the more you program yourself to do that automatically. That means in many ways your personal and professional success is intentional, but it also means a large amount of your success is automatic. You begin to say, think, and do things automatically that are of a premium nature. Ask yourself, "How much do I trust myself?" and "How can I start to trust myself more?" "If I did trust myself to the highest degree, how would I act?" Take a second right now and think about three things you could make decisive decisions about today. Remember they can be both things you have control over, like going somewhere, or doing something, or they can be things like, the path you take on your drive into work, or the weather. Either way, you are in control!

Take Action!

Making decisions does not have to be something that scares you. In fact, it can be something that empowers you. Begin to view each decision you make as an opportunity to let your bigger and better self come out.

How can you create a ritual out of Decisive Decision Making?

How can you decide in advance that you are going to get the most out of each experience?

How can you trust yourself more so that you can stop worrying about your decisions and enjoy each moment to its fullest?

Put this book down and take action now!

Positive Belief Power

The acquired habits you have, more often than not, are simply a reflection of the beliefs that you have. Habits like overeating, binge drinking, and procrastination can often be traced back to some type of negative belief. Luckily two of the most powerful tools for changing your core beliefs have already been laid out. Self-love and BTFAR are the keys to changing your personal programming and putting a stop to negative beliefs.

A very interesting thing happens when you begin to love yourself more and adopt new beliefs. Your overall standards and expectations go up, and you reach new levels of self-respect. This newfound respect for yourself changes your perspective on the habits you have. You transition from a place of becoming aware of your negative habits once and a while to becoming fully conscious of the negative habits you have and how out of congruence they are with your current expectations for your life. The habits that you were once willing to let slide are now things that absolutely disgust you. Changing your neurological association to your bad habits is by far the greatest way to put an end to them forever.

Let's look at why most people fail to change their bad habits long term. Changing your behavior and replacing your bad habits with something new and more positive sounds nice, however unless the core belief is changed, the underlying problem will still exist and find a new way to manifest itself. And that is exactly what most people do. They decide that they want to change their bad habit or at least stop it. So they try and DO something new. They give up smoking, and they start eating healthy and exercising. All fine and dandy until that core negative belief that was causing the negative behavior rears its ugly head.

When the negative belief shows up, this is where most people "fall off the wagon" and never get back on. You see it all the time. Someone quits smoking for a month . . . six months . . . a year, and then starts again. A person will go on a healthy diet and after a few weeks, then they are right back to their old eating habits. And exercise, oh man... we've all heard that one before. That's the age old New Year's resolution that almost never comes to fruition. How about more extreme cases, like how a large percentage of people who have heart surgery due to clogged arteries as a result of over eating, are right back to their unhealthy eating habits as soon as they have recovered. It all leads back to the core programming.

In these cases, everything has changed outside the person, but the most important aspect of change is on the inside and it remains the same. It was no different for me after I read hundreds of books and listened to countless hours of self-help information. My life did not radically change because although I knew more, I had not become more. Changing beliefs that are tied to bad habits is so important because with that new belief comes with a certain perspective. That perspective or outlook defines how you think feel and react to certain things.

As an example, imagine a person at work is disrespected by a co-worker and afterwards this person is left feeling beat up. They wish they had stood up for themselves. They wish they had been stronger, but they weren't. This leads them to make statements like, "Why am I such a coward?" This question escalates the negative emotions they are already feeling to an even higher level and puts them into a state of self-loathing. The self-loathing becomes the activating event that causes their negative behavior whether it is smoking, drinking, or etc.

As you can see, the disrespectful comment from the co-worker was merely the trigger to make this person bring up their harsh negative belief about themselves. So imagine if this person had a very strong self-love and powerful respect for themselves. How would that chain of events been different? The initial comment that started the whole domino effect would have been perceived in a completely different way. The negative comment would have been completely disregarded all together, or upon self-questioning, this person would have asked a completely new set of questions. Questions like, "What can I do to make that person's day better?" and even if the questions were self-directed, the process would be more like, "I know who I am and that is what matters. I am not going to listen to what someone else has to say."

Whamo! Now all of the sudden the negatives feelings, self-loathing, and negative behavior never happen. There is no chance for them to exist because there is no belief or perspective in place that would cause those types of thoughts, feelings, and actions.

Just think about what your life would be like if you could view the current negative habits you have in such a way that it ensured you would never do them again. How much more powerful would you feel? How much more control would you have? Begin to question the habits you have. What is the root belief behind them?

Take Action!

Once you understand the core belief that is causing the habit, ask yourself these three questions:

- "How can I love myself more?"

- "How can I raise my standards?"

- "How can I shift my current belief to a better one?"

Revisit the chapters on Self Love and BTFAR if you have to. Keep in mind that habits are merely actions and results, which stem from your core beliefs. If you can build up your love for yourself and install powerful beliefs, you will see that your current bad habits will not fit into your criteria for how you want to live your life. And that will make using the following tools a snap!

Put this book down and take action now!

Self-Talk

We've been talking about literal habits, which are things that you actually do, but I'd also like to spend a little time and talk about verbal habits because just as much as it's important to be aware of the actual things you are doing, it is also important to be aware of what's called your self-talk. Self-talk is the communication you have inside your mind. It is the constant dialogue going on inside your head. Long after the conversations with friends and family and colleagues are over, our mental chatter continues. The interesting part about self-talk is that most people overlook what a powerful role it plays in people lives.

Did you know that three people could all have exactly the same experience, but the way they end up feeling about that experience drastically changes due to the type of words they used to define that experience? The same is true for you in your life. The words, phrases, questions, verbs, and metaphors that you use on a daily basis are currently one of the biggest factors controlling the quality of your life. Even if you shift your core beliefs, you must also go out of your way to re-establish a new and more positive attitude. Changing your outlook will afford you many positive benefits. What about the predictions and interpretations you have about life? How do you think those would be affected if the overall quality of your self-talk was positive?

Now you may be thinking to yourself, "Come on, the words I use can't really have not much of an impact on my life, right?" Wrong! It is time to stop looking at words as simply a string of letters and start looking at them as something that, when used correctly and completely, transform your life. Let's look at a few examples to show you what I mean.

"This will never work!"

"I can't believe I'm going to be late for work again!"

"How dare she talk to me like that! Who she think she is?"

Using self-talk like this not only decreases the quality of that moment but often times negative self-talk like this will leave long-lasting negative impressions on how we feel about ourselves. That means you could be seriously affecting your future and not even know it. Research across the world has shown that people with predominantly positive attitudes tend to live longer than people with more negative pessimistic attitudes.

Heavy negative self-talk generally leads to unnecessary worry and needless stress. And as many of us know, large amounts of stress can have serious short-term and long-term effects on our mental and physical well-being. The key here is to restructure the way you think so you have a more lighthearted overall view on life, as well as an enhanced ability to think from a problem-solving and realistic standpoint.

In order to master your self-talk you have to understand how it works. There are three levels of self-talk:

- Precursors

- Programming

- And procedures.

Precursors: Precursors are internal or external events that are the catalysts of your self-talk. Internally they may be thoughts or feelings memories or sensations. Externally they could be something like looking at the clock and realizing that you are late for work, or leaving the house and realizing that you have forgotten something important. Precursors activate your nervous system and tap directly into the third level of your self-talk. This leads us to the next level.

Programming: Programming is the hardwired beliefs you have in reaction to a given event. This is where the actual self-talk begins. The beliefs you have give you a specific interpretation when certain events unfold. For example, if you were to see a snake, the type of self-talk you would have in reaction to seeing that snake would differ depending on what type of programming you had about snakes. If you had a snake as a kid growing up, the quality of your self-talk will likely be positive. On the other hand, if you had a fear of snakes and what you said to yourself and the quality of that communication would be much, much different in that instance. This brings us to our third level of self-talk.

Procedures: If you think that self-talk is entirely mental, then think again. The way that we talk to ourselves has a direct impact on how we feel and how we act. In the case of seeing a snake, undoubtedly you would have some type of emotional and physical reaction whether it was excitement and curiosity, or fear and aversion, the chain of events would extend themselves much further than the chatter in your mind. This is why it is so important to master your self-talk. It is such a shame to think that you could be in a perfectly happy state and have your mental, emotional, and physical well being potentially shattered by an unexpected event. On the flip side, it is inspiring to think that the same random event could cause an unforeseen opportunity to exercise your champion qualities, given the right programming.

Similar to BTFAR, the primary tool for shifting your self-talk is awareness. Because there are so many different programs in your mind and combinations of unforeseen events to which they can be connected, I do not suggest that you sit down and try to reprogram them all. That would take you forever. But if you can begin to be aware of your reactions, both internal and external precursors, you will be able to change your procedure in any given circumstance.

There are two types of awareness you must apply to yourself when restructuring your self-talk. The first is mental awareness. This means being able to listen for certain things that would act as a would-be precursor. Being able to be aware and identify these internal and external activators gives you the power of choice.

Once you have the power of choice, you are able to control the end result of the situation. Most people would believe that self-talk is a stimulus and response condition that cannot be controlled. Luckily, that idea is a total hoax. That is because the core of your self-talk comes from your programming. And anything that can be programmed can be reprogrammed. Think of your awareness as your mental police and it's their job it is to monitor the quality of your mental communication.

In order to help you prepare for some of the self-talk modification that you're going to be doing, you will need positive alternatives to your negative statements. Just like changing any other habit, if you have a specific replacement for the old behavior you increase your probability of success by leaps and bounds. Not only will you be prepared when you hear negative chatter, but you'll have a concise statement prepared and ready to fire off. I have created a quick reference guide for you that highlights some of the major negative self-talk fundamentals.

Think That Not This

Negative self-talk: "Things make me mad."

Positive self-talk: "Things cannot affect me; only I have control over how I feel."

Negative self-talk: "I lose control when I get upset."

Positive self-talk: "I can control my reactions."

Negative self-talk: "My negative self-talk is a result of my upbringing."

Positive self-talk: "I am in control of my self-talk and have the power to change it for the better."

Negative self-talk: "It is too late for me to change now."

Positive self-talk: "I can always change, if I set my mind to it."

Negative self-talk: "I will only be okay if things are perfect."

Positive self-talk: "I will be okay no matter what; I can make the best out of any situation."

Negative self-talk: "I can't believe this is happening to me; I don't get it."

Positive self-talk: "I take responsibility for my manifestations, and am determined to learn their positive lesson."

Negative self-talk: "This is going to be horrible."

Positive self-talk: "Nothing is ever as bad as it seems."

Negative self-talk: "If I fail or do not meet my goals it means I am a failure."

Positive self-talk: "I accept myself for who I am and know that as long as I learn from my mistakes, I will always be successful."

Negative self-talk: "Other people think little of me."

Positive self-talk: "If I put my best foot forward people will view me in a positive way."

Negative self-talk: "I feel hopeless and doubt things will ever improve."

Positive self-talk: "I must always have hope. It is what will carry me through the hard times."

The second type of awareness is a reactionary awareness.

That means being aware of your procedures in any given moment. This ability is just more important, possibly more than internal awareness. Because sometimes we have such strong visceral programming about a given subject, when triggered we will instantly react to it. This means is that cognitive level of internal awareness is completely bypassed.

Imagine the stereotypical scene of a woman who sees a mouse. As soon as she visually becomes aware of the mouse, the precursor has fired off such a strong emotional jolt that even though she may want to get over her fear of mice, she instantly reacts without thinking and screams "mouse!" and jumps onto a chair shrieking and pointing.

This is where reactionary awareness comes in handy. Though the woman may not have had control over how she reacted, what she does have control over are her decisions after she has reacted. Once she realizes that she is up on the chair, she has the ability to shift her self-talk in a way that will limit her procedure so that the undesired effects of the event can end at the initial reaction, rather than progressing into an overreaction.

Often, it is not our reactions that get us into trouble; it is our overreactions. Think about all the damage that is done in society to people's friends, family, coworkers and so on due to our rash overreactions. It is when we get out of control that we say and do things that we often regret and cannot take back. Our personal lives are no different. Getting to a state where we have hurt ourselves directly or indirectly generally comes from an overreaction of some sort.

Just imagine how much damage you could spare yourself and others if you are able to shift your reactions from positive to negative, if internal awareness is the police of your mind and reactionary awareness is the police of your physiology. Remember, reactions do not have to mean large physical actions that we take. A reaction is any shift in your physiology can be anything from your breathing, body language, muscular tension, and facial expression. You can use any one of these as clues to help you become aware of your reactions.

For example if somebody says something hurtful and you begin to feel your breathing become shallow, your arms cross, your shoulders and fists tense up, and your smile turn into a scowl, these are all signals that you need to take control of your physiological state. You may not have been able to stop them from saying the hurtful words, and you may not have an ability to control your initial reaction to them, but you can definitely control how you are going to proceed. Imagine how much better you would feel if, as soon as you begin to feel those physiological cues, you instantly took measures to reverse them. By doing this, the power stays in your hands and you can return to a positive state much more easily.

Now that we have covered the main areas of self-talk, I would like to focus on some of the more acute areas, such as your personal vocabulary, metaphors, and questions to be specific. The metaphors, questions, and vocabulary we use also have massive influence over how we feel and we act.

Let's start by analyzing two aspects of your personal vocabulary. The quality of the words you use in general and the size of your word databank. Is the quality of the words you use on daily basis primarily positive or negative? In any given conversation, approximately how many words do you have at your disposal?

Make a list of the ten most common words you use from day to day. Review the list and look for any words that are negative or dull. Let me give you a story from my personal life to illustrate why this exercise is so powerful.

When I was in the early stages of my personal revolution, I distinctly remember making great progress and suddenly from time to time having major setbacks in my progress. Though I was changing the core of myself and how I perceived the world, much of my self-talk and personal vocabulary remained the same. So when I would do something like celebrate a victory or go see a great movie I would use the phrase "pretty good" to describe my experience. I adopted this phrase because early on, I had believed that I did not deserve to experience anything more than "pretty good." By using that phrase, I was able to keep myself in a state of mediocrity successfully, even if the experience I was having in that was extraordinary.

As my beliefs about myself changed for the better, I would catch myself still using this phrase. I realized that simply because I had changed my beliefs about myself that did not mean that my self-talk instantly changed. Although my self-talk was related to my beliefs, they were separate habits, therefore they had attacked separately. Since my new belief was to love myself and experience the best that life had to offer, the old phrase of "pretty good" needed to be exchanged for something that was more fitting.

I was excited to realize that I no longer had to be limited and I could choose from thousands upon thousands of words. I also realized that I could expand my personal thesaurus so that I could use a handful of different words to describe how I was feeling.

From there on out, I had many more powerful and colorful words I could use that were much better at defining how I was actually feeling. At that point my beliefs, self-talk, and experiences were all congruent with one another.

I have put together a list of words that will help you expand and enhance your personal vocabulary.

A
Able
Ageless
Assent
Abundance
Agree
Assert
Accelerate
Agreeable
Assist
Accept
Aid
Associate
Acclaim
Aim
Assure
Accomplish
Alacrity
Astir
Accrue
Alert
Astonish
Ascend
Alight
Attain
Accord
Alive
Attempt
Achieve
Attentive
Action
Always
Attest
Accolade
Amaze
Attraction
Accredit
Amazing
Attribute
Activate

Amiable
Attune
Active
Ambition
Augment
Add
Amity
Auspicious
Addition
Amuse
Authentic
Adept
Anew
Available
Admirable
Appealing
Avid
Adorable
Applaud
Awake
Advance
Appreciate
Award
Advantage
Aspire
Aware
Adventure
Approve
Awash
Affable
Arouse
Awesome
Affirm
B
Beatific
Blessed
Beatify
Blessing
Beatitude
Bliss

Beauteous
Bloom
Beautiful
Blossom
Beautify
Benefaction
Bonanza
Beneficial
Bonus
Befriend
Boost
Benefit
Bountiful
Benevolent
Bounty
Beauty
Bright
Beloved
Brighten
Best
Brill
Bestow
Brilliant
Better
Bubbly
Betterment
Budding
Big
Buddy
Bijou
C
Calm
Compliment
Can
Confidence
Capable
Confirm
Care
Congenial
Celebrate

Congratulate
Certain
Conscious
Charitable
Consciousness
Charity
Consider
Charm
Considerate
Charmer
Constant
Charming
Constructive
Cheerful
Content
Cheers
Contribute
Chirp
Cool
Chirpy
Cooperate
Choice
Cope
Chortle
Cordial
Chuckle
Correct
Cinch
Cozy
Civility
Could
Classy
Courage
Clean
Courteous
Clear
Creative
Comely
Credit
Comfort

Cuddly
Comfortable
Cushy
Comic
Cute
Comical

D

Decency
Decent
Delectable
Delicate
Delicious
Delight
Desirable
Do
Dreamy
Dynamic

E

Eager
Engage
Equity
Ease
Engaging
Equivalent
Easily
Engross
Erudite
Easy
Enhance
Especial
Economic
Enjoy
Essence
Ecstasy
Enlighten
Essential
Edify
Enlist
Establish
Educate

Enliven
Esteem
Effective
Enormous
Ethic
Efficiency
Enough
Ethical
Efficient
Enrapture
Euphony
Elate
Enrich
Euphoria
Elegant
Ensure
Eureka
Elevate
Enterprise
Evolution
Eligible
Enterprising
Exalt
Emphasis
Entertain
Exceed
Emphasize
Entertainment
Exceedingly
Emphatic
Enthrall
Excel
Enable
Enthuse
Excellence
Enchant
Enthusiasm
Excellent
Encourage
Enthusiastic

Excite
Endear
Entire
Exotic
Endearment
Entrust
Expert
Endeavour
Equal
Expertise
Endorse
Equality
Exquisite
Endow
Equally
Extensive
Energetic
Equilibrium
Extraordinary
Energize
Equitable
Exult
Energy
F
Fabulous
Flexible
Fair
Flower
Faith
Focus
Faithful
Fond
Fame
Fondly
Family
For
Fancy
Foresee
Fantastic
Foresight

Fare
Forever
Fascinate
Forgive
Fast
Forgiveness
Favor
Forward
Favorite
Frank
Feasible
Free
Felicity
Freedom
Fellowship
Fresh
Festive
Friend
Fetching
Friendly
Fine
Friendship
Finesse
Fruitful
First
Fulfill
Fit
Fully
Fitting
Fun
Funny
Flashy
G
Gallant
Goodness
Galore
Goodwill
Game
Gorgeous
Generate

Gosh
Generous
Grace
Genial
Graceful
Genius
Gracious
Gentle
Grand
Genuine
Grandeur
Gift
Grateful
Gifted
Gratify
Giggle
Gratitude
Gist
Great
Give
Greet
Glad
Greeting
Glorious
Grow
Glory
Guarantee
Glossy
Guest
Glow
Guidance
Go
Guide
Going
Good
H
Handy
Homely
Happily
Honest

Happy
Honestly
Harmonious
Honesty
Harmonize
Honeyed
Harmony
Honorary
Healthy
Honor
Heart
Honorable
Heaven
Hooray
Heavenly
Hope
Hello
Hopeful
Help
Hopefully
Helpful
Hospitable
Helping
Hot
Highly
Humane
Hilarious
Humanitarian
Hilarity
Humorous
Hip
Humor
Handsome

I

Idea
Ingenuity
Ideal
Initiate
Ideally
Initiative

Immense
Innocent
Immerse
Innovate
Immune
Input
Impartial
Inspiration
Impeccable
Inspire
Impress
Inspired
Impressive
Interest
Improve
Interested
Improvement
Interesting
Increase
Invitation
Incredible
Invite
Indeed
Inviting
Ingenious

J

Jest
Joke
Jolly
Jovial
Joy
Joyful
Joyous
Jubilant
Jubilation
Juicy
Just

K

Keen
Keep up

Kind
Kind-hearted
Kindly
Kiss
Kudos

L

Large
Lively
Lark
Lovable
Laugh
Love
Lavish
Lovely
Learn
Loving
Learned
Loyal
Learning
Lucid
Leisure
Luck
Leisured
Lucky
Leisurely
Lucrative
Liberate
Luminous
Liberation
Luscious
Life
Lush
Light
Luster
Lighten
Lustrous
Light-hearted
Luxuriant
Likable
Luxuriate

Like
Luxurious
Liking
Luxury
M
Made
Mediate
Magnificent
Meditate
Magnify
Mellow
Magnitude
Mercy
Maintain
Merit
Majesty
Method
Major
Miracle
Majority
Miraculous
Make
Morale
Manage
Most
Manifest
Motivate
Manner
Much
Many
Multitude
Marvelous
Must
Master
Matter
N
Neat
New
Newly
Nice

Nicety
Nifty
Nippy
Nirvana
Noble
Nod
Normal
Notable
Note
Noted
Notice
Noticeable
Nourish
Now
Nurse
Nurture
O
Obliging
Offer
OK
On
Onward
Oodles
Oomph
Open
Openly
Open-minded
Opportune
Opportunity
Original
Outgoing
Outstanding
P
Pacify
Perfection
Practical
Palatable
Persevere
Praise

Palpable
Perspective
Precious
Paradise
Placid
Prize
Paragon
Pleasant
Pro
Pardon
Please
Produce
Par excellence
Pleasurable
Productive
Passion
Pleasure
Proficient
Passionate
Plenitude
Progress
Passive
Plenteous
Promote
Patience
Plenty
Promotion
Patient
Plus
Prosper
Peace
Plush
Peaceable
Poise
Pure
Peaceful
Polite
Purify
Peak
Positive

Purity

Pep

Possible

Perfect

Potential

Powerful

Q

Quality

Quiet

Quick

Quackery

R

Radiant

Reliable

Rapture

Relief

Ready

Remarkable

Real

Remedy

Really

Reputable

Reason

Respect

Reassure

Responsible

Receive

Rest

Reception

Restful

Receptive

Restore

Reciprocate

Result

Recommend

Reward

Refreshing

Rewarding

Regard

Rich

Relax

Release

Right

S

Sacred

Simplify

Sufficient

Sacrosanct

Simply

Sumptuous

Safe

Sincere

Super

Safety

Smart

Superabundant

Salubrious

Smashing

Super

Satisfaction

Smile

Superior

Satisfactory

Sociable

Supple

Satisfy

Social

Supply

Save

Special

Support

Saving

Spectacular

Supporter

Savior

Splendid

Supporting

Self-assertive

Splendiferous

Supportive

Self-
confidence

Splendor

Supreme

Self-discipline

Steady Sure

Self-esteem

Straightforwar
d

Sweet

Self-help

Succeed

Swell

Sense

Success

Swift

Sensible

Successful

Sympathetic

Share

Succinct

Sympathize

Simple

Suffice

Sympathy

Simplicity

Sufficiency

T

Tact

Timeless

Teach

Timely

Teacher

Top

Teaching

Training

Team

Tranquil

Testament

Tranquility

Testimonial	Upbeat	Wonder
Transcend	Upgrade	Wholehearted
Testimony	Uplift	Wonderful
Transient	Upstanding	Wholesome
Thank	Urbane	Wonderment
Transparent	Useful	Wholly
Thankful	User-friendly	Wondrous
Triumph	Utmost	Will
Thanksgiving	**V**	Workable
Triumphant	Valid	Willing Worth
Therapeutic	Validate	Win
True	Valuable	Worthwhile
Therapy	Value	Winner
Trust	Venerable	Worthy
Thorough	Veracious	Winning
Trustworthy	Verify	Would
Thoughtful	Versatile	Winsome
Trusty	Very	Wow
Thrill	Viable	Wisdom
Truth	Vibrant	**X**
Thrive	Virtue	**Y**
Try	Virtuosity	Yearn
Tidy	Virtuoso	Yes
U	Virtuous	Yippee
Ultimate	Vitality	Young
Ultra	Vivacious	Youth
Unconditional	Vivid	Youthful
Uncritical	**W**	Yo-Yo
Understand	Warm	Yours
Understanding	Wise	You said it
Unequalled	Warmth	**Z**
Unequivocal	With	Zeal
Unerring	Welcome	Zealous
Unfetter	Witty	Zest
Unflagging	Well	
Ungrudging	Won	
	Wellbeing	

Let's move on now to explore personal metaphors. A metaphor is when you compare or match two things together that are normally not related. A common example of a metaphor is "life is a journey." The metaphors you use in life play a large role in how you define your reality. This is another area where you will want to become specifically aware of the metaphors that you use, so you can make sure that they are making your life better and not worse.

Below is a list of common negative metaphors and their more positive counterparts. If you look at this list and see that you use one or more of these negative metaphors, begin to make a habit of using the positive counterpart instead.

Negative metaphor: "Life is like a war."

Positive metaphor: "Life is like a dance."

Negative metaphor: "Life is a gamble."

Positive metaphor: "Life is a roller coaster."

Negative metaphor: "Life is a race."

Positive metaphor: "Life is a stream."

Negative metaphor: "Life is a prison."

Positive metaphor: "Life is an open road."

Negative metaphor: "Life is a joke."

Positive metaphor: "Life is a funny joke."

Sit down and think about the metaphors you most commonly use and write them all down. If they are the same or similar to any of the negative ones in the list above, adopt a positive counterpart instead and begin to use those as your new metaphors for life.

Next, we move on to questions. I cannot stress to you how powerful questions are in your life. The reason why questions are so powerful is because, due to the way that your brain is programmed when you ask a question, it *must* give you an answer. This becomes a double edge sword because one simple negative question can cascade into a whole entourage of negative thoughts and feelings and actions. On the other hand, one single positive question can ignite your possibility thinking and unlock hidden potential and solutions, instantly amplifying your mental and physical state.

Let's look at the difference between these two phrases;

"I am such an idiot."

"Why am I such an idiot?"

On the surface, the difference between these two statements is minimal but the emotional impact between these two is huge. The first phrase is a statement where the person is simply stating that they are an idiot. That type of self-talk is obviously detrimental, however, the damage ends once the statement ends. The second phrase is different, because it is a question its sends a message to your brain asking for more information. Your brain can only give you information that is of the same quality as the questions that you ask it. That means is if you ask your brain a negative question, it *must* give you a negative answer.

What's worse is if you ask your brain and negative question like, "Why am I such an idiot?" most of the time you will not only get one answer but you will get many. All of a sudden, what started out as a seemingly harmless question has now turned into a bombardment of negative information about yourself. Because of the law of BTFAR, everything from your mental to your physical state are affected. How unfair is that?! The good news is that it is a two way street and as soon as you begin to ask new powerful and positive questions, you instantly begin to get powerful and positive feedback.

Just like reprogramming your vocabulary, you must become aware of the negative questions that you are asking yourself and instantly ask new and more positive questions. By asking new and more positive questions, right away you are interrupting the previous signal that it has been sent to the brain and you are asking a new one that requires completely different information. This is a pattern interrupt, which you learned in the previous chapter. Remember a bad habit can only be detrimental if you allow it to get to a harmful stage. Here is a list of some of the common negative questions that you may be asking yourself and their positive counterparts:

Negative question: "Why is life so unfair?"

Positive question: "How can I even the odds?"

Negative question: "I always fail, so why should I try?"

Positive question: "How can I learn from my past, and put my best foot forward?"

Negative question: "Why does this always happen to me?"

Positive question: "How can I change my approach?"

Negative question: "How can I proceed if I don't know what to do?"

Positive question: "If I did know what to do, how would I proceed?

Negative question: "Why is God punishing me?"

Positive question: "How can I use this moment as an opportunity to grow?"

Questions are also good for reframing negative statements. For example:

Negative statement: "That's just the way that it is."

Positive question: "How can I change the things I am not satisfied with?"

Negative statement: "No matter what I do I will never succeed."

Positive question: "How have I succeeded in the past and how can I use that to help me be successful now?"

Negative statement: "I can't do it."

Positive question: "How can I do it?"

Negative statement: "I can't handle this."

Positive question: "How can I handle this?"

Negative statement: "I hate traffic!"

Positive question: "How can I practice gratitude in this moment?"

Now that we have spent some time focusing on your personal vocabulary, metaphors, and questions, I would like to drill down even further and focus on three words in particular that can drastically increase the quality of your life instantly, once you start using them, or not using them, as you will see.

Those three words are yes, no, and sorry. I am willing to bet that you do not say yes enough, and when you do, it is for the wrong reasons. I am also willing to bet that you do not say no enough, and when you do, again, it is probably for the wrong reasons. And if you're the kind of person who tends to think that everything is your fault I will bet the farm that you say the word sorry too much. Those three statements may be pretty bold on my part but as long as you have room for improvement, which everyone does, I believe they are accurate.

Let's start with the word yes. I would like you to become a "Yes Man" (or woman, for now we'll take Yes Man to mean either). I definitely do not mean that I want you to become an order taker, or a butt kisser. Since we're revolutionizing everything in your life anyway, let's completely redefine your definition of a Yes Man. Traditionally a Yes Man is a submissive unquestioning individual. From here on out, the new definition of a Yes Man is an individual who is not only open to new opportunities but actively seeks them out.

Think about all the things in your life so far that you could have said yes to but didn't, and now regret because you wish you would have. Isn't that a horrible feeling!? You see, most of the things in life that we end up regretting are not the things we do, as much as they are the things we don't; the things to which we didn't say yes. Imagine how much better your life would be if you had said yes to all the good opportunities that you passed up. Unfortunately, you can't go back in time and change those decisions, but you can commit to becoming a Yes Man and taking advantage of all of the opportunities that come your way in the future.

The great thing about restructuring your self-talk as a whole is that it makes being a Yes Man much easier. Chances are, the reasons why you turned down opportunities in the past were because of your beliefs and your negative self-talk. Something came your way and because of how you interpreted this situation, you placed a negative expectancy on future events and therefore you passed them up. For example: your friends invite you to a concert and both the opening band and the main event are groups that you have never heard of before. So, you say to yourself, "I have never heard of either of those bands and they probably aren't any good, so I'm not going to waste my time or money."

Lo' and behold, you catch up with your friends the next day and they are all raving about how awesome the concert was and how much the two different bands rocked. And now you feel like the clown of the century for passing it up. Now that you are shifting your self-talk and becoming more aware of the conversations in your head, the previous example would go something like this: your friends invite you to a concert and you've heard of neither of the bands playing. You say to yourself, "I have never heard of either of those bands and they probably aren't any good so I'm not going to waste my time or money." And then, because you are monitoring your thoughts and ready and willing to rephrase your negative questions, you say to yourself, "What if I discovered a new band that I really like, and went out and spent some quality time with my friends?"

All of a sudden, you have changed your negative expectancy to a positive expectancy. Everything, from the images, feelings, and emotions that you have about this event, becomes exciting. Now rather than having a sense of avoidance, you are literally compelled to go. The more you say yes to the opportunities in life the more richness you add to it. Also the more you say yes, the more you open yourself up to the unexpected bonuses that life has to offer. Think about all the beautiful stories out there of couples that met and fell in love simply because of a random string of events. Or someone who stumbled upon an idea for a business because they were invited out to dinner and were struck by an ingenious after being exposed to something they saw. There are millions of stories like that and it is time for you to be the main character in some of those stories, rather than sitting at home reading about them.

Making a habit of saying the word yes has other hidden benefits, as well. The more you say yes and the more you begin to experience all of these bonuses that life has to offer, the more your subconscious begins to get inspired and you get to a point where you say yes to things automatically. To add fuel to the fire, whenever you say yes to something, you say no to something else. By saying yes to adventure, you say no to mediocrity. When you say yes to being bold you say no to being small. When you say yes to success you say no to poverty. Speaking of the word no, let's explore that a little bit.

As I said before, most people who say no often say it for the wrong reasons. They say no to change. They say no to opportunities. They say no to adventure. And, in the end, what they are truly saying no to is their ultimate-self. Ironically, the same types of people are the people who would be considered mice, pushovers, saps, easy targets, softies, and suckers. These people say yes for all the wrong reasons. They think little of themselves and often have a victim mentality, which keeps them from respecting or standing up for themselves.

Just like the word yes, the word no can be equally as positive and powerful. The word no gets a bad rap because it is negative by nature. However when used properly, the word no can produce very positive results. If you are the type of person that is more of the traditional Yes Man, a person who puts yourself last and tries to please everyone else, then this section is especially for you. If the idea of putting your foot down and saying no to friends and family and coworkers seems bold to you, then I am excited for you, because that means as soon as you start saying no, your whole world is going to make a quantum leap. A second century playwright named Terrence once said, "Fortune favors the bold." This has become a model by which I have learned to live and it should be one of yours as well.

Let's look at the facts - if you are the kind of person who always says yes, the chances are the majority of the time you don't really want to say yes. You only say it because you're not willing to stand up for yourself, and/or you are afraid of what people might think of you if you say no to them. Let's look some of the common thoughts from people who do not say no enough.

"If I say no, they might not like me."

"If I say no, they might not respect me."

"If I say no, they might think I don't care."

"If I say no, they might not be willing to help me in the future."

Let's do some analysis here, shall we? Let's look at the first statement: "If I say no, they might not like me." My first question would be, if you've never said no, then how can you be certain that's how they will feel? That leads me to believe that if you have never actually said no and experienced this negative response than means your theory comes from your imagination, which is not based on facts or reality whatsoever. And, therefore a very unreasonable place from whence to draw conclusions about the real world. Also, what if we turn the tables, how about a time when somebody said no to you? Just because they said no, did you abruptly stop liking them? I doubt it.

What about the second phrase: "If I say no, they might not respect me." As a matter of fact, more often than not, when you put your foot down and say no, it shows people that you have respect for yourself and that they cannot take advantage of you. That shows you have strong character and that is a very respectable trait. If you want to take it one step further, you may actually start to inspire other people who observe you. If they see you as a person who was once a lamb, begin to act like a lion they very well may be inspired to do the same. By saying no, you may just make your life better and someone else's at the same time. What a concept!

Let's study the third statement: "If I say no, they may think I don't care." This is another example of an assumption that comes from your imagination. You think that because you always want to try to make people happy that if you say no, your drastic change in behavior will tell people that you don't care. Wrong! I think it's time to start giving the people in your life a little more credit. It is not like they are on the verge of completely writing you off at any moment and if you say no you are banished for life.

More realistically, if you say no to your friends, family and coworkers chances are they will understand because they say no sometimes too. It actually makes more sense to other people for you to say no from time to time than it does for you to say yes constantly. And what about some of the thoughts you've had when someone has said no to you. I am guessing you didn't take it personally and that you logically concluded their reasoning about why they said no, rather than blatantly thinking that they didn't care.

Last but not least: "If say no, they might not help me in the future." This one is a doozy. That statement means that the only way for you to get help in the future is for you to *always* say yes to people. That statement also simultaneously takes a lot of credit away from your friends, family and coworkers, as well. It is human nature for people to want to help. And people generally want to help those who are closest to them, so if anyone is going to want to help you out is going to be your friends, family and coworkers. People who tend to say no often think that if they ask for help they are being a burden, or that they are bothering people. When in reality the same people would actually love to help you out with something. And, by not asking them for help, you are robbing them of their opportunity to do something nice for you.

The final word that I want to focus on specifically is the word "sorry." Have you ever known someone who apologized for practically everything and it didn't matter what it was. This person would apologize for anything from the weather, to the traffic, and everything in between. They've said they're sorry so much that whenever you talk to this person, you can predict they will apologize for a multitude of things at least a handful of times. Doesn't it drive you crazy?

At this time, I would encourage you to think about how much you say, "I'm sorry." Although what I really want to know is why you feel like you have to apologize for everything. Is it an inferiority complex, low self-esteem, need for attention, programming from your parents, or an overall feeling that everything is your fault? Take advantage of this moment and do your best to uncover what is causing you to apologize so much.

Remember, this is about liberating yourself. This is about stepping outside of your comfort zone and being bold. Imagine how much confidence, certainty, and overall empowerment you would have if you could stop apologizing for everything. Keep in mind that this is not about dodging responsibility. In fact, it is just the opposite. When you make a commitment to be 100% responsible for your life, you realize it is only appropriate to apologize for things over which you have direct control.

There are a few different ways you can overuse the word "sorry." The first is in how you initiate conversation with others, for example, saying things like: "Sorry sir, but do you have the time?" "Sorry, can you tell me how to get to Walnut Street?" "I'm sorry to bother you, but can you give me directions to the grocery store?" These are all classic examples of a person apologizing for things that they have no control over. The other type of apology abuse is in your reaction to conversation. For example, it would be bad if you were to apologize for any of the following statements: "Too bad it's raining outside today." "I had trouble with my car and it made me late to work today." "I am having a bad day."

There is a chance you may not have any type of negative personality complex at all. There is a chance that you over-apologize just to be nice. Saying you're sorry may help you feel like you're being thoughtful, considerate, and agreeable. This is nice in theory but playing "Mr. Nice Guy or Gal" you often sacrifice how you really feel, and will agree to things, just to avoid conflict. On top of that, you will find yourself becoming angry when people do not appreciate or respect your kindness. This can lead to negative thoughts, resentment, and passive aggressive behavior. None of which are going to help you or anyone else. Nor do they have anything to do with being nice.

My greatest wish for you, if you apologize too much, is to get to a point where you never apologize for anything that is not your fault ever again. The truth is, people don't want apologies. They want solutions. You might think that saying sorry in a given situation will make you or the other person feel better, but helping that person find a solution is a much more prudent option. And, as far as how you speak to other people, I want to challenge you to drop the words "I am sorry" from the beginning of all your sentences. You will start to feel more respect for yourself, and from others.

Now that you have the tools for eliminating your bad habit and creating powerful rituals, it is time to face the ugly habits you have and decide whether you can replace them with a positive ritual or if they need to be erased all together. Go down the following list and identify any of the bad habits that you have and write down on a piece of paper exactly what combination of tools you are going to use to put them to rest.

Stress

Hot headedness

Impatience

Narrow mindedness

Taking on too much at one time

Worry

Guilt

Fear of the unknown

Doubt

Working too hard

Overeating

Emotional eating

Poor self image

Laziness

Procrastination

Lying

Cheating

Un-natural state changers (i.e. drinking, smoking, hard drugs, Tylenol, coffee, soda, etc.)

Gossiping

This is obviously a fraction of the bad habits that exist in the world, but this will at least get you thinking about the current bad habits you have. Chances are you know what many of them are already; you have just never had the correct level of personal power to be able to get rid of them. Now you have the tools and identity to start doing the things you really want and to put an end to the things you really don't want to be doing. Your perception of your actions, habit, and rituals and what they mean, change as you begin to live in line with your ultimate-self. Your rituals will inspire you to take action, although to be able to unleash all your personal power you must fully master motivation.

Take Action!

The quality of your self-talk is huge! Now is your opportunity to build a strong positive foundation for your self-talk.

What is/are your:

- precursors?

- programming?

- procedures?

How can you become more aware of the current self-talk you have?

What needs to happen to improve your self-talk?

What is the quality of your personal vocabulary?

What kind of personal metaphors do you have?

Put this book down and take action now!

Congruent Expectancy

If Positive Belief Power is the number-one key to eliminating your bad habits, then Positive Expectancy is second. Positive Expectancy means shifting your assumptions and expectations from negative to positive. Another huge reason why people fail to change their bad habits long-term is because of the negative mental association they have regarding what the new reality would be like. An example of this would be a person who wants to eat healthy but isn't. What are some of the typical excuses they use?

> "Eating healthy is a hassle"

> "It's expensive."

> "Health food tastes like cardboard."

> "Eating healthy food takes too much time to prepare."

All of those phrases are directly connected to a negative expectancy. As I mentioned earlier, people by nature move away from things they expect will bring them pain. This is one of the leading reasons why people say, "I know what to do but just don't do it." If you believe that eating healthy is going to involve pain, then why on earth would you ever want it to be a serious part of your life?

Let's turn the tables and look at people who have made eating healthy a ritual. They do not have any of the complaints or negative beliefs about eating healthy like the people with unhealthy eating habits have. When they think about eating healthy, they see it as something that is part of who they are. They use some of the following words to describe eating healthy:

> "Preparing healthy food is fun."

"Eating healthy is worthwhile."

"Eating right can taste good and be healthy."

"The cost of healthy living is priceless."

Do you see how these two types of people are worlds apart yet talking about the same thing? That is how powerful your mental associations can be. Either they will help you find a reason to stay away from something or they will help you be fully committed to it.

You may have a list a mile long of positive reasons of why you "should" eat healthy, but if you expect the process to be painful, especially long term, then you're sunk. Negative expectancy is one of the biggest factors that will lock you into your bad habits. Along with that comes the positive associations that you may have about the bad habits you have. The wires become crossed and people will develop negative expectancy about the things that will make their life better and positive expectancy about the things that are constantly making their life worse.

The positive expectancy a person will have that is connected to a given habit has a few sources. One is the certainty that the given habit creates. It is not the habit itself, most of the time, to which a person is so attached, as much as it is the effect that the habit has. Whether the habit helps reduce stress, numb, or distract that person, it is certain a given habit will produce these results time and time again so they build a dependency to them. Therefore, even the thought of going without this habit can be painful, even if the habit is a negative one.

In order to have totally mastery over your habits, you have to develop what I call Congruent Expectancy. That means that the positive rituals you would like to create have a deeply positive and compelling expectancy attached to them. This way you literally become propelled toward success in those areas. Along with that, there must be a strong negative emotional expectancy attached to bad habits you have. This where your sense of morals and identity come into play and can help you more easily shift away from negative habits.

Shifting your beliefs about the current habits you have, and the future rituals you would like to have, is easier than you might think. Let's say that exercise is one of the rituals that you would like to add to your daily life. But, you have had bad luck with it in the past, either because you were overwhelmed at the gym, fell off the wagon and didn't get back on, or avoided exercise all together because you thought it would be just too painful.

This is where you get to have some fun. Your challenge becomes figuring out how you can make exercise something that is fun, enjoyable, pleasurable, and something you look forward to. This transition in thinking will open up your possibility thinking and start creating new positive associations with working out.

Remember, working out should be something you love to do! For example; rather than thinking about how it is going to be painful, think about how great you'll feel after. Rather than thinking of it as a waste of time, begin to see it as an investment of your time. Do whatever you have to do to shift your attention onto the positive aspects of working-out.

You can use a scale of one to ten to help you modify your beliefs and associations. Using this scale is a great way to quantify your progress in your transition from negative to positive, regarding positive rituals or positive to negative regarding your bad habits. Start by specifying what the most extreme sides of the scale are. For example, one might be something like you totally hate the idea of fitness and have an aversion to it and ten could be something like you absolutely love fitness and are always compelled to exercise.

Once you have a scale defined for your given habit that you would like to transform into a ritual, then you have to decide where you are specifically on that scale. The point here is to be as clear and honest as possible. I use this tool all the time with my clients. The dialog usually looks something like this:

Me: Ok Brad, on a scale of one to ten, with one being you totally hate eating healthy and ten being you absolutely love it, where are you?

Brad: I would say that I am about a five or six.

Me: If you had to choose one, would you say you are a five or six?

Brad: I am a five.

Me: Ok great, now in your own words, describe the new beliefs you would have to have in order to live as a ten.

Brad: Well, I suppose that I would believe eating healthy was an important part of my life and realize I owe it to myself and my family to be strong and healthy.

Me: Great! If that is the belief you would have as a ten, what is your belief now?

Brad: I guess I just don't really care right now. My belief is that eating healthy is not a big deal.

Me: Ok, if our goal is to get you to be at a level ten, how can begin to adopt this new belief that you do care and that eating right is a very big deal?

Brad: Maybe I could use eating healthy as an opportunity to respect myself more, and then I'll start to take eating healthy more seriously.

Me: That is an awesome idea! Tell me more, what would it feel like to be eating healthy and know that you are respecting yourself at the same time?

Brad: Oh man, it would feel great. I would have more energy, I would lose weight, and my self-confidence would go up.

Me: I love it! Now let's look into the future a little bit. What would a day in the life of Brad living at level ten look like? Walk me through it.

Brad: I would start my day off with a really healthy breakfast and a tall glass of water. I would take my lunch out of the fridge that I had prepared the night before, because I hate the idea of buying pizza or a burrito at lunch. And, after work, for dinner I would come home and make something I knew I would enjoy and that was also healthy rather than something that was quick and easy.

Me: That is great! You would be thinking ahead and planning your meals. Having your meals prepared is a great way to set yourself up for victory and respect yourself at the same time. Can you see how that would create a positive expectancy toward eating right?

Brad: Oh yeah! That will be awesome!

Me: Brilliant! I am curious; can you tell me how the idea of you having an unhealthy eating habit makes you feel now?

Brad: It makes me feel sick. I would feel like I let myself and my family down. I would feel like I disrespected myself and my family and I would never want to do that.

Me: Ok, so tell me what is something you could do today right after this conversation that will be in line with getting you to a level ten?

Brad: I am going to go to the grocery store and stock up on healthy food for the rest of the week and buy some containers, so I can have my healthy lunches prepared and ready to go in the morning. I can't wait to get started!

Me: Brad, I'd like to congratulate you on your decision. I am excited to see how things go. Great work!

This dialog shows how the client went from a clear understanding of the scale, with one being totally hating healthy eating and ten being that they totally love it. It shows how Brad got clear about where he was on the scale. From there he defined what a ten was to him personally and what beliefs he would have to have in order to live at that level. He then discovered how he could shift his current belief to a level ten and it opened up his vision to how rich and compelling that future would be. This causes him to adopt a positive expectancy about eating healthy automatically. After that, he cannot help but feel the overwhelming feelings of excitement and richness that this new way of life will afford him.

The great thing that happened almost secretly was that because of Brad's strong positive believe and perspective of what living at a level ten would be like, he also created a strong negative expectancy about what would happen if he continued with the negative habit in the future. By tying his sense of morals and family into the ritual, the idea of unhealthy eating became something he now has an aversion to.

Every aspect of the one to ten scale process is important, but the most important part is to find a way to begin to seed this new belief into your psychology now. This way the new belief becomes real, it becomes a place that you can actually think, feel, and act from rather than being just an exciting idea. Being able to buy into the new positive belief is what is going to give you the positive expectancy you need in order to create a powerful ritual.

Take Action!

In order to have powerful rituals you will need to have a positive expectancy about rituals. The way you feel toward your new ritual must be congruent with the quality of that ritual. Make sure you do not have any conflicting beliefs or habits that will sabotage your new rituals. Remember the reason why so many people fail to keep New Year's resolutions – they fail because even though they know their new ritual is better for them, they still have negative beliefs about it and what it means.

How can you create a positive expectancy about the rituals you want to develop?

What type of belief do you need to have in order to support your new ritual?

Put this book down and take action now!

Triggers

The pesky part about bad habits is that they are mostly automatic. Often times it can be difficult and frustrating to break a bad habit. This constant challenge and frustration can lead to feelings of defeat and eventually lead to giving up all together. One minute you're fine and the next you are neck deep in some type of unhealthy behavior. When it comes to bad habits, stopping them for good is the goal, and hopefully you have been able to see that the secret to putting an end to bad habits lies in preventative measures. It is better to erase a bad habit all together than to try to manage it when it comes up.

Although sometimes even though you may have new beliefs and expectations for yourself, it can still be hard to break a habit. Habits become hardwired into your nervous system, which makes them hard to get rid of even if you have some of the previous preventative tools in place. Imagine if you had a tool that would catch all the slip ups, a tool that was like a trained watch dog ready to attack at the first sign of a bad habit. That is exactly what triggers are.

Triggers are mental and/or physical alarms that you attach to a negative thought, feeling or action. Triggers are very similar to Reactionary Awareness, which you will learn about in the self-talk section coming up. Triggers help you program your brain and bring awareness to the moment so that you can take control of your thoughts or actions. This way the power remains in your hands and you do not have to worry about the negative repercussions of your old habit.

In order to instill a trigger, you have to be very clear about the precursor or activating event that causes the bad habit in the first place. This originating event can be anything from a thought, word, phrase, action, or feeling. A more specific example of this would be a person who has had a long week at work and on Friday they get home and they are tired, frustrated, and feeling like they want to cut loose, so they say, "I deserve to have a drink." The first thing they do is head for the alcohol, be it the wine rack, liquor cabinet, or refrigerator, with the idea that they will have only one drink. That one drink turns into five or six and sooner or later becomes regret. The precursor, in this case, would be the thought that they "deserve" to have a drink. This thought becomes the beginning of the end. This thought sparks all sorts of different emotions and thoughts. They begin to rethink the negative aspects of the week, which allows them to feel justified in their "I deserve" statement.

The trigger would be attached to the phrase "I deserve." This would make that specific phrase become the magic word, which activates a mental alarm. The alarm consists of a high level of awareness and a positive replacement for the negative behavior. You must have a positive replacement when shifting from bad habits to positive rituals, because the brain needs something immediate to grab onto in order to steer you in a better direction. The positive replacement in this case would be a drastic new definition of the word "deserve."

Ideally, you would have instilled some new beliefs about who you are, what your purpose is, and why you should be dedicated to loving yourself more. That means if the old statement was, "I deserve to have a drink," then the new statement would be something like, "I deserve to respect myself and treat myself right." This becomes powerful, because even if the person has not yet fully adopted this new phrase to a point where it is natural and automatic, as long as it is in place as a trigger, the positive effects can still be realized.

Triggers become reminders that allow you to interrupt your pattern at the perfect time. They remind you to drop your current thought and to focus on the one that is more fitting for what you really want in life. Think about how helpful it would be to have a strong yet positive reminder each time an old habit tried to flare up. On top of that having a trigger that redirects your energy, and focus, would begin to condition your brain in a way that lets your brain know this new positive ritual is the new operating system that is in charge. Very powerful!

Let's look at a verbal example of triggers. Let's say a man has a bad habit of saying the word ain't. Because this habit is an acquired habit, there is very little awareness around it. It is not connected to a negative belief or feeling. It is merely the result of years of conditioning from outside influences by friends or family. In this case, the person must install a verbal trigger so that when they hear themselves say the word ain't, it reminds them to replace it with something else. In this case, the positive replacement would be "is not." This person may not be able to stop him or herself from saying ain't but as long as he or she has attached a trigger to it each time they say it, they will be reminded of the correct wording. This will transfer the balance of power from one side to the other. Soon the brain gets sick of being corrected all the time and phases out the word ain't all together. I can still remember doing this myself when I was transforming my vocabulary. I grew up saying, "How 'bout it?" and when I caught myself saying it to someone, I would stop and repeat the sentence by saying, "What do you think?" Even though it was awkward to have to go back and say the correct phrase out loud to whomever I was speaking, it helped me create and solidify that new pattern of speech.

The last type of trigger is a physiological trigger. Sometimes the bad habits we develop can be purely a physical thing. An example of this would be habits like:

- Foot tapping

- Nail biting

- Fidgeting

- Knuckle cracking

- Playing with hair

- Back/neck cracking

These can often be related to feelings of stress, nervousness, or anxiety. If that is the case, they can be reversed by addressing the underlying feeling or belief, which causes the negative physical manifestation. Physiological habits can also be acquired habits that you have developed over the years from observing people who are close to you. Physiological habits are directly tied to your nervous system. They can be tough to break because on a cellular level, your body engages in this physical habit and many times the level of awareness and control we have over it is very low.

Installing a trigger to a physical habit comes down to becoming aware of the initial thought that prompts the physical action. Consequently, this gives you an opportunity to stop the physical action before it starts. If the physical habit is an acquired habit and does not necessarily have a source thought or belief at its root, then you must attach the trigger to the physical movement itself. It is important to identify the earliest symptom of the negative physical habit. A few examples of this would be putting your hands together in preparation to begin cracking your knuckles, raising your hand up toward your head to play with your hair, or creating a certain stance in order to crack your back. All of these early warning signs can be used as triggers that will make you aware of the action and allow you to take control over what you are doing. Rather than executing the habit and then feeling bad for doing so, say instead something like, "I really need to stop doing that!"

The positive replacement in this case does not have to be anything drastic but it does have to be something specific. For the best result, it should be a combination. It should include a question to yourself - one that will encourage you to get back on track and focus on whatever it was that you were doing - and a physiological movement that will interrupt your pattern and help you refocus. The question can be something simple and direct like. "What am I focused on right now?" or, "How can I get back on track?" The action can be as easy as taking your hands apart if you are about to begin cracking your knuckles, lowering your hand if you are about to start playing with your hair, or moving your body back into a normal position if you were going to crack your back. Whatever the combination is, the key is to know specifically what you are going to say and do for each one.

Once you have your new triggers in place, some repetitive exercise is a foolproof way to extinguish the old habit for good. As goofy or awkward as this part might be, trust me, if you actually **do it** you will have a higher level of mastery over yourself and your habits.

Start by performing the initial movement, and then immediately ask yourself the question you have put in place to get you back on track. Then execute the physical action you have set up to detour the negative one. I will use back cracking as an example. From a normal standing position move into whatever your stance is to crack your back. As soon as you are in the stance, since it is the trigger, you ask yourself your question to refocus yourself. "What am I focusing on right now?" Then move your body back into a normal position. This creates a formal system that you can repeat; the sequence would look like this:

Perform initial movement connected to bad habit

Movement triggers awareness

Redirecting question is asked

Reforming physical movement is executed

Repeat this pattern for five minutes and do it exactly the same way each time. It reprograms your nervous system more quickly. Your neural network will literally begin to reshape itself. You will begin to develop what is called muscle memory or motor memory. After an action is repeated enough times, the muscles begin to memorize the motion and therefore less awareness and intention is

necessary to prevent the unwanted habit in the future.
You can see examples of muscle memory in your everyday
life - anything from typing on a keyboard, riding a bike, or
driving a car. These are all things you have trained your
body to do in such a way that doing so becomes almost
automatic.

You may feel silly standing in a room repeating these
movements over and over for five minutes straight.
However, as the old saying goes, "Practice makes perfect."
By actually practicing refining your habit, you do not have to
live in such a reactionary state, plus you build up your
confidence in regards to being able to take control of
yourself. That way, when you are in the moment and you
have much more power. No matter what type of trigger you
are, instilling, you must include some kind of repetition.

Another great tool for refining your habits is forcing yourself
into situations or environments where you are prone to
demonstrate your bad habit. At first glance, this might seem
like you are setting yourself up for failure. In reality, this
turns into a real world opportunity for you to practice your
trigger and build your self-discipline. An example of this
would be a person who wants to build up their confidence in
public and therefore forces themselves to attend more social
or public events. The beauty here is that the old habit of
being shy will naturally arise, which would then cause the
trigger for that person to go off, redirecting their thoughts
and energy in a direction that will help them be talkative and
engaging.

When it comes to breaking habits, I do not believe in
avoiding situations that generally trigger those bad habits. To
me that's like putting a Band-Aid on a broken leg. To have
true mastery, you must be able to insert yourself into the
environments that once caused your bad behavior and be
able to have total control in that moment. That means if you
are afraid of going to parties because you have a bad habit of
drinking too much, then going to parties can actually be the
thing that cures you of your bad habit. Because in reality it is

not the party of which you are afraid. It's drinking too much. And as long as you have a powerful belief and the trigger to match, you will react completely differently in that situation, while still being able to enjoy the personal and social benefits of going to a party.

The more opportunities you give yourself to exercise your beliefs and triggers, the better off you are going to be. Just imagine the great sense of personal power that you'll have when you find yourself in a situation where you would generally be a slave to your bad habit. This time, instead you turn the situation around completely act from a place of personal integrity. And, the more situations you get into where you have those types of victories, the more you will ingrain that certainty of character into your life.

Take Action!

Installing triggers will allow you to take control over your
negative emotions.

What negative emotions require the need for you to install a
trigger?

What would the mental and or physical trigger(s) be for that
specific habit?

How can you practice this trigger?

Put this book down and take action now!

As If, Even If

A very dangerous phrase floats around in the self-help world. This phrase by its very nature sets people up for failure and disillusionment. That phrase is, "Fake it, 'till you make it." At firstglance, you might not think much of it. However, by now you should have a good understanding that even the smallest words can make a big difference in your psychology and your overall results.

When people say, "Fake it 'till you make it," they are generally referring to modifying some type of behavior. It can be anything from eating healthy, to exuding confidence, to relationships. The idea behind fake it 'till you make it is that all you have to do to adopt a new behavior is to pretend like that behavior is part of who you are. The biggest bone of contention that I have with this phrase is the word "fake." If you have to pretend as if you enjoy eating healthy, have confidence, or are wealthy, then you are basically starting a race with your shoelaces tied together.

When you fake something, all you're doing is changing the exterior. If you watch people who try to pretend as if they're happy when they're not, what happens? It not only fails every time but it is evident to everyone around. Have you ever seen somebody fake a smile? There is no comparison between to a genuine smile and a fake one. But more importantly, what is going on behind the scenes internally is where the real difference lies. The brain is just way too smart and it knows when a thought, feeling or action is genuine or not. And if your brain does not believe that what you're doing is real, then what you're pretending to do will never transition itself into who you are.

What's even worse is that people will try this idea of fake it 'till you make it and when it doesn't work out, they feel even worse about themselves and become disillusioned about the area of their life upon which they wanted to improve, making it more difficult to make progress in the future. As you can imagine that is a very dangerous combination, cause the one thing that is going to help that person become better, slowly becomes something they lose faith in. Self-improvement is enough of a challenge as it is and a person having to renew their belief in self-help only adds to that challenge.

The largest flaw with this whole idea is that there is a disconnect between what your brain believes in connection to your identity and what you are saying or doing. Identity, mastery, and change all have to do with being congruent in your beliefs, thoughts, feelings, and actions. As we know from BTFAR beliefs are at the top of the list for a reason.

I ended up stumbling upon the solution to the "fake it 'till you make it" riddle in a very ironic way. I studied acting. I know what you must be thinking, "How on earth did you find the solution to faking it in acting, which is the highest form of pretending?" That, my friend, is where you are wrong. True acting is not about faking anything. A real actor becomes their character and for that brief moment, when they are on film or on stage, they truly are that person. The actor gets into the mindset of his character and finds out exactly what their beliefs are, so that they can adopt them. The greatest actors you've ever seen or heard are so good and are so convincing, because they have transformed themselves into someone new. They dig deep down and discover parts of their character inside themselves.

After further thought, I stumbled upon an even bigger breakthrough. First and foremost, I realized that your ultimate-self is not someone that you become, rather it is someone that you uncover. This means the deepest truth of all is that you are pretending to be lamb when in fact you are a lion. If the beliefs, thoughts, feelings and actions you currently have are not congruent with who you really truly are, then they are fake. I know that sounds like a very bold statement but stick with me on this one. Think about it. Imagine a lion walking through the jungle acting like it was a lamb. One of the greatest forms of self-love is knowing who you are and acting like it.

The things that you're afraid of, the bad habits you have, none of the negative beliefs you have about yourself have anything to do with who you really are. Therefore, if you discover that eating healthy is a ritual that is in line with your true identity, then instantly you also discover that from then on eating unhealthily would just be pretending you don't care about your health.

So, I modified the idea of fake it 'till you make it into the new and improved version: acting "as if, even if." When you act "as if, even if," you are telling yourself that you are going to act as if you were your ultimate-self, even if you haven't been in the past. That means if you are someone who is overweight and you realize your ultimate-self is someone who weighs 100 pounds less, then you can begin acting as if you were this person who weighed less, even if that's not who we've been lately.

I once worked with a man who was obese and he wanted nothing more than to shed the weight. He had tried literally everything from pills, to crash diets, fasting, and fads and none of them worked. He came to me down on himself because of all his previous failures, yet at the same time he was so determined to change his life for the better, that he told me he was willing to do whatever it took.

We went to work right away on his core beliefs. And found out that he had a belief where he thought he did not deserve to be healthy. Unfortunately, this belief came from his childhood where his mother and father would constantly tell him that he was no good. I asked him what new belief the ultimate version of himself would have. He said that the ultimate version of himself would believe that he should be his greatest source of love and respect.

After he realized that his current belief was just an echo of his parents and that it had nothing to do with what **he** believed deep down, he started to think differently. Although I knew this was an extreme case, which required extreme tactics. I asked him to go into his bedroom where he had a full-length mirror (which he avoided looking in at all costs) and I asked him to stand in front of it. He told me he hated standing in front of that mirror because he felt embarrassed and ashamed of what he looked like. I told him all of that was about to change.

I asked him to take off all his clothes down to his underwear. After a few minutes of resistance, he did so. He and I had discovered the belief that his ultimate-self would have but he wasn't totally sold on it yet. So I asked him to look into the mirror and see past the excess weight and shame and to find the version of himself that was fit and proud. He slowly but surely started to think and feel differently from the inside out. And then like a bolt of lightning, it hit him. He found himself staring at his ultimate-self. The man in the mirror was full of self-love and someone outstanding, who also had positive beliefs about healthy eating and exercise rituals.

In that moment he realized that all that extra weight had nothing to do with who he really was and that all along he had been a fit man stuck in a fat man's body. He understood that acting "as if, even if" made total sense. He was not pretending to be someone else anymore, he WAS that person. And just because eating right and exercising had not been part of his daily routine, that didn't mean it shouldn't be, in fact he realized that eating right and exercising must be part of his daily life in order to live in accordance with who he really was. From then on, he just kept acting as if he was fit even if his physical body was not there yet. He ended up losing all the weight and continues to work out and eat right to this day.

The whole key to acting "as if even if" relies on your ability to have a light bulb moment and understand that the new belief or ritual that you would like to have in your life is actually already a part of who you really are. This will eliminate the inner conflict of feeling as if you are faking it. You will realize that your new beliefs or rituals are what you would have in the future once you had totally uncovered and transformed into your ultimate-self and therefore must be the same beliefs and rituals you have now.

Rather than looking at the additions to your life as alien, or something that you have to put on and take off like a mask. You look at them and say to yourself, "I *AM* that." Just like the fit man in the fat man's body. He looked in the mirror and saw that even though he was obese that he was that fit man on the inside. His beliefs, thoughts, and feeling about himself were all in line with those he would have if he were fit and healthy on the outside. His body simply needed to catch up.

The greatest part about acting "as if even if" is the moment you start to feel more real, more genuine. You feel like you are really who you're supposed to be. There is this feeling of lightness that comes over you and you have more passion and energy. Being your true self is effortless when you truly embrace it. Acting as if you are a lamb every single day when in reality you are a lion robs you of the natural power a lion is meant to have.

Take Action!

Your new rituals are going to feel foreign to you, and that's OK. Remember the new rituals you want to take on are those that your ultimate-self WOULD be doing. So, even though they are not natural or even comfortable at first, you must act AS IF they are normal, EVEN IF they aren't quite yet.

How can you begin to act "as if, even if"?

How can you use some of your ultimate-self to allow you to act "as if, even if"?

Remember: Acting is NOT faking! It may feel fake because your new ritual may be the total opposite of your current behavior. But that does not mean it's not how you WOULD be behaving if you were your ultimate-self. Now can you look at the new behavior even if it's foreign and say "I am that!"

Put this book down and take action now!

Motivation

It seems that motivation is something everyone wants more of, yet no one ever seems to have enough of. So what gives? If you know all the tricks and tips that the gurus use, then why is it that you struggle to be constantly motivated? The reason is simple; true motivation comes from inspiration, purpose and identity. If your goals are not tied to those three areas, then your motivation will be mild at best. That said, what is your motivation like on a regular basis?

Motivation at its core is not a tip or trick. Real motivation is not something that happens every now and then. I believe to be truly motivated you must understand what motivation is at its deepest level. When you are able to do that then you are also able to reap all of the glorious benefits. Motivation may be what you want but it is not what you need.

True motivation is directly connected to your sense of purpose. If there are certain aspects of your life that tie directly into your identity, then you will always find yourself with adequate amounts of motivation to accomplish anything you desire. I believe the best way to illustrate motivation and how it works, is to provide you with a contrast between people who are constantly motivated and those who are not.

Let's say there are two groups people that want to get physically fit. The first group has a list of all of the hallmark reasons of why they want to get fit. The list would look something like this;

Lose 25 pounds

Look better in a bathing suit

Build muscle

Lower my cholesterol

Decrease heart attack risk

Lower my stress level

At first glance, this list seems like it would be more than sufficient for giving this group ample amounts of motivation. It has both internal and external motivators; the desire to look good in a bathing suit, the desire to lose weight and build muscle would be tied into external motives. The desire to lower cholesterol, stress, and risk of heart attack would be tied into internal motives.

Yet, even with all of these seemingly powerful reasons why this group should get physically fit, they fail to produce any substantial or long-term results. This group represents the majority of people who want to be fit but are not. It is this group of people that go on yo-yo diets, and will stay with an exercise routine anywhere from three weeks to three months and then lose "motivation" and quit. When this group falls off the wagon, they have a tendency to beat themselves up about it. And, the negative effects of beating themselves up make it even harder to be motivated in the future.

The primary reason that someone in this group fails to produce any significant results is not for lack of motivators. We can clearly see those listed above. Rather, it is that those motivators do not have a strong enough source. They do not come from a burning desire and commitment to live congruently within one's personal expectations and life purpose. For example, think of something that you would never do no matter what. Maybe it's lying, cheating, or stealing.

Now think about why it is that you would never do that thing. You wouldn't consider it because it's something that is against your character. On the other hand, think about some things that you would absolutely never give up on and always be committed to. What are those things? Maybe they are your wife or husband, your kids, your family, your friends. Or maybe they are something more like your beliefs, religion or morals.

Whether it is something that you will never do or it is something that you will always do, when it comes to these types of things there is definitely never a lack of motivation. With that being said, let's look at the second group. The second group is a very interesting bunch. And unfortunately, they are a very rare group, as well. The second group has no problem whatsoever being motivated and committing to fitness. These are the people that will go out of their way to make sure that they exercise. What's even more interesting is, even though they may be aware of all the common reasons of why people work out and realize those benefits (like the ones listed above), their number one reason for working out is much different. This group works out constantly, without fail, simply because they believe it is the right thing to do. They are inspired to get up and go.

After comparing these two groups, we can see the differences between them, and in doing so, it is easy to discover that motivation has very little to do with what you *know* and has everything to do with *who you are*. Isn't it true, if you think about it? Out of all the people in the world who want to do something but are lacking motivation the majority of them know just about everything that is involved with attaining that goal. People who want to get fit know that being fit is good for them. They most likely know where they could go to exercise. They know all the reasons of why they should exercise and chances are, even though they are not a fitness expert, they still probably know at least enough exercises to get started. Yet, this is the same group that consistently fails to commit to exercise for the long run or even worse, never gets started.

Let's look at the other group, they're not necessarily smarter than anybody else is and they don't necessarily know more than the first group. In some cases, it is even the opposite. They may not know the first thing about fitness, but they have made the decision that fitness is such a key part of who they truly are that they go out of their way to find the right information and resources to allow them to fulfill this burning desire that they have. The idea of fitness has become integrated into this group's moral code and therefore becomes part of their identity. It makes fitness one of the things that they will always be committed to, while at the same time, something they will never turn their back on.

This idea really cracks the whole motivation code wide open. As overly simplistic as it might sound, the quality of motivation is directly related to the quality of the motive you have for the goal you desire. Ultimately, it boils down to understanding how you can be inspired by the things you want to be motivated about. I am reminded of Tony Robbins when he made his decision to get fit. He decided enough was enough and he simply started running down the beach. He didn't let what he did not know about fitness slow him down. He just went for it. His natural inspiration to be a better a person took over and off he went.

This really shows us something powerful about how easy or difficult it can be to be motivated. Another large component of motivation is focus. As we can see in the formula BTFAR whatever you focus on, greatly influences how you feel. If that is the case, then it is no wonder that people who focus on the negative and painful sides of exercise have a hard time being motivated. If a person has negative beliefs about what fitness means, naturally their thinking from day to day will be unsupportive. What are some of the beliefs you currently have regarding things about which you are trying to be motivated?

If a person is truly motivated to do something, then reasons and resources don't matter. Their greatest reason is close to their heart and whether they have the resources or not, they will find a way or make it happen. Real motivation is unstoppable and inexhaustible. Imagine how it would feel to never again wonder if you were going to take action or not. Pretty liberating feeling, isn't it?

Motivation is a great place where you can see the forces of pleasure and pain at work. If you were to look at all the different categories of your life and think about the things that you do and do not do, you could easily apply this theory. The reason why you watch movies, spend time with friends, read books or play games is that they make you happy. The reason you avoid doing the dishes, taking out the trash, doing homework or whatever it is that you avoid is because you associate pain with that task.

There is nothing mystical about motivation. When you are truly tapping into your motivation, there is no need for a list of reasons why you should do something…you just do it. A child does not sit down and create a list of reasons to help them get motivated to go to the playground. They just go. Playing, to a child, is part of their identity; they are directly inspired by the idea of having fun and thus automatically are compelled to do so. Are you starting to draw some correlations between fun, beliefs, congruent expectancy, and rituals?

The ironic part of this theory is that sometimes we do things that we know are painful and continue to do them anyway, as we saw in the rituals chapter. For example, people who smoke cigarettes and know for a fact that they are bad for them, yet continue to buy them. Or someone who is in an abusive relationship and knows for a fact that it is bad for them, but continues to remain in it. Why do people do that? If we are wired to move towards things that make us happy and away from things that make us sad, why do we consciously do things that cause us pain? As I am sure you have put together by now, it is because there is a dueling reality between what that person wants and what they get.

Fear, your comfort zone, the chimp brain, and a dueling reality all contribute to killing your motivation. They are the primary reasons why someone may want to change, yet stays stuck. The great news is that if you are not as motivated as you'd like to be, there is most likely some fear involved along with an improper motive to do whatever it is that you want to do. Luckily, as you know fear is your friend and as you are going to discover, the things that you want to be motivated about will ultimately become part of your makeup.

If we look back at the two groups, the group who constantly struggles with motivation does so because, although they may want things to change, their mindset is not severe enough. If they tell themselves they are going to work out on Monday and end up failing to do so, they say something like, "I will go tomorrow." This is what is called the ultimate tomorrow syndrome, because ultimately tomorrow never comes. In this case, there is a mediocre expectancy or even a negative one.

The group who is constantly motivated allows the natural laws of pleasure and pain to work for them. They have a very black and white mentality. They also have a very extreme understanding of what it will mean to go workout. And attached to that understanding is a high level of positive expectancy along with the naturally occurring source of inspiration to work out, due to the way that this group has learned to define fitness. On top of that, because the morals and expectations of this group are so high, the concept of not following through on what they told themselves they were going to do is so painful and disgusting to them, that they actually create a brief negative expectancy for what will happen if they do not work out. Do you see the key differences between these two groups? At its core, intrinsic motivation is the most powerful way to inspire yourself to take constant wholehearted action.

This is why many of the older theories of motivation do not work. External motivation does not tap into the core of who a person is and therefore has inconsistent results. You can see examples of this everywhere. Companies will try and "motivate" their employees with things like benefits, bonuses, and store discounts or stock options. Likewise, they will motivate them with fear by punishing unfulfilled work, being late and under performance, even to the extent of being fired.

While these carrot and stick methods may work to a
degree, they rarely produce the *best* kind of results. Though
pleasure and pain may be motivators, they cannot create the
same quality of power that intrinsic motivation can. Not
everyone is motivated by money, benefits, and discounts.
And not everyone is motivated by the fear of being fired.
The overall flaw in this approach is what leads companies to
high levels of turnover and a lower bottom line.

We see unsuccessful approaches to motivation in parenting
as well. A parent will often bribe a child with a new toy or
treat if they behave and punish them with a time out,
spanking, or taking something away such as a play date,
movie, etc. This approach is equally ineffective. I'm sure
you have seen proof of this before in your own life, either
when you were a child or simply by observing this in
society. Just because a child is bribed with a toy or treat, it
does not ensure that they will act a certain way. And it also
goes for punishment. Simply because a child is threatened
does not guarantee that they will be good. In fact often times
we see an opposite reaction.

In relation to the child being good or bad when it comes to
intrinsic motivation, they are motivated to be good not
because of toys, treats or punishments, but because of
something deeper. The child will feel driven to be good out
of the personal value they have for what being good means.
They know that if they are bad, they will personally feel like
they are a bad child. They will also be perceived that way in
the eyes of their parents, which ties greatly into their
decision-making process. Similarly, an employee who is
driven by an intrinsic motivation does not need bonuses and
does not respond well to being threatened. An employee who
has a high level of intrinsic motivation is compelled to do a
good job at work because they believe in the overall vision
of the company. When the mission statement of the company
can be linked to an employee's sense of purpose and
identity, then that employee is filled with a sense of value
and contribution. If the employee feels like they are part of
something they truly want to be involved with, there is an

inherent desire to contribute to the overall big picture of the company. Thus increasing the value of the company and feeling that individual employee has.

This means that if the ideas and goals you have are not linked to your sense of identity and purpose, then the fear you feel when beginning that task or ritual will not be matched with something even more powerful to ensure that you move forward. Therefore, the fear you have about a given goal directly ties into your levels of motivation to which it is related. This shows us why it is so important to have our goals tied into who we truly are. Until we do that, the fear of the unknown and the comfort zone will simply be too much and it will keep us in a stagnant state.

Where do you need to find motivation?

School?

Finances?

Health?

Relationships?

Your career?

Whatever you want to be motivated about, make a list. Start at the top of the list and find a way to attach intrinsic motivation to each and every one of those things. Look at the areas of your life you want to improve. It's time to get real and see things for where they are. Don't fluff it up and make it something that it's not. If you're not happy with your job, get real about it. If you're not happy with your weight, get real about it. Think about what it's costing you to stay the way that you are.

Now think about actually doing the thing that requires motivation. Think about in detail. What it would be like to have a new job or what it would be like to lose weight? Grab onto that picture and get excited about it. Think about the beliefs you have attached to those goals. Do they support you or do they defeat you?

Don't say, "Well, things aren't too bad," or, "Things could be worse." Get drastic and say, "This has got to stop and I'm going to start moving towards new future!" Stop trying to motivate yourself with the ideas of reward and punishment and allow the pure intrinsic motivation to take over. Real motivation is just a side effect of living with passion. Start asking how you can be more inspired and motivation will flow freely.

Take Action!

If you are going to be the architect of your destiny, then you are going to need enough motivation to constantly build and rebuild your world. Real motivation is not something you should have to fight with. It should flow from the core of who you are. Motivation at its core is a side effect of inspiration, which is the most pure form of intrinsic motivation.

How can you tap into your inspiration?

Do you have beliefs and actions that support the rituals you want to be motivated about?

Put this book down and take action now!

Goal Setting

As I mentioned earlier, I believe that no matter what, people will feel a certain level of pain if they are not growing. Setting goals and achieving them is part of the self-improvement process. More than that, it's just part of the growing process. Setting goals is a way to allow the ultimate-self to come out. The great thing you'll find about goal setting is that if your motivation is under control, setting goals and achieving them will be much, much easier.

Even still, it doesn't hurt to have some useful tools that can help you set goals and achieve them. The first tool I want to share with you regarding goal setting is SMART goals. A SMART goal is a goal that is:

- Specific

- Measurable

- Attainable

- Realistic

- Timely

Specific: If there's one thing that you've got to know about goal setting, it's that the more specific your goal is, the more likely it is for you to attain it. Think of it like this, if your goal is to get in shape, an example of a non-specific goal to get in shape would be: "I want to get fit." That goal is not at all specific. Because that goal is not specific, it is not something you can easily get excited about and it therefore becomes very easy to slack off on.

On the other hand, an example of a more specific version of that goal would be something like, "I am going to start working out at the gym and work out three days a week." That goal is much more specific and so thus it is much more easily attained. When it comes to your goals, you have to be specific in every category.

For example, you should know:

> Who is going to be involved?

> What are the results that you want to accomplish?

> Where are you going to partake of this goal?

> What type of time frame are you going to establish?

> What are the requirements and restraints about this goal?

Most importantly, why do you want to achieve this goal? What is the purpose or benefit that you would receive by accomplishing this goal? As we discussed before, having a strong purpose of why you want to do something can be one of the most powerful tools to person can have.

A powerful goal must create a strong sense of positive expectancy. That means that when you visualize the goal you can clearly see a positive outcome - one that makes you believe achieving this goal would be far better than letting it slide. If you do not believe reaching your goal will greatly benefit you in some way shape or form, then why would you ever feel motivated to get off your butt and do anything about it?

You must have clarity, not only about the goal itself (i.e. "I am going to start working out at the gym and work out three days a week."), but it also means you have to get clear about what positive benefits and results you are going to get when you achieve this goal

Measureable: Next, a goal must be measurable. That means there must be some way to break the goal down into realistic parts. If the goal is to lose 30 pounds, how can you break

those 30 pounds down into a weekly or daily amount?
You have to be able to measure your progress along the way
towards your ultimate goal. This allows you to be excited
about your progress along the way.

Most people have the ultimate goal of losing a certain
amount of weight, yet they don't keep track or measure their
results along the way so they get discouraged. They don't
see that 30 pounds coming off right away and they are
unclear about the results they have gotten so far. It makes
them feel as if they realized any results at all, which is a big
bummer and a major reason why people quit their fitness
programs and fail to achieve any long-term results.

You have to be able to do two things here. One, you have to
have a goal that is very attractive and you have to be very
clear about what that goal is why you want it, but more
importantly what it's going to be like when you achieve it.

Along with that, you have to be excited all along the way.
You're going to be excited each morning when you get up
and start doing something to move you towards your goal
because you have such an exciting and clear vision of what it
could be like when you get there.

You have to have the ability to celebrate your small victories
as well. This is part of measuring your success. That's
what's going to ensure that you stick with your goal. As
exciting as the idea of losing 30 pounds is, that's not going
to be tangible or realistic right away. You have to be just as
excited about losing one pound as you are about 30.
Ultimately, you'll know, each day if you can lose one pound
or even half a pound and as it will take you to your goal of
losing 30 pounds. That's why it's important to have
measurable goals, so each time you reach one of those
benchmarks that is your cue to celebrate.

I can't stress to you enough how important it is for you to
take time out and celebrate your achievements along the
way. It's the ability to celebrate your achievements along the

way that is going to keep you motivated from day to day. As much as it is good to have a long-term view and understand all the benefits of what you are working towards in the future, it's important to be able to be stimulated and excited in the moment, as well. There may be goals where you will have to be clever about how you measure them. Exercise again is a great example. You may work out for multiple weeks and not **SEE** any results, although you may **FEEL** amazing.

If you can focus on parts of your goal that set you up for victory, then you will always have something to measure and celebrate. The natural high and feelings of disciple and accomplishment are always available to measure even when literal numbers on the scale or inches lost around your stomach are not. Remember this is your game, if you make the rules, set them up so that winning is easy.

What I would recommend is that you find some very specific way to celebrate. Something that you can do each and every time you reach one of your benchmarks to signify that you're making progress. If your goal happens to be losing 30 pounds, I would not recommend celebrating my going out and eating cake. Remember to be realistic about how you celebrate. You set yourself up for even more victory this way because you know exactly what you have to look forward to once you accomplish your given task.

Celebrating your victory is important on a subconscious level also. If you are putting in all this effort to makes changes in your life yet you don't celebrate, then your mind will think you are doing all this work for nothing. Your brain is not set up in a way to do something for nothing. If your brain does not attach some happiness or accomplishment to what you are doing along the way, it is very likely it will sabotage you and influence you to give up.

Attainable: Along with being measurable, a goal must also be attainable, so what does that mean? What that means is that your goal has to be a combination of something that you can realistically achieve yet something that is slightly out of your reach. That will begin to shift your mindset because you will have a deep understanding of why you want this thing and why it's important to you, even though it might be out of your grasp. Your mind will shift in ways that will allow you to start believing, thinking, feeling, and acting in a way that is conducive to achieving your goal.

When you put your goal just slightly out of reach, it allows your ultimate-self to come out. It is that self inside of you that is more than who you currently are. The key word here is attainable. Often times, people set goals for themselves that are not attainable. Their goals might be things that they want but they are not things that they can realistically attain. They put their goals too far out in front of them or they make them so big that it becomes impossible for them to break them down into tangible realistic steps. I am certainly a fan of dreaming big. I do it all the time and I recommend it to everyone. However, every big dream must then be zoomed in on so that it becomes something that you can actually move toward.

Have you ever wanted to achieve a big goal, then were immediately discouraged by how overwhelming and complex it was? Imagine what would have happened if directly after you come up with this big idea, you had narrowed down your thinking into a handful of very simple easy-to-follow steps that you could use to get started. Think about how many goals or dreams you could have followed through on just by doing that one simple trick.

It is fine for a goal to be large as long as it is not beyond your beliefs. If you're trying to attain a goal in which you don't believe you can reach, then that goal will always remain five feet in front of your face. That ultimately is a way of setting yourself up for failure. When you're creating your goals, make sure that they make sense from an action standpoint. You must be able to look at your goals and be able to see exactly how you can reach them. There is an old saying that goes, "If you fail to plan, then you plan to fail."

Sadly, that is what most people do. They get all excited about their goal but they do not make a plan that allows them to easily and clearly begin.

When creating a goal that is attainable, it is important to think about two things:

What do I need in order to get started?

What type of system or plan do I need to have in place to allow me to take action on this goal consistently?

An example of that is someone that wants to become a martial artist. They would first need to decide what you needed to do to get started (a.k.a. find a school, buy gear, etc.). Then they would have to decide on a training schedule that they could commit to each week. This would allow them to take the grand idea of being a martial artist and breaking it down so that their dream was honestly attainable.

Realistic: Realistic does not necessarily mean that the goal has to be easy. Realistic means that your goal can actually be accomplished and that it's not just some pipe dream that remains in your imagination for the rest of your life. You must be honest with yourself. The goal that you're setting up must be realistic for where you currently are in your life. For example, if your goal is to be a marathon runner and you decide that you're going to go out and run 20 miles tomorrow to start training, I'm here to tell you that you're probably do end up in the hospital. Not because I don't believe in you, I absolutely do. Although, I also know that you have to work up to running 20 miles a day. The realistic version of that goal might be something like this: "I want to be a marathon runner and I'm going to start by running a mile and a half each day." That is much more realistic because that is more fitting for what your body can actually do at this moment in time. As you improve, your goal will improve as well. Soon you'll be able to do two miles a day, and then five, then ten etc. Remember you must walk before you can run.

Attainable goals go hand in hand with realistic goals. Some times because you are so excited to start in on a new ritual or idea, you may have the tendency to believe your levels of passion and enthusiasm will be matched by your body, which is not true. It can be embarrassing if you aren't able to do what you want to do right away.

Last, a goal must be timely and this ties into the other aspects of goal setting, We've been talking about and that is that if the goal is not timely. There is no sense of urgency wrapped around it.

You have to know if you give someone enough slack to hang themselves with, nine times out of ten they are going to do it. Think about your job or career. I'm sure to some degree there are deadlines or time frames established with what you do. If things didn't have deadlines or time frames attached to them to create a sense of urgency, there is a very high probability that many of those things would never get done, especially if you hate your job.

Think about it, if there was no urgency about paying taxes, how many people do you really think would do it? Although because we know that's not the case, many of us pay our taxes on time, because we know it's an urgent matter to do so. That brings up an important point. It is crucial to have deadlines and time frames wrapped around your goals, because that gives you a sense of reference and accomplishment. It also helps you to crank up the urgency, but deadlines and time frames alone will not create a sense of urgency. You have to figure out why it's important to get the goal finished at a certain time and determine what the consequence might be if it didn't get finished on time. We talked earlier about using happiness and sadness as a motivator and this is definitely a place where you can use it.

A large factor why people fail to accomplish their goals is because they don't really feel like there are any strong ramifications if they don't. They know that if they don't accomplish their goal by a certain date, nothing drastic is going to happen to them. At least that is how they feel about it.

You've got to change that mindset so you must to get into a state where for one, you want to accomplish that goal and secondly, you know that by not accomplishing that goal you would be creating some serious unhappiness for yourself. That ties into getting real and getting drastic. When you get real and you get drastic you also become urgent.

You also want your timetables and deadlines to be realistic (for you) and you don't want to set up a deadline that's too short, because then you can defeat yourself. This will cause you to beat yourself up and feel like a failure. It's about setting yourself up for victory, not tragedy. Now you also don't want to give yourself too much time, because then it becomes easy to slack off. Be honest with yourself and figure out what a realistic amount of time is going to be for your goal. Whether you have current goals or you are in the process of creating new goals, you want to ensure their success. Make sure that they are smart goals. Additionally I would like to emphasize the importance of making sure that each goal is emotional.

A lot of times people share their goals with me and a lot of the reasons for why they want to do something are very logical. For example, they want to lose weight because it will lower their cholesterol or because it will lower their blood pressure. Those are both great reasons to want to exercise, but those things specifically are not very emotional. The long-term effects of having high blood pressure and high cholesterol can be very emotional which is a good start to move you out of your current state, so that you are uncomfortable and want to move forward but you also want to couple it with a positive and compelling emotional idea. One that really gets you excited.

Along with that, you want to make sure that your motives

are personal. Now, we talked a little bit about this earlier, and I'd like to cover it as far as goal setting goes, because it's important. When people create a list of why they want to reach their goal, they tend to come up with a list that has very little to do with themselves. They want to lose weight to look good for someone else. They want to lose weight, because they're going to a wedding. They want to lose weight because they are going on vacation and want to look good in their bathing suit.

It's motives like that those that make it very easy to fall short on your goals. For one, those goals are somewhat moment oriented. Think about wanting to look good for the wedding. What happens to your motivation after the wedding is over? Suddenly you no longer have a drive to continue to go to the gym. The drive that was compelling you to get out of bed no longer exists. What about the drive to exercise for your upcoming vacation? You lose some weight, are able to fit into your bathing suit and feel good about yourself while you are away. But when you get back, it's the same thing. Your motive for exercise is gone and so therefore you do not feel the need to work out any more.

I do want to add that having other people involved can be a great motivator - a great reason to quit smoking, for example, would be because you don't want your children to be exposed to secondhand smoke. That's a great reason to want to quit smoking although that reason alone is not going to be enough to quit. You personally have to want to change. You have to want to change because *you* want to change. You want your life to be better not because of what other people are going to think about you or your loved ones.

Your subconscious knows when you're doing things for the right reasons and for the wrong reasons. If your subconscious knows you're doing things for the wrong reasons, it will be very difficult if not impossible to achieve those things. However, if your subconscious knows that you are doing something for the right reasons, it will do everything in its power to help you accomplish those things.

You need to be conscious of that.

To go along with smart goals and being emotional about your goals I'd like to give you a tool that can help you move towards your goals with much more ease. This tool is called The Moving Force Analysis.

The Moving Force Analysis

This is a literal paper and pencil tool, so get out a sheet of paper and draw a line down the middle of it. On one side, you write down all of the potential things that are going to help you achieve your goal (skills, abilities, talents, resources, etc.). Write-down anything that you think will help you make this goal a reality. On the other side, you want to write out what you feel your opposition is. What are the things potentially that are going to hold you back from this goal? Do you need to learn something new? Do you need to change your beliefs? Do you need to make some new connections?

This is powerful because it gives you a clear understanding of the things that are going to help you accomplish your goals and the things that are going to get in your way. It allows you to look into the future to get an idea of some of the things you might be up against and gives you the chance to do something about those things beforehand so that you can either make them less of a barrier or remove them completely. This is similar to being aware of a pothole in the road and swerving to avoid it, thus allowing you to reach your destination (or goal for our purposes) as planned.

Being aware of your strengths and weaknesses while you are creating your goals will do wonders for you. Undoubtedly, with each new goal there will be challenges and solutions along the way. I cannot stress how important it is to have confidence when you are even doing something as simple as creating your list of goals. When you actually begin to take action steps, your initial confidence creates momentum that pushes you forward. Likewise clarifying any barriers in the beginning will save you a lot of time and energy along the way. Imagine how much more smooth and successful your journey will be if you can identify potential stumbling blocks before you even get started, and then to find solutions to them before you even take your first step. If you want to talk about setting yourself up for victory that is exactly how you do it!

Not to mention there are going to be enough unforeseen challenges along the way. These are complications that you would have never been able to see coming, no matter what. Therefore, by taking the time to identify the dips in the road that you CAN see you will be able to take all the time and energy you will save and put it towards the tricky ones you weren't able to see. By no means is this tool designed to try to eliminate all the problems on your path to success, in fact, in a way you should look forward to at least some tough spots in the road. Those tough spots help you get better, they force you to be creative, and ultimately what was once a stumbling block becomes a stepping-stone.

This is where you have to combine your ability to look down the road and foresee what is ahead with your ability to take a leap of faith. You will never be prepared enough and you can never learn everything you need to know. There are always going to be elements for which you aren't ready, simply because you have never been down this path before. So how could you possibly know exactly what to expect? The answer is you can't. Although the good news is that because there is a bigger better version of you inside, that means you are capable of doing much more than you think you can.

Imagine when you were forced into a situation where you were given no choice but to rise to an occasion. Maybe there was an emergency, something you forgot about or something you weren't expecting. You might not have been prepared or educated in that area but it was so urgent and important for you to respond in that moment, that you surprised yourself and everyone around you. There is a secret you can learn there.

If you can harness your own ability to throw yourself into situations before you are totally prepared, it can actually be a good thing. Sometimes you just have to dive in when things are at 90% and just make the best out of it. Most times in life, no one is going to come along to throw you into a situation where you must become someone better. That means if you want to get better or accomplish something you have to step up and dive off yourself even if you're not totally ready. Be bold!

There is one other part I would like to add in here and that is that sometimes people have a hard time taking action because they spend too much time in their head. They think too much, they know what they want to do. They know why they want to do it. They're clear; they're determined to their emotional path and yet because they think so much, they never go from their head to their feet. They never make that transition and take the action to get started on their goals.

Even if someone is truly inspired, full of motivation, and passionate to get started on their new goal, often times because they have not built up the ritual yet, it can still be very difficult to take action. I know this to be true. Personally, I had a very hard time taking action, even when I had everything figured out. It was simply because I had such a strong habit of not doing anything. All the passion and excitement was there but it was like a small muscle that had not been built up yet.

Countless results have been left by the wayside because of a person's inability to take action. They spend too much time thinking about things and not taking action on them. Here's the important thing to remember about taking action, thinking and taking action have nothing to do with each other. Once your goals are clear, once they're emotional and once they are completely prepared to go, the truth is, there's nothing more to think about at that moment. You literally don't need to think about anything else. You know exactly what to do. The only thing that's left is to do it.

Here's a small tool called "Three in a Row Good to Go" that can help you get out of your head and into your feet. You must make a list of the first most basic steps possible. Here is an example of what that might look like:

Paint the fence

Step #1 Go to garage

Step #2 Get paint can and brushes

Step #3 Walk over to fence

I know…This sounds almost insulting. Nevertheless, trust me even some of the smartest people I know have trouble getting started on their goals. This tool changes the balance of power on the scale of thinking and action. By the time you have taken the third step, you have some momentum built up and as Newton says, "An object in motion stays in motion." It just makes sense that you have to get a little running start, then you're actually up and moving around and your action taking brain is in control.

With all of the information, tools, and systems from the above chapters, taking action should be easy. However this little trick helps you literally get moving so your body matches what is going on inside. The trick here is to do something with your physical body that will get you moving in the right direction. So, this is another place where you can set yourself up for victory. Remember, being in your head vs. your feet are two very different places. No amount of thinking will ever get you into your feet. It takes initial action to get the ball rolling.

Take Action!

Think about the goals that you currently have. I want you to examine them with all of these things in mind.

Are your goals smart?

Are they emotional?

Are they personal?

Do you have a very specific and clear way to celebrate your benchmarks?

Do you have a clear understanding of the things that are going to help you accomplish your goals and do you understand what things might be in the way of your goals?

Finally, how can you strengthen those assets and weaken the barriers or break them down completely?

When you find yourself in your head for too long remember:

"Three in a Row Good to Go"

Quickly think of the first three simple action steps you can take to get yourself moving. Sometimes it is as easy as just standing up!

Put this book down and take action now!

Time Mastery

Ok, now that you're motivated and you have a clear understanding of what goals are and how to set them, it's time to look into time management. How are your time management skills? Are they where you want them to be? Well if they're not, then it's time to listen up. I would like to take this moment to get something off my chest. Time management is a joke. There, I said it. I have been studying personal improvement for over 13 years and I have seen this enormous trend - everyone wants to learn how to get better at time management but nobody knows how to do it. That's because time management is a hoax. Let me explain what I mean by that. By the way, from here on out we are going to be calling it time mastery I believe that is a much more fitting description for what it actually is.

If you observe people who try to learn how to "manage" their time, you will find that the majority of them fail. It's not because they aren't smart, or passionate, or serious about mastering their time. It simply comes down to the fact that most people do not understand what time is or how to take the greatest advantage of it. There are two secrets to effectively mastering your time; you must monetize and ritualize your time in order to get the most out of it. Both of these aspects are equally important and, when used together, complement each other in a way that allows you to have more control over your time than ever before.

Monetizing Time: Monetizing your time does not necessarily mean putting a dollar value on it, although it can. Monetizing your time has to do with valuing your time. More than that, monetizing your time is about changing your beliefs about what time it is. So many people squander away their time because they believe it's not very valuable. They waste countless hours doing things that will never amount to anything. If you have ever used the phrase, "I'm just killing time," then you know exactly what I mean. After you have learned to monetize your time, I can promise you that you'll never say that phrase again.

To get the most out of your time your new belief about time must be:

"Time is your most valuable asset."

You may have heard that phrase before but now it is time to incorporate it into your sense of identity. The truth is, we might not all have the same opportunities, connections, resources, and finances. The one thing that we all have in common is time. No matter who you are, no matter where you are, we all have the same amount of time. Time is absolutely your most valuable asset. Time is more valuable than your TV, your car or even your house. Without time, you would not have been able to get your TV, car or house. More importantly without time you would not be able to enjoy your car, house, or TV.

Time is mankind's greatest luxury and without it, the value of life declines to nearly zero. The root of effective time mastery is an understanding that your time is your most valuable possession. Therefore, it is the last thing on earth that you should ever want to waste. At the end of life, everyone wishes that they had more time, and that they had not wasted so much of the time that they were given. You should be fired-up with excitement about the idea of mastering your time, for no other reason than an understanding that most people get to the end of their life and wish they had more of it.

What about regret? We never ever regret taking advantage of our time. We never regret utilizing it or making the most of it. What we regret is spending hours upon hours doing nothing and then looking back and realizing what a waste it was. If you have ever felt bad about wasting your time...you should! That bad feeling is your ultimate-self telling you that you are letting your most precious asset slip right through your fingers. Learn how to master your time and you will never have to regret wasting it.

Effective time mastery comes from an understanding that there are going to be many things in this life that are out of your control. What is important to keep in mind is that time is the one thing that you can control. You might not be able to control how much of it you have, however, you can absolutely control what you do with the time you do have. You'll find the time mastery is a huge separating element between people who are successful and people who are not. People who are successful understand that their time is very valuable and they also understand that they have to take full advantage of the time that they have.

People who are unsuccessful do not think of their time as valuable at all, so they waste it. They do not treat it like their most valuable asset, and because of that, they can never seem to have enough of it. Think about people who are wealthy - they treat money with the utmost respect. To them, a dollar is worth way more than a hundred pennies. That's why they have a lot of money - because they respect it and they know how to value it properly. What about the people that are constantly broke? Their beliefs about money are the opposite. They do not respect it and they do not know how to value it. Therefore, they never have much of it. Time is exactly the same.

Think about how many people you know who wish that someone would invent the 25-hour day. Yes, there is no doubt that people are busy, but when you have a strong enough sense of time and what time means, you can accomplish everything you need to get done in the amount of time that you've been given. There are three keys to monetizing your time.

Value: First, you must value your time. When you value your time, you're not willing to waste it. On top of that, you begin to use your time more wisely. You start thinking about time in a different way. You begin to look at your time as a luxury so you begin to work smarter and not harder. Your mind begins to see new possibilities of how you can maximize your time, and how you can optimize it. How you view and define time makes a huge difference in your personal and professional success. The more you value your time the more you're going to take advantage of it.

Protect: The second key of time mastery is protecting your time. If you truly view time as your most valuable asset, then you will protect it more than any other asset in your life. Successful people absolutely protect their time. They know it's worth more to them than their money, car, and house put together.

What would your life be like if you treated your time as if it was your most valuable asset? What would happen to the quality of your life if you treated your time as if it was more valuable than anything else was? When you protect your time, your perception of the things you do changes dramatically. As the quality of your perception of time goes up, simultaneously so does your perception of the time wasting things you do from day to day. You look at those same time wasters with total disgust. You start to see the little sidetracks as absolute killers. Soon they fall into the same category as the other things you would never ever do.

On the other hand, once you start to value your time to a high degree and you protect it, then your mind starts to shift into more productive manner and you start to think about things in a more efficient way. You start seeing opportunities to use your time in a more useful way that you didn't see before. Your possibility thinking gets activated.

That is because once you're vision and perception changes about what time is, your vision and perception about how you use your time changes, as well. Think about successful people that you know. They do two things with their time: they use their time wisely and they enjoy it. Successful people would rather find ways to maximize their time rather than live in an imaginary world where they hope for more of it. If you look, there is a huge difference between people who protect their time and people who don't.

People who protect their time, have time and use it to their advantage. People who do not are slaves to time, always having to conform to what their time allows them to do. You hear it all the time… "I'll do that if I have enough time." "We can go there if time allows." Wait a second!? Who's in charge here? You or your time? Your time is yours, and if you want the life you deserve, you'd better start treating it as such!

Prioritize: To master your time successfully, you must be able to prioritize it effectively. When you have a clear understanding of what time is it becomes very easy to prioritize your time. You can look at a list of potential things to do and you can instantly see which ones are the most important things to do on that list. For example, if you have a list of five things to do and on that list you have:

Finish writing Chapter 1

Walk the dog

Take out the trash

Pay the bills

Go to the gym

Return important phone call

You can easily look at that list and know what the first and most important thing to do on that list. Once you have that established, then you can look at the next thing on the list and decide how important that is, until you have your list rearranged in an order of maximum importance.

The ability to prioritize your time is a huge asset because we all have the same amount of time, although we don't always know what to do with the time we have. Sometimes it's hard for us to know which things are more important and sometimes we get overwhelmed with all the things we have

to do which can lead us to a state of option paralysis.
That means that because we have so many options we end up
getting overwhelmed and ultimately fail to do any of the
things on our list that we set out to do.

Also, it is important to prioritize your time, because no
matter how much you value it or protect it, there will always
be things that catch you off guard. That's life. As they say,
"Life happens." There will always be unexpected things that
will steal some of your time. Sometimes these unexpected
things are good, and sometimes they are bad. Either way
these unexpected things will make it so that not all of the
items on your list will be accomplished. Therefore, if you
have gone out of your way to make sure that the most
important things get done first, when those unexpected
moments happen, the idea is that the only things that get
sacrificed on your list are the ones that are on the less
important side.

They are only 24 hours in a day and, when you really get
down to it, that's not a lot of time. One way to help you
prioritize is to set up the coming day the evening before. Just
before you go to bed each night you should have a very clear
understanding of what you're going to be doing the next day.
So when you wake up in the morning, you don't have to
think about anything or wonder if you're doing the right
things or if your time could be used in a better way. Instantly
as soon as you wake up, you know you're doing the most
important thing and your whole day has been already
predefined for you so that you know exactly what things to
do and when. Talk about a ritual...

Taking advantage of tools like planners and calendars can
help you do this as well. For example, when you go to bed at
night you can look at all the things that you have to do
tomorrow - get out your planner and you schedule things
accordingly. If you don't have a planner or a calendar, I
recommend getting one now. If you really want to be
extreme about it, this is what I personally do along with my
calendar in my planner, I also have a big white board

(actually I have six) and I write my goals up on my white board. Generally, the goals that I put on my white board are the goals that are to be accomplished the next day and I write them in big bold letters. That way there's no way that I can avoid seeing my list and I know exactly what needs to be done when I wake up.

This leads us to the second secret of time mastery, ritualizing your time.

Ritualizing Time: As you read about in the 13 Traits of Champions, being religious is an absolute must. The quality and amount of daily rituals that you have is nothing but a mirror of the quality of your life on a whole. Look at the people in your life who are absolutely ritualistic about something, anything really, maybe they exercise every day, maybe they read every day, or maybe they practice some other type of IPIDD each day. No matter what it is, chances are the quality of their life is extraordinary because of the great benefits they get from their daily rituals. Think about your own life, what type of daily rituals do you have? I hope that by now you are well on your way to creating some powerful rituals. But what about your rituals related to time? Being able to effectively master your time comes down to the daily rituals you have around how you spend your time. Time mastery is not about being able to produce great results every now and then. It is about being able to create daily magic. There are plenty of people who can come up with an idea, set some goals, get excited and then take action, but without creating rituals they will fail to get the kind of results that they want long-term. What is important to know as far as time mastery and rituals are concerned is, "How can I begin to create daily rituals that will allow me to master my time?"

Ritualizing your time ties into many of the other areas we have touched on so far. Clarity - being clear about who you are and why you are here - is taking advantage of your time and enjoying part of who you are Will getting the most out of your time allow you to fulfill your life's purpose more easily? What about self-love? Don't you think that by valuing, protecting, and prioritizing your time, you are at the same time valuing and ultimately loving yourself? Self-nurture? By using your time wisely, don't you also take care of yourself at the same time? What about personal patterns of excellence? By knowing how you personally get the most of your time, don't you also set yourself up for victory? The answer to all of these questions, as you know, is yes. The more you begin to incorporate the above into your life, the more the lens by which you view your world and your time will change. And change for the better.

Take Action!

Think about your current ability to manage your time.

On a scale of one to ten, how well do you manage your time?

Do you need to reshape some of your beliefs about time?

Do you need to create some systems and strategies so that you can better manage your time, or maybe a combination of the two?

Figure out what you need to do in order to be a master of time mastery and start reforming your approach right now. Keep in mind the two secrets to all time mastery are monetizing and ritualizing your time.

Think of this moment right now as an opportunity to once and for all get your time management under control. The reality is most people look back on their life and regret, not the things they did, but the things they never got a chance to do. Don't let that be you, take time right now and answer the following questions.

How you can start to view time as your most valuable asset?

How you can make that belief true for you?

How you can start to protect your time?

How can you optimize it?

What are your three biggest time wasters?

How can you limit or even eliminate those time wasters from your life?

How can you start to be aware of how you can use your time more wisely?

How can you ritualize your time?

Put this book down and take action now!

Money Mindset

I'd like to change gears a little bit and talk about money. No matter who you are, money is a very serious and emotional subject. Whether you love it or hate it, are obsessed with getting more of it or you go to the ends of the earth to avoid it, everyone's got something to say about money.

The interesting thing about money is that your relationship with it generally is a direct reflection of how much or little of it you have. That's pretty simple. If money is something that you avoid and have a negative relationship with, then it's pretty safe to say that you probably don't have a lot of it.

On the other hand, if you think of money as a positive thing and you have healthy beliefs about it, then most likely you have a fair amount of it or at least enough to get by. What type of relationship do you have with money? Is it a positive or negative one?

What's also important here is to keep in mind what your goal for money is. Some people truly are interested in money or creating more of it. For those people, that's fine but if personally you are not happy with your financial situation, then now is the time to do something about it!

What is the quality of your beliefs about money? If you can answer that one question, it will give you significant insight into how you can change your financial situation. There is no doubt that times are changing. The economy and global finances are shifting so rapidly that even experts themselves are unsure of what to do. It's in a time like this where you want to have your money mindset completely mastered, so that you don't have to be a victim of the economy or its downturns.

Did you know that during the Great Depression there were more millionaires created than ever in US history? When most people were standing in the breadline, upset about what was going on with the economy, other people out there decided that they were going to focus on what they could do to change their personal finances rather than worry about what the economy was doing.

Hopefully, you are starting to notice that your life is about options. It is about choice. Just like the story of the two women who almost get hit by the taxi. One of them made a choice that impacted her life in a negative way. The other made a choice that had a positive impact, but the important thing to remember is that they both had the exact same experience.

The power of choice, when it comes to money and your financial situation, is everything. We can prove this idea by looking at people throughout history that were born in to poverty yet they made the decision not to stay there. This happens not only on a small scale but often times it happens on a large scale as well. Think about some of the most famous and powerful people in the world: Andrew Carnegie, John Rockefeller and Oprah Winfrey. The truth is these people accomplished amazing and great things and there is no doubt that they made a serious impact on the world, yet they all came from VERY humble upbringings.

As a society, sometimes the world tends to see wealthy people as different from the rest. And to a degree, they are different. They had to be different in order to do what they did. The danger here is that because we see this huge difference in income, free time, and overall lifestyle, we begin to think they are capable of something we aren't. This automatically creates a disconnection between people and the amount of money they believe they are able to generate. Most of what you see is the result of years and years of struggle. Yet for some reason, people don't make that correlation. They just tend to think that wealthy people woke up that way.

If you want to revolutionize your financial situation, along with your life, you're going to have to realize that there is literally no difference between you and the successful people you admire. In fact, you probably have it easier than they did!

Anyone in any given situation can become wealthy. That's a tough pill to swallow because most people don't believe that they can do anything about the situation in which they find themselves.. You have exactly the same brain, heart and potential that anyone great in history had. The fact remains that as long as you're not willing to give up and you are willing to do whatever it takes to get what you want, you can reach any goal that you set for yourself. However, wealth is like health. If you want it, there are certain rules and laws you must follow in order to have it. And, when it comes to building wealth, the biggest and most important factor that will determine your financial success or failure is the Law of Attraction.

The Law of Attraction

The Law of Attraction says that the things that you consistently think about with intention and emotion manifest into your literal reality. This is a very important law to be aware of because all of the things you have in your life right now are a representation of the thoughts that you have around those things. You have attracted everything you currently have into your life.

Just like the brain, the Law of Attraction can only manifest into your life things that are of the same category as your constant emotional thoughts.

It's pretty safe to say that most people do not intend to find themselves in a negative financial situation. Although most people also don't understand how the Law of Attraction works. For example, people will say things like:

"I don't want to be in debt."

"I hate having to pay bills."

"I wish I wasn't broke all the time."

One of the things that all of those statements have in common is that they are all negative. That is why people who don't want to be in debt continue to be in debt. That is why people who are broke all the time continue to be broke all the time. Like attracts like. Even though you might not want to be broke all the time, if that is what you are consistently thinking about and focusing your attention and your energy on, that is the only message that the law attraction has to work with. Therefore, it continues to bring you more of the same.

What you also have to understand is that because you create your reality, in this way some people tend to think that they are bad creators or bad at using the Law of Attraction. When in fact this is not true at all, The truth is everyone is a master of using the law attraction. They just primarily use it the wrong way. Think about people who have tons of credit card debt and are consistently broke all the time. You can't just get there overnight it takes work. Those people were very powerful creators indeed.

It's not about becoming a better creator. It's simply about shifting your focus so that you can create more positive things. You do that by thinking about what you *do* want rather than what you *don't* want. It's so funny how we get conditioned to think a certain way. I ask people all the time what they want and they'll say, "I don't want to live like this anymore." I'll reply, "Well, that's great, but tell me what you do want." And, they get this puzzled look on her face because they feel like they just told me what they want. But really, they are focusing on what they *don't* want.

They say the rich get richer and the poor get poorer. Because we know ultimately there's no difference between those two groups of people, the only reason that statement rings true is because those two different groups of people are thinking about and attracting two very different things into their lives. It makes total sense if you think about it. Anything that you have or achieved in your life, even if it was something you obtained because you focused all your thoughts on achieving that thing and even if it was something you had never had before, your thoughts and emotions got you so excited and curious about that thing, that you could feel what it would be like to have it before it was even part of your reality.

What happened? Because you directed your thoughts in a consistent and positive way, the thing that you wanted, whatever it was, eventually came into literal existence in your life. The fact is, you have used the law attraction before. The truth is, you're using it all the time. That is one very important aspect of which you need to be aware. That no matter what, the law of attraction is always working. You need to know that and you need to be aware of the thoughts you're thinking on a consistent basis. Just because you're not aware of the things that you're thinking that does not mean your thoughts are not constantly manifesting themselves.

The more conscious and intentional you can be about your thoughts, the more you can have control over the things that you're manifesting your life. Here are a few ideas to help you master the Law of Attraction.

Beliefs: The first thing that you must have in place as far as building wealth is your beliefs. You can have all the wealth building ideas and tools in the world but if you do not have healthy positive beliefs about money, then you are sunk. An example of that type of sabotage is people who want more money, yet have some of the following beliefs:

"I don't deserve to be wealthy."

"To be wealthy, I have to become a monster."

"If I am wealthy, I will be less spiritual."

"If I am wealthy, people will try and use me."

Even if you have great intentions for money, if you have some underlying negative beliefs about what money is and what having more of it will mean for you, then you'll surely never have the amount you deserve. What's worse is that is if they happen to get more money, somehow, they will almost undoubtedly sabotage that, as well, and the money they get will be lost.

A great example of that is what's called "the curse of the lottery," which is the majority of the people who win in excess of $1 million or more. Within one year, they return to the financial situation (or worse) that they found themselves in before they won the money. The reason for that is, even though they wanted the money, some part of them still did not have healthy beliefs and habits built up around having massive amounts of money. Once they got the money, their

subconscious knew it was something that they weren't
comfortable with, so they would blow it or give it away.
Thus, they could end up back to the financial comfort zone
that they were used to have, in order to be consistent with the
beliefs that they have.

Building wealth takes work as it is and it would be a total
shame for you to lose it due to your financial programming.
As you can see, there are two major forms of sabotage at
play here. One of them is sabotaging yourself before you can
even reach your ideal financial destination. The second is, if
somehow you got there with the current beliefs and habits
you have about money, you'll sabotage that as well.

Due to the immense power that both forms of sabotage can
have on you, it is paramount that you examine your current
beliefs and habits regarding money. After you discover the
core negative beliefs you have about money, then it is time
to push your comfort zone. Find a way to shift the polarity of
the beliefs you have about money. For each concrete
negative belief you have about money, choose an equally
opposite positive one. Remember the key here is not to
simply create new beliefs but to create new beliefs that you
can truly buy into and engrain into who you are. Therefore,
the above negative beliefs about money could transform
into:

> "I am worthy of unlimited wealthy."

> "It is in line with my ultimate-self to have
> abundance."

> "Having wealth will allow me expand myself
> spiritually."

> "I will be able to donate to my favorite charities."

Clarity: Be as clear as you possibly can about the things that
you want. The reason for this is very simple. If I was to tell
you to go to the store and get me some stuff and that's all I

said, what would you come back with? Who knows right? Yet if I said go to the store here is a very specific list, then all you have to do is go to the store and get what's on the list. The Law of Attraction works the same way. The more specific you are with your thoughts, the more specific your results are going to be.

In regards to money by simply saying, "I want more money," that alone is not enough because that's not very specific (although it is positive). However saying a specific amount is better, just like the grocery list. Remember, it is the Law of Attraction's job to bring you whatever you desire in life but if you can't be specific with it, it can't bring you the things that you want. You have to ask in a certain way.

Next, you must be clear about the amount that you want, because clarity lends itself to emotion. You also have to be emotional about the amount of money you desire. You have to get into the mindset of what it would literally feel like to have that amount of money. You cannot just think about wanting $10,000. You need to be able to feel what it would feel like to have that amount. By doing that, you're letting the Law of Attraction know that you are ready to receive an experience that is identical.

The trick here is to be sending a consistent *positive* message about money that is in line with having not wanting. The difference between the emotional level of wanting something and having something are two totally different feelings.

For the most part, people who "want" continue to want. Yet the people who can translate that wanting into a having feeling attract exactly what they need.

I believe that emotion is one of the least talked about yet most important parts of the Law of Attraction. Everyone wants more money, although the emotion that generally comes along with it is negativity, understandably so. Unfortunately, the reason that people ask for money the most is in reaction to a moment where they do not have enough of it. Their car breaks down and they don't have the money to fix it; they have to go to the hospital and can't afford the medical bill; they find out they owe the IRS money...whatever it is, the majority of the time, instances like these will cause people to want more money. The dangerous part is because there is negative emotion attached to the experience, that negative emotion gets translated into the quality of the emotional state they have and the overall connotation of how they phrase what they are asking for.

Also, it is important to get clear about how you would like to have more money. This one is important. Let's say your wish is to have more money but you also would like more free time. However, when you state your intention, if you leave out the part about the free time, then you may attract more money, however, it will most likely not be in the way you would like it. An example of this would be getting a promotion at work in which you would be making more money, although it would require you to work MORE hours every week. Not cool.

Yes, you may want more money, but unless you're 100% specific with HOW you want to have that money come into your life, then what you manifest may be even worse than what you currently have. The lesson here is to think of all the details that are involved with the money you desire. Besides the obvious part of having the money, what will be different about your life when you get this money and what will that FEEL like? You may say, "I want more money doing what I love." That way if you don't love your current job, what you end up manifesting will be something new that is in line with your passion, rather than some bogus promotion you don't want.

This is a great place to use the "As if, even if" tool. If becomes very difficult to have more money in your life because if you've never had, it can be difficult to know how it feels. And if you don't know how it feels, then it is a challenge creating that feeling of having more to send out to the Universe. This is where you can get creative. This is where you get to have fun. If more money is what you want, then it is your job to find a way to uncover that new wealthier version of yourself.

The first and best tool I have seen and used with my clients is imagination. The better you can imagine what your life would be like to have this money, the more you can start to take on that character and become it. Most people just stop at thinking about having the money, and they miss the whole boat of feeling what it would be like to have it. Think about what you want personally. How much is it? But more importantly think about what a day in the life at that financial level would feel like. View it in your mind from a first person perspective. See yourself doing whatever it is you would be doing, even if it's nothing. See it. Feel it. Experience it in your mind. You'll know the feeling once it hits you and when it does, it's your job to grab it and hold onto it. That feeling is the "vibe" that you need to create around this reality you see in your mind.

Other people may not have such strong imaginations. In that case, you can create what is called a vision board. A vision board is a large piece of paper, cardboard, or poster board that you can put pictures on. Find magazines or advertisements that have compelling pictures of the things you desire and cut them out. Arrange them on the board in a way that is the most appealing to you. The point here is to be able to look at this vision board and ignite the feeling place of the life you desire. Seeing pictures of that new car, house, or boat may be exactly what you need to kick your imagination into gear and help you reach the emotional place of having these thing. This section is on money. However, you can use a vision board for anything you want, relationships, careers, family anything.

If imagination and vision boards are not up your alley, then you may be the type that has to really get out and touch it. In that case, I would encourage you to find some way to get as close to the things you want in order to create the sense of having them. This may include going to the dealership and looking at your dream car. The experience of actually seeing it, touching it, sitting in it and even test driving it can help you drum up that feeling of owning it. Maybe it's a house you desire. In that case, the strategy there would be finding a house you like that is on the market and going to see it. Real estate agents are more than happy to show property. By actually being in the house, you can get a sense for what it would really be like to live there. If you are the type of person that needs the hands on experience, I would encourage you to think about the things you want and get creative about how you can become exposed to them. It could be anything from a day pass at an elite spa, gym, or country club to a fancy dinner out at a ritzy restaurant. Have fun with this but remember to be smart about it. There is no need to break the bank on any of these adventures. You do not want to feel bad about experiencing any of them. You should feel happy and excited to do them. From here, it's time to constantly activate that feeling on a continuous basis.

Consistency: Once you know the exact feeling of the vibe, then it is time to exercise it. Consistency and quality of your vibe are the one-two combination you need to attract the kind of money you really want. The things you think about all the time are the things that become your reality. The things you think about every now and then even though you might want them are the things that never happen. Mastery in any area of your life comes from being consistent.

In order to constantly send this new and powerful money attracting vibe, you are going to need to create a ritual around it. You must be sending out the same message each and every day. Go out of your way to find a way to ritualize your money getting transmission. I recommend the following approach.

Morning: The morning time is the most ideal time of the day. The morning is the start to your day and therefore whatever type of start you get off to in the AM is generally going to decide what the quality of the rest of your day is going to be. That means you want to take advantage of this time so you can get the most out of it. Start by setting your intentions soon after waking up. You ideally want to be in a fully active and aware mental and physical state when you do this. Stating your intentions while you are groggy or sleepy can dampen the emotional effects of the exercise. It can work in reverse though, sometimes you can use intense affirmation along with an equally powerful physiological movement to get you jump started. This is called an incantation. By igniting the feelings and movements of your wealthier self, you can snap yourself out of your befuddled state and seize the day.

Afternoon: Once the clock hits noon, that is your cue to give yourself a quick evaluation of your thoughts, feelings, and actions. Think about the thoughts you are having. Are they helping your intention along? Or is they are out of alignment with your morning intention. How can you turn them around and get them back on track? Ask yourself, "How am I feeling?" Is how you're feeling at noon the same as how you were feeling in the morning? If it's not, then you have an opportunity in that moment to make it that way. What about your actions? Are they money-getting rituals or are they money-wasting habits? The middle of the day is a great time to do a quick recap on yourself and make sure you keep yourself moving in the right direction. This is in line with self-nurture because unfortunately you do not have someone who is magically going to appear midday and make sure you are on track. And since you don't, you must be able to do that for yourself. Think about how powerful it will be to have a ritual in place that forces you to continue your positive money attracting vibe transmission.

Night: All day long, your conscience and subconscious mind are influenced. And if you are going out of your way to project your powerful intentions all through the day, by the time night rolls around you have already hopefully been the largest source of influence on your mind. The important thing to remember is that just because you go to sleep does not mean your mind stops working. In fact, it is just the opposite. When you are asleep, your brain's ability for creation and imagination are many times more powerful than they are when you are awake. You can take advantage of this by stating your intentions before going to sleep.

No one fully understand dreams at this point, although what is known is that the thoughts you have that are both highly emotional and closest to the time you fall asleep generally are the ones that influence your subconscious and your dreams. The average sleeper will have three to four dreams per night, each dream lasting approximately five minutes. The interesting part is that time in the dream state is not the same as time in general reality. This is why an entire story will play out while you are dreaming that may seemingly go on for hours, yet only last five minutes. Due to the quantum nature of dreams, it is important to be able to take advantage of them as much as possible. Though it may be hard to measure how much dreams influence a person's conscience reality, there is no doubt that they have an impact. I once had a dream that I could do a back flip and I had never done one in real life. Yet that dream was so vivid on an emotional and physiological level that when I woke up I executed a perfect back flip off the side of a dock and was able to do them from that day forward.

The possibilities are endless, and there is no saying what you may gain out of your dreams. In regards to wealth, it could be anything from beliefs, mannerisms, business ideas, etc. You never know what may happen as a result of your lofty dreams, however, what is for certain is that the more you intentionally program them the better it will be. That said, for the most optimal results, you want a very specific system for how you influence your dreams. This is where you can use your imagination again to create a short yet vivid movie that you can mentally watch as you fall asleep. The great part here is that you have total freedom over this movie. You are the creator. Anything can happen, so do not hesitate to make your movie as glorious as possible.

By creating a ritual morning, noon, and night around attracting money, you put yourself on the fast track to manifestation. Each part of your day has a large impact on how the next part will go. By being intentional and stating your financial goals during these pivotal moments, throughout the day you become the greatest and richest source of influence on yourself. Put this book down and put together your daily ritual for your daily wealth creation.

Action: The truth is, even if your beliefs, clarity, and rituals are on par with attracting more money into your life, a sack of cash is not going to fall out of the sky and fall on your head. You have to do more than just sit in your house and think about these things that you want. You have to get out and start taking some action. The Law of Attraction is more like a guiding force than a magic trick. When your thoughts and feelings are in the right place, the Law of Attraction will lead you in the right direction. This is why it is so important to actually get out there and act. You may meet someone you wouldn't have met otherwise. You might go somewhere you have never gone and get inspired by something. The Universe will open up new doors for you, but you must be present at the time they do.

No one fully understands how the Law of Attraction works. Sometimes the Law of Attraction will bring you exactly the things that you want. Other times the Law of Attraction will bring you the essence of what you want. But most of the time the Law of Attraction will bring you opportunities that will help you create what you want. The more action you take, the more you set yourself up for success, because you have raised your probability for allowing the Universe to present you with an opportunity. They say you have to be in the right place, at the right time and for the most part, that's true. A lot of people think that phrase has to do with luck. Well it has nothing to do with luck and it has everything to do with being in a place where you can receive the fruits of your labor.

If the Law of Attraction has created some powerful and positive opportunities for you out in the world and you don't show up, guess what. You miss out on them. Use that knowledge to your advantage and take as much action as possible. And when these amazing new opportunities begin to come your way, don't mistake them as a fluke or a stroke of chance either. When opportunity comes knocking, don't forget that you invited it over! Sooner or later, if you turn your back on the gifts the Universe is trying to present, you it will begin to think you don't truly want them and cease to send any more your way. It is also crucial to make sure that you have expanded yourself, so that you are capable of receiving the new abundance the Universe has to offer you. This goes back to the curse of the lottery. Wanting something is one thing. But actually being prepared for it to arrive is another thing all together. Most people want a big life but are only capable of handling slightly *less* than what they currently have. In order to have more, you must become more as a person. The amount of joy, abundance, and money you can attract is in direct proportion to the amount of space you have created inside yourself to allow it.

Taking action in this sense comes down to two things: one is allowing and the second is creating.

Allowing: In order to allow yourself to accept the fruits of your labor, you must be in a position to do so. That means one of the biggest beliefs you must have in place regarding wealth is excepting it. You must say YES to wealth. There are many ways to say yes to wealth. Sometimes it's indulging in an idea. Sometimes it is allowing yourself to be spontaneous. Other times it can mean being open minded about an opportunity. Remember, whenever you say no to one thing you simultaneously say yes to something else. And likewise, when you say yes to something, you are at the same time saying no to something else.

Think about that for a moment. Think about the things that you have been unknowingly saying yes or no to in regards to your wealth. Let's use saving as an example. When you have thought about saving in the past and you said no to it, what you said yes to at the same time was the continuation of your current financial situation. Before you reach a new level of

financial achievement, you must say yes to it and when
the moment arises where you life goes to that next level you
must say yes to that as well.

Since you do not know exactly how the Universe is going to
present you with your opportunity, you have to take action
and find out. Now is the time to start going to events, parties,
charities, etc. Start saying yes to more things than you ever
have before. For there to be a massive change in your bank
account, there has to be an equal or greater change in what
you DO. If all you do is wake up, go to work, come home
and sleep, how on earth can the Universe present you with
anything new? It can't! Shake things up! Get out and use the
tools from the section on fun to help you do this.

Imagine what would happen if you combine imagination,
spontaneity, curiosity, and adventure along with a wealth
mentality. That is seriously powerful! You would be sure to
allow any and everything the Universe has created for you in
that were the case.

Have fun with this. Think about exactly how you can allow
more wealth into your life. I know for me, one of the greatest
things I ever did to help me was to find out where wealthy
people hung out and go there. I realized that all the places I
normally hung out had zero wealthy people. So, I got
creative and started to think about where I could find them.
As intimidating as the idea of being around people who had
leagues more money that I did was, I realized that is what I
needed to do. First, as a way to shake myself out of my old
habits, and second as a way to get accustomed to my new
wealth rituals.

Creating: This part takes some guts but the rewards are well
worth the effort. Anyone who has achieved great wealth will
tell you that they were solely responsible for creating it. This
is where the Law of Attraction has a twist. Wealth is
generally not automatic and most of the time, it requires
work. That means on top of all the internal work you are
doing with your beliefs, clarity, and consistency, you must

also create new mechanisms for money. Being specific about HOW you want to receive more money is important. When you know how you want to make more money, then it will be clear to you what needs to be done in that area of your life to create it. For example, if you want to begin making money from your passion, then you have to find a way to be able to monetize it. What are you literally going to do allow money to start flowing to you in that area? Maybe it's starting a website. Maybe it's making a prototype. If it relates to your job, then you need to think about what needs to happen to allow that next level of income.

The point here is to create a ritual that will allow you to do something that moves you closer to your financial destiny each and every day. You certainly cannot make more money doing the same thing you've been doing. That means you are going to have to find an additional way to make it, or a whole new way all together. Keep in mind that often times the amount of money you make is in direct correlation with how much you enjoy the work you do. Sit with that thought for a moment before you move on.

Take Action!

Mastering your finances is no small order. Answer the following questions in order to get yourself aligned with the right mindset and habits that will allow you to create the wealth you deserve.

What is your current financial situation?

What beliefs or patterns caused your current financial situation?

What new beliefs and rituals do you need to create in order to allow more abundance into your life?

How can you get into the feeling place of HAVING the things you desire?

Put this book down now and set yourself up for financial success once and for all!

Put this book down and take action now!

Quit Your Job!

That's right. I said it. Let's look at the big picture here. You will spend approximately one third of your life at your job. One third of your entire life... at your job! That is a lot of time and if you are not in a career that allows you to be fulfilled and live your passion, then that means one third of life is essentially wasted.

It doesn't make any sense for you to be going through this massive revolution and continue to stay in a job that holds you back. The real kicker is that the effects of staying at a job you don't love are far more severe than just robbing you of one third of your life. The truth is, if you hate your job, there is a good chance even though you despise it, that you think about it and complain about it all the time even when you're not there, sucking up more of your precious time that you will never get back.

When that alarm clock goes off in the morning do you cringe at the sound of it as it taunts like a cruel joke, all the while knowing you are giving up numerous hours of your precious life every single day? You hit the snooze button once, twice, three times. You're out of bed with just enough time to be late you grab a cereal bar (if that) and off you go. You get to work just barely on time. You swipe your rinky-dink timecard, you put on your rinky-dink name tag and you get behind the counter. You sit down at your desk, you take a deep breath and the first thing that you do is look up at the clock and tell yourself you can't wait until it's time to go home. That, my friend, is no way to live.

Aren't you sick and tired of being sick and tired? Don't you wish each and every day that you could earn the kind of money you deserve? Aren't you fed up with being treated like you are just a number that is as disposable as the trash? You should be! None of the above has anything to do with loving yourself, being true to your identity, or following your purpose. As a matter a fact, it's all in direct opposition. The quality of how people treat you is in direct correlation to

how well you allow them to treat you. How well you
allow others to treat you is in direct correlation to how well
you ultimately value yourself. At the core, I'm willing to bet
you don't get upset because someone treats you badly, but
more so that you let them do it.

Think about it…you want more respect at your job. But do
you demand it? People will only give you what they perceive
you're worth. And unless you show them what you're really
made of, how can you expect anything better? I can
guarantee that if you are not happy with your job, you are
getting paid less than what you are truly worth. That sense of
being shortchanged each and every day burns you and it
should! At this moment, more likely than not you're excited.
Your heart is beating faster. There is literally electricity
coursing through your veins. Yet, if I said to you, "Ok, then
the first thing you need to do is quit that measly job that
holds your potential hostage," instantly all that power would
fade and fear would set in. All of the negative "what ifs"
descend and you wouldn't be able to see how you could pull
this big idea off. This is where it's crucial to remember that
the fear in this case is saying, "Yes! Now we're talking!" but
it's that negative "what if?" thinking that holds back the
possibly thinking, which in turn could allow you to create
the solutions to how you CAN pull this whole thing off.

Then if it's not the "what ifs" that get people, it is the
rationalization. They say things like, "I can't leave my job
because:

"I have bills to pay."

"I've invested so much in this job already."

"I have to support myself."

"If I quit, I'll lose my work benefits."

"My job pays very well"

"I have to take care of my family."

"Things might get better."

"If I quit, my jerk of a boss wins."

"I'm not a quitter."

"The economy is down and there are no other jobs."

"Quitting will look bad on my resume."

Let's be bold and dissect each and every one of those statements to show how pathetic they really are.

I have bills to pay: In the great adventure of life, risks must be taken. So what if you fall behind on your bills? They're not going anywhere. Is the value of keeping the lights turned on really worth keeping your dreams in the dark?

I've invested so much in this job already: While I can appreciate all the time and effort you put in your job, sinking more time and energy into a job that will not give you back what you deserve is not worth it. Just because you have spent a lot of time doing something does not justify continuing to do it.

I have to support myself: That is where you are wrong. The idea of supporting yourself is synonymous with making a living and getting by. Staying stuck in a job that does not serve you is certainly not a way to support yourself. The reality is that by staying in a job that does not suit you in many ways, you are not supporting yourself in fact you are destabilizing yourself.

If I quit, I'll lose my work benefits: Did I just hear you say comfort zone? Because I'm pretty sure you did. Listen, your current job may afford you some nice perks like a salary, company car, and healthcare. But deep down those are all simply happy-face stickers that are stuck to the inside of your cage. You get to enjoy them to a degree, but the reality is that rather than helping you grow, they're helping you to stay stuck. You should rename them shackles and believe that is a much more fitting word that describes what they actually are. The value of these benefits may make staying at your job seem worth it. However, I would challenge you to think about what the long-term cost of sacrificing the great masterpiece that is your dream. And healthcare? There's a very good chance it is your job itself that is making you sick. Did you ever think about that?

My job pays well: Whoop-de-friggen-doo, you cannot put a price on happiness. No amount of money is ever worth having to sell yourself out every day. Let's get real, if you're unhappy with your job, then all of that money really isn't doing you much good is it? This is another scenario where the money becomes a secret metaphor for a prison. Do you want to know the real kicker? The people who live their dreams get paid more than anyone else. So if you really want make a lot of money, do what you love and you'll make more than you ever have. And just food for thought, even if you ended up making less money but were absolutely punch-drunk in love with your job every day, wouldn't be worth it? The truth is you can have both.

I have to take care of my family: I personally love this one. I certainly admire a person's desire to take care of their family. I believe taking care of your family should be one of your biggest priorities. Although that does not mean that you should give up on what you love for them. In fact, it is just the opposite. Supporting your family means much more than just keeping the bills paid and putting food on the table. Supporting your family means giving them the best version of yourself. It means giving them the best in life that you can possibly give them without sacrificing your own dreams and it also means giving them your time. Your time is the most valuable thing you have to share with your family and if you are working all the time in a job that you hate, you will hardly have any time for your family. You owe it to yourself and to them to create a life that is significant and magnificent. That's how you take care of your family.

Things might get better: This is what I call hopeless hope. Deep down in your soul you know things are never going to change. And even if they do, will it really make things that much better? The answer is no. Hoping and wishing for things to change while you maintain the same routine is like hoping a sinking boat will magically patch itself up and begin to float gain. You're sunk. Fortune favors the bold and those who create their destiny do not use words like "hope" or "might." Instead, they use words like "will" and "must."

If I quit, my jerk of a boss wins: Who cares? Let's put things in perspective here. If you quit your job and end up living a life full of passion and fulfillment, who really wins? The truth is that right now, your boss has control over you and currently that makes him or her the winner. Your boss didn't ask you to trade in your dreams for a name tag. You offered. At the end of the day, it is not about winning or losing; it's about living your purpose in being happy.

I'm not a quitter: Up until this point, I'm not so sure about that. If your dreams could talk, what would they say? In a lot of ways, you have already quit. You have to get over the idea of being perceived as a quitter or thinking of yourself as a quitter. Some of the most happy and successful people in history are also people who either quit multiple jobs, dropped out of high school or quit collage. Dr. Seuss once said, "Be who you are and say what you feel, because those who mind don't matter and those who matter don't mind."And, from a personal perspective, if you quit your job and went on to achieve something much greater, in reality you having quit anything means the truth is you have been promoted.

The economy is down and there are no other jobs: That is 100% false. There are plenty of jobs available for those who are willing to seek them out. And, the great news is, if the dream career that you are looking for is not available in the job market that means you get to create it. If you are dead-set on achieving your goal, you will either find a way or make one. Remember what I said about the Great Depression creating more millionaires than ever before in history? Well it is more possible now than ever. With the level of technology and resources that are at your disposal, it is easier than ever to make your dreams a reality.

Quitting will look bad on my resume: Well if you stay at your job for the rest your life, your resume won't make much of a difference will it? On top of that, I sincerely doubt that your dream employer will care about a job that you hated. If you look at the people who follow their dreams, what they end up doing generally looks nothing like what they did in the past. They are often hired because of their passion, talents, and abilities, none of which are acquired or exercised in a dead-end job. As you can see, there is really no excuse to stay at your job if it is making you unhappy, while, in fact, there are a multitude of reasons for you to quit. They say that time waits for no man and it is absolutely true (that goes for women too). The longer you stay at your dead-end job, the less time you will have to bask in the glory of your life's dream. Goethe once said, "Whatever you can do, or dream you can, begin it. Boldness has genius, power, and magic in it." I would encourage you to take his words to heart.

As you can see, there is really no excuse to stay at your job if it is making you unhappy. While in fact, there are a multitude of reasons for you to quit. They say the time waits for no man and it is absolutely true. The longer you stay at your dead-end job the less time you will have to bask in the glory of your life's dream. Goethe once said "Whatever you can do, or dream you can, begin it. Boldness has genius, power, and magic in it." I would encourage you to take his words to heart.

Now you know you will never be able to live large if you continue to think small. You must embrace the fear as positive and allow it to unleash the flow of brain and will power that will carry you from your current position to a bigger and better place. That's the only way it'll ever happen! I'm telling you now, if you quit your job yet are still fearful and hopeless, then I promise you that will be the beginning of your demise, because you will have no vision or juice to move you forward. The great news is, at this point, you should have an understanding of what fear really is and how it can work to your advantage. Let's get real; the majority of the world calls their job the daily grind. What kind of metaphor is that!? You know what the rest of us call it, the daily glide (Ok maybe that's just what I call it).

What about the phrase, "Get a real job." Let's think about what a real job is. Is what you do at your job now real? I doubt it. The smile you put on, the outfit, the attitude, none of it is real. Your parents and authorities tell you to be realistic, sensible and practical. Well guess what. A lot of those same people that told you that are probably living way below their potential and sold out on their dreams in a long time ago. Just like relationships, you basically have one or two types of careers. Those are that are toxic; that literally damage your life. Then you have careers that are helping you become a better person and adding to your ability to be fulfilled and make a difference.

I either quit or was fired from every job I ever had. I had every type of job imaginable from modeling to sales to scrubbing toilets. I would meet a customer or a passerby, get involved in great conversations and eventually get to the point where I was giving them some type of advice or tool they could use to help them in their life. And bad because I would blatantly disregard my duties so that I could help people, I was either reprimanded or fired. I reached a point where I realized that I could be out helping people and making a difference rather than doing something that did not serve my purpose. Those were the times where I would literally walk out. It had nothing to do with me being irresponsible or immature and it had everything to do with being bold and following my heart. As it should be with you, as well.

You are here to learn that which you do not know. You are here to do that which is your destiny and the greatest of your achievements shall be the ones that scare you the most. You must stretch yourself beyond which you think you can do. You must risk more than you believe you should. You must unleash yourself upon the world and you'll never do that behind the bars of a job that does not allow you to do so.

Creating Value

Just like time, wealthy and successful people have a very clear and healthy understanding of what money is. Successful and wealthy people understand that money is simply a representation. It is a representation of their ability to produce value for other people. Let's look at that a little bit more closely. The reason you get paid what you get paid currently is in direct correlation to the amount of value that you produce for your company and ultimately for other people. If you want to start making more money, you have to find a way to do one of two things. First, how can you start to increase the amount of value that you can produce for other people? And, second, how can you reach more people with the valuable product or service that you have? As simple as it is, those are the only two ways of making you more money, increasing the value you can produce and increasing the amount of people you can reach without value.

Take someone like Bill Gates or Steve Jobs. They are some of the richest men on the planet. That is because their products are of great value. Without the Windows Operating System or Mac OS, your computer would be nothing but a pile of junk. It might as well be an oversized paperweight, although because of what the Windows Operating System or Mac OS allows you to do, it is very valuable to you. Not only that, but millions upon millions of people use computers. Therefore, millions upon millions of people see the value in the Microsoft or Mac programs and are willing to pay for it.

Wealthy people understand this. They understand that you must be able to produce a product or service that is valuable and you must be able to reach a large number of people with that product or service. There are two potential directions you can take with this information: first, you can start to think about how you can increase your personal value in your current career, so that you can produce more value for your company and ultimately the customers that your company serves. If you can demonstrate that you are more valuable than what you're being paid, your salary will increase.

The second direction you can take with this information is that you can decide to start your own business. The wealthiest people throughout history all had their own businesses. The difference between working for someone else and working for yourself is night and day. When you work for someone else, there is always going to be a limit to how much you can make, however, when you work for yourself the amount of money that you can make is unlimited.

I may be personally biased, but I believe owning your own business is the way to go. There are of course all of the classic reasons to be your own boss, which are:

- Making your own schedule

- Having more freedom

- Work becomes fun

- The attractive paycheck

- Nice vacations

All of these are very true when it comes to being an entrepreneur. However, there is an even deeper and more attractive side to being an entrepreneur. Those are things like:

- Achieving your dreams

- Living with passion

- Being fulfilled

- Living your purpose

- Contributing to your friends and family society and world

- Inspiring others to follow in your footsteps

This is the real juice when it comes to being an entrepreneur. Rather than barely making it through the day, you have the time and energy to do the things that really matter. Your life becomes something that is much more effortless and successful for you.

If you are planning on going into business for yourself, there are few important things that you have to think about:

What are your skills passions or abilities that are going to allow you to create a high level of value?

Is there a current market for your product or service?

Can you effectively reach your market?

If you are not earning the kind of money that you would like to be in your job or your business, rather than asking yourself, "How can I make more money?" the question I would encourage you to ask is, "How can I produce more value?"

Investing

Another aspect of building wealth that I want to talk about is investing. The absolute truth is that your finances are either rising or falling. You're either making money or you are losing money. Even if you're fairly smart, with the state of inflation and the economy, the money that you have today is very likely going to be worthless tomorrow.

There is a very important idea that wealthy people understand when it comes to their money and that is "use it or lose it." If you're not using your money in a way that helps you to have more of it, then in one way or another you are losing the money that you have. Unfortunately, for most people, that's not difficult because they use their money on things like clothes, shoes, TV's and other stuff. None of those things helps people to build their wealth. If anything, those are things that help people lose the money that they do have. This idea of investing is very powerful when it comes to building your wealth because investing is taking your money and putting it into something that will ultimately give you a return, which is called an ROI or return on investment.

There are a lot of big misconceptions about investing, as well. People tend to think that investing is only for smart and wealthy people. We'll how do you think those people got to be smart and wealthy? They knew that they wanted to invest their money. They found something that they wanted to invest in. They learned more about it and educated themselves, and eventually became wealthy.
Can't you do exactly the same thing? Of course you can.

The great thing about investing is that there are many different
options for you as well. There are stocks, bonds, mutual funds, futures, and the foreign exchange market to name a few. I am not going to suggest one or the other. I am not here to advise you on what to invest in, rather to get you inspired on the idea of investing so you can put it to use in your life.

They all might seem a little bit intimidating at first.
Although if you at least get it started and pick one of them
that you're interested in, then you can begin to get the basics
of that method of investing. You can begin building your
knowledge about it. What is also great is a lot of companies
will give you what's called a demo account so that you can
invest play money in the beginning so you can get the hang
of it. There's really no excuse not to be investing.

This entire revolution is an investment. The more you put
into your into it, the more you are going to get out. Don't let
your money get left behind while the rest of your life
transforms. The same goes for your career. Don't stay stuck.
Be bold and take control of your future today.

Take Action!

Think about what your relationship with money. Is it primarily positive or negative?

What type of beliefs do you have about money?

If you have negative beliefs, how can you start to take on some more positive beliefs about money?

Remember the keys to the Law of Attraction are:

- Clarity

- Emotion

- Consistency

- Action

- Your beliefs

If you hate your job then it's time to quit. Ask yourself these questions:

Is my job helping me or hurting me?

What are my current excuses for staying at my job and how can I eliminate them so that I can move on?

How good would my life be if I followed my dreams?

There is no doubt about it - your finances and your career are two of the biggest and most important aspects of your life.

Put this book down and take action now!

Transform Your Relationships

"We need to talk." Have you ever heard that line before? I think most of us have. And I am fairly certain almost all of us get a sinking feeling when we hear that line. So, what is the deal with relationships? Why are they so scary? Why are they a struggle? And why in the world do over 50% of all marriages end in divorce? These are all very good questions. Questions that most people do not have the answers to. Ironically, I believe we all have a need to be connected. In the game of life there is absolutely no doubt that being a master of your self is important. The real magic happens when you are able to master the ability to have an outstanding relationship with not only yourself but all the people around you.

No matter who you are, no matter what your goals are in life, to some degree or another we are all in relationships. It is important for us to have the ability to create and grow healthy relationships it is my personal belief that regardless of the amount of success or money that you have, it is your relationships that make you truly rich.

That's not to say, that money is not important or should not be sought after, although the benefits of money can only go so far. However, the benefits of true powerful relationships are endless.

What's important to remember here is that as much as you should be interested in the benefits of great relationships, equally you should be interested in how you can add substance to your relationships.

The power of a truly great relationship comes from the synergy of two or more people. The more personal power that you have and that you can potentially bring into a relationship, the better that relationship is going to be. In many ways when it comes to successful relationships, you are the key.

You will notice that the people who have successful relationships, across the board, can be successful in those relationships because they have a very strong and powerful relationship with themselves.

They can understand and relate to other people very easily because they have a very deep understanding of who they are as an individual. It is that strong understanding of who they are that allows them to communicate and to connect to other people very effectively.

One of the biggest components of relationships that I want to talk about is dating. I believe, to some degree, that everyone wants to love and be loved. Yet dating still seems to be an area in many people's lives where they have some serious challenges. When it comes to dating, an important question to ask yourself is, "What am I looking for?" A lot of times, people tend to rush into relationships because they feel like it's what they should do or they feel like they are fulfilling their need to love and be loved.

The problem here is that when people rush to relationships without knowing exactly what they want out of that relationship, it creates a potential formula for disaster. It would be like going to the grocery store just because you're hungry and filling a shopping cart full of food but not really being aware or certain of what you wanted to eat. And, if you weren't careful, you may accidentally throw some things in your cart that you are either allergic to or that are bad for you.

It is important to know what your goal in a relationship is. As we know from before, the more clear you are about what you want, the easier it is to produce that result.

Here are some dating ideas:

Are you clear about what you want in a relationship?

Are you looking for a long-term relationship?

Are you looking for a short-term relationship?

Do you want to get married?

Are you looking to just go out and have fun?

Each one of these questions represents a category and each relationship category requires a very specific type of person. If you don't know what the goal of your relationship is, then you could easily attract into your life the wrong type of person. Needless to say, if you get two people in a relationship that have contrasting criteria for what they want out of it, you can almost be 100% certain that that relationship is going to fail.

Similarly, it is important to ask yourself if your motives for getting into a relationship are healthy or unhealthy. For example, some people want to get into a relationship because they're looking for love, which is very understandable, although sometimes, people end up looking for the wrong type of love.

What I mean is a person could be looking to get into a relationship so that the other person in that relationship can fill them with love because that person is lacking self-love. Now the problem here is that no matter how many people you get into relationship with and no matter how much any of them love you, no one can ever fill you with self-love.

Self-love is something that has to come from within you. Another example is some people are looking for respect, which makes sense but some people are looking for the other person to fill them with respect because they have low self-respect. No matter how much respect someone gives you or how powerful you make yourself seem in a relationship, if you do not have high levels of self-respect, you will continue to feel unhappy about things.

What's worse is the other person that you're in a relationship with will begin to feel bad. That is because they will feel like they are doing everything in their power to love, care for and respect you. Yet, they will feel like in the midst all of that, nothing is working. That can be a very negative and harmful feeling for them. And eventually it can lead to the demise of the relationship.

For the sake of your mental and emotional state, along with the other person's, you owe it to yourself and to them to make sure that your motives for getting into a relationship are healthy. If you are looking to get into a relationship because you are seeking love, then make sure it is a healthy kind of love. If you're looking to get into a relationship because of respect, then make certain it is a mutual and positive respect.

Also, when you're thinking about what your goal is for your relationship, get specific about the type of qualities your ideal person would have. The more specific you are about the qualities that they would have, the more that is going to orient your mind in a specific direction and allow you to know when you have met the right person. Therefore, if you're looking for someone who is smart, witty, and classy, then that gives you a good idea of the kind of places where you can go to find that type of person. Also, an equally important benefit is it gives you an idea of the places you should avoid like, the local hole in the wall bar.

One of the biggest benefits to having crystal clarity when it comes to your relationships is growth. Like we said before, there's really no such thing as neutral in life and it's especially true when it comes to relationships. The quality of a relationship is either increasing or declining. People are always going to be growing or they are going to be resisting their need to grow. And, that means couples will either become closer to one another or further and further apart.

The more clear you are about what you are looking for in a relationship, the better your chances are of meeting someone that you'll really be able to grow with. You have two aspects to the synergy of your relationship. The first is the current excitement and power of your relationship. This is the juice and rush you get in the initial stages of a relationship. This where were you are learning about who each of you are. Everything between you two is new and adventurous. This is where the foundation of the relationship is built. That is why it is important to be very clear about your motives and actions during this time. If a relationship starts off with a weak foundation, it will be difficult for anything substantial to stand on it after that.

The second aspect of powerful relationships is the future and the growth of that relationship. A truly powerful relationship is like wine, the older it gets the better and more valuable it becomes. The greatest couples I have ever been able to observe were couples who got past the new and exciting stage and were able to create something that was in fact more meaningful and rich, than what they had in the beginning. So many people worry about losing the fire or spark, meanwhile they are forgetting completely about connection and love.

They say that opposites attract and to some degree, that is true. Although it is important to keep in mind is that it's very helpful if you have it least similar qualities and beliefs. What does that mean? That means if you are looking for someone who is a good listener, ask yourself if you are a good listener. If you are looking for someone who is spontaneous, ask yourself if you are spontaneous? Some people might say, "But, Shannon that's the point. I want to find someone so they can bring some new dimensions to my life. Someone that is not exactly the same as me." And, I would agree with you hundred percent. However, what I would add to that is that is this person, I can almost guarantee, if they really are what you're looking for, is going to add to your life in numerous different ways. If there are a few key categories where you guys can really connect, then that'll make things even better.

As much as relationships are about synergy, they're also

about compromise. This can be a challenging idea for a lot of people because a lot of people believe that their life should be exactly the way they want to be; that they shouldn't have to give up anything. The word compromise for a lot of people makes them think that they would be losing something. People think that if they compromise on something, that one person gets what they want and the other person doesn't. The true meaning of compromise is coming to a decision or a conclusion where both people are happy. It is what's called a win-win situation.

I would challenge you to think about what your personal definition of compromise is and if you think of it in a way of giving something up, then my question to you would be how can you think of compromise as creating a win-win situation where both people are happy with the result?

I've worked with hundreds of people and I have seen potentially amazing relationships fall apart simply because of people's inability to compromise. Remember, relationships are about working together, not working against each other. Relationships are about adding value to each other and growing together.

Imagine what kind of richness you would be able to create in your relationships if you constantly had a mentality where you were looking for the mutually beneficial solution. This would keep your personal integrity intact as well as clearly demonstrate to the other person that you honestly cared about producing favorable outcomes for them as well. This type of win-win thinking is exactly what will become the adhesive power when things get rough.

Along with compromise comes commitment. Anything in life that is valuable and truly worthwhile is going to take some serious commitment. Commitment can be tricky for a lot of people because people have been damaged from past relationships, so they are less willing to commit themselves one hundred percent to a relationship. That becomes a double-edged sword. By not opening yourself up in committing one hundred percent to a relationship, you will indeed avoid getting hurt. Yet you will also avoid getting one hundred percent of the potential glory that the relationship has to offer.

Because of that, people have what's called the 50-50 rule. I'm sure you've heard it or used it to some degree before. It's when people say, "I'll make an effort when they make an effort," or something like, "I'll meet them halfway." This is a dangerous principle to live by. That is because you're ideally going for a relationship that is synergistic; something that is more than the sum of its parts. Yet, if you're only willing to put in fifty percent effort, it becomes nearly impossible to reach that result. The person that you're in the relationship with is only getting a fifty percent commitment from you. And sooner or later that's what they will begin to think is the most you have to offer. That is why it's so important to give your all and be one hundred percent committed.

Did you know that to create steam, you must get water to a temperature of 212°? Anything less than 212° will not produce steam. Not even 211°, yet if you can get water up to 212°, you can create steam. With that steam, you can power a locomotive. Relationships are exactly the same way. If you are giving less than one hundred percent of your commitment, then that is the same as you wanting to power a locomotive, yet stoking the fire to a temperature that is less than 212°.

You might be thinking, "That sounds good in theory, although what if somebody breaks my heart again. I don't think I could go through that." Well, let me lay out your options for you very clearly.

Option #1: Give fifty percent effort and most likely never reach your relationship goal because you're not willing to give what it takes to create such a thing. Ultimately, you never get what you want.

Option #2: Even though a person might break your heart, you realize that it's not the end of the world. It's kind of like the lottery. You can't win if you don't play. Yes, you might get hurt along the way but if you don't give it one hundred percent - your best effort - you'll never know. You will potentially miss out on all the glory that a truly great relationship has to offer you.

Some of the biggest rewards in life come from taking some of the biggest risks. You are rewarded by putting your heart and soul on the line. When it comes to relationships, putting everything on the line is just one of those risks that you must take. You have to get yourself to a level of commitment where you're willing to do whatever it takes to get the type of relationship that you want.

First Date Syndrome

The runner up in the first place in the relationship blunders is what I call First Date Syndrome. I believe to some extent we have all suffered or will suffer from it at some point. Example: It is the first date and you really want to make an awesome first impression, so you put your best foot forward and keep it out there. The result? You make an exceedingly powerful mark on the other person. Now you're in trouble, why? Because the person who you portrayed is not an accurate representation of who you really are and the more comfortable you become with your new mate, the less you feel like you have to put on a show. Then one day, WHAMMO! You are up the creek without a paddle because this oh so dapper character is just that, a character and not a genuine picture of your real self. The real kicker happens when the person you have been fooling starts to figure things out. They start saying things like, "Where is that guy I fell in love with?" Guess what, sweetheart? He doesn't exist. This is a total trust killer and ultimately makes you look really bad. This ends up giving you the opposite effect of what you wanted.

It is one thing to want to make a good impression and I think that is a healthy motive to have. Although it is important to make sure that, even though you may want the other person to like you, you should want them to like you for who you really are. And as much as that sounds like an after school special, it's true. Deep down you want someone who can see and accept the real you. But if all you do is show them what you think is going to impress them, then they get an inaccurate vision of who you are.

So many people do this! They bust out their best dance moves, hottest outfits, and they put all of their coolest toys on the table. And after they have created enough of a WOW factor, they ease off. And they stop doing the things that made them so special and amazing. My advice here is to pick a side. If you meet someone that makes you want to raise your standards as much as I believe you should want to do that for yourself, I don't think there is anything wrong with having some outside help. Just remember that if you are going to do awesome and amazing things once, you'd better be prepared to do them forever.

If doing those flashy things and it's not really part of who you are, then commit to not doing them. You will save yourself the pain of having to be someone you're not and you will also paint a much more genuine picture of yourself. The more straight forward you are in the beginning, the more solid you allow the future to be.

When it comes to male/female relationships, there is a challenge. That challenge is that males and females have very different needs. Have you ever noticed how most men think that a lot of the things that women do are crazy? Similarly, have you also noticed how most women feel like a lot of the things that men do are stupid? So there is certainly some type of disconnect here. There is clearly a misunderstanding of the needs of the opposite sex.

For example, most males have needs that are related to being dominant, powerful, and competitive. Therefore, they do things like jump out of airplanes and watch football. The reason they do those things is because they meet a specific need that man has. When a man watches football, many of his male needs are being met all at the same time; the need for power, competition, and dominance.

On the other hand, you have the needs of women. The needs of women are much different than the needs of men. Some of the primary needs of women are to have attention, be in touch with their emotions, and to feel special and safe. Thus, things like reading romance novels will fulfill many of a woman's needs.

Often times, people will be frustrated with the opposite sex because they believe that the things that they are doing serve no purpose. For example, most men can't understand why women watch soap operas, but rather than try to understand what needs they are fulfilling by watching soap operas they write them off as silly and a waste of time. What most men are missing out on is if they understood why women watch soap operas, the male could have a better idea of how he personally could fulfill some of those needs in the female's life.

Likewise, if women made a better effort to understand why men do the things that they do rather than writing them off as pointless and stupid, then they could understand the needs that, that male is trying to fill. And could start doing things with him that are related to those needs, which would incorporate her into his need rather than have his need be a source of distraction, which would take time away from her, and more importantly them.

No matter what, both males and females have needs. They will always find a way to fill those needs one way or the other. Of course, ideally if they can fill those needs by doing things *with* the person that they are in a relationship with then of course they would. If they can't unfortunately they will surely fill their needs *without* that person.

It is in your best interest to understand what your personal needs are. The same goes for trying to understand what the needs are of the person you are in a relationship with. The better you can understand and meet their needs, the more happy and more fulfilled they are going to be with you. That means they will be more likely to do things that include you.

The only way that you're going to understand the needs of the person that you're in a relationship with is to communicate. This can also be difficult when it comes to male/female relationships because males and females have very different ways of communicating and expressing themselves. You must realize that the quality of your relationship relies on the quality of your communication. Communication is definitely one of the aspects of relationships that takes some practice and commitment. As long as you have two different people who express and interpret information differently, then you are almost always going to have miscommunication somewhere along the line.

The real trick that I've come to learn about communication is to focus not so much on what the person is literally saying (the words, etc.), rather to focus on the essence of what they are saying.
The absolute truth is that communication means nothing without connection. I am going to say that again because I think it's important: communication means nothing without connection!

Two people can be in a relationship and they can communicate but it doesn't mean for one second that that communication brings them closer together as a couple, nor does it mean that that communication helps connect them. I've worked with couples who had been married for over 20 years and yet they felt like they hardly knew each other because they had such poor communication. So, the amount of time that you spend communicating, as you can see from that example, means very little.

You'd be amazed at the deep level of connection you can get

with someone when you have a rich and powerful communication with them. This is important when it comes to communicating because often people will get into arguments and fights and even potentially end up breaking up because of a lack of connection.

What we can learn from this is that if you are trying to communicate a point to someone and they're not getting it, I'll tell you right now that raising the volume of your voice and treating that person like a two year old is not going to help them get the point. In that case, you are only changing the volume and demeanor of your voice. And you are most likely making the other person more upset and they are far less apt to want to listen to you.

Obviously, that person does not understand the way that you are presenting the information. Imagine if you went to a different country where you didn't understand the language. It wouldn't matter how many times you said the same thing or how loud you got. A person who does not speak your language wouldn't understand what you're saying. What's the answer? The answer is to be committed to your intention, but not to your approach.

For instance, if you're trying to tell someone that you really love them then that is your intention. Your intention is to show them how much you care. If for some reason you're not getting the result that you want from them or you don't feel like they completely understand you, then you should take that as a cue to change your approach; to change the way that you are saying what you're saying. Remember it's not what you say that is important. It's getting your intention across to that person in a way that they can fully understand that makes the difference.

If you're trying to express how you feel to someone and they're not getting it than rather than getting upset and raising the volume of your voice and blaming them for not understanding. You can simply say exactly the same thing in a different way. It tends to be our instinct to blame other people when they don't understand but the fact is it's not that they can't understand the essence of what you're trying to say. It is simply that they can't understand it in the way that you are saying it. Don't give up on them. If anything, give them the benefit of the doubt. Figure that they can understand what you mean as long as you're willing to change your approach and say things in a way that makes sense to them. This idea is especially important when it comes to male/female relationships because the way the two interpret and express things is very different.

By showing your partner that you are willing to communicate effectively, they will see that you truly care. It will also show them that you are patient and that you have them in mind. You would be amazed at what an impact you can have on a person when they know you are going out of your way to be thoughtful of them.

Trust Building

We now move onto the infamous building block of all relationships which is trust. I have put together what I believe are the core ingredients to building trust.

Say it. Do it: One of the essential components of trust is doing what you said you were going to do, when you said you were going to do it. This should be a value you have for yourself personally but it becomes even more important in relationships. If you consistently do what you say you are going to do, then you prove to that person that they can count on you. The confidence that comes along with being able to rely on someone is immeasurable. Keep in mind that in a relationship, nothing is little. Even the small things matter and often they matter just as much or more than then big things. This is why you must do your best to be consistent all the time. If you say it…do it.

Tell the truth: This is a big one. Relationships live and die based on truth. Even the littlest lie can damage a relationship. When you lie to someone, they trust you less and feel like they need to protect themselves from you. There is a combination here of not lying which means always being honest and when you are honest, always being fully honest which means not omitting any details or information. The quality of communication goes through the roof when you are totally honest with someone. The truth may not always be pleasant, however, to your surprise, you will find your partner will respect you more for telling the truth, even if it's ugly, rather than telling a pretty lie.

Be vulnerable: When there are opportunities for you to be vulnerable, take them. The relationship you have with another person should be a special one. And if a person knows that you are willing to be vulnerable in front of them, that makes them feel extremely special, because they know you do not do that for everyone. This also shows them that you trust them in your weakest state. If you can show a person that you are not afraid to be open, then you will be trusted in a way like never before.

Speak your feelings: This one can be tough for men because they often feel like they aren't supposed to show their feelings. This relates back to being vulnerable. The person you are in a relationship wants to see the real you. They want to know that you have feelings. This is how they will relate and feel close to you. No one can relate to a person that only talks about facts and figures. And because women generally find it easier to talk about their feelings than men, they can feel alone in that area. Speaking your feelings also has to do with issues that concern you. If your partner does or says something that you do not like, it is your responsibility to tell them. Being passive-aggressive is the opposite of effective communication. Do not keep your mouth shut just to avoid a fight. If you are walking on eggshells, there is a good chance that the relationship is on the rocks as it is. Communication will only help either make it better or help it end faster. Either could be a good thing, depending on what is right for that couple.

Promises: Always keep your promises. The idea of keeping

your promises is similar to doing what you said you were going to do when you said you were going to do it. The difference is that a promise is even more powerful. When you promise something to someone, you are giving them your word that you will do it. If you don't, much of the trust you have built will go away. Promises are intimate things that mean a lot to the person they are being kept for. Follow through on your promises and you will ensure some serious trust in your relationship.

In the end, trust can only be gained by giving it. Trust builds certainty in a relationship. The more trust there is, the stronger your relationship will be. All relationships have tough times and one of the only things that will pull you through is your ability to trust that the person is going to weather the storm with you and that you will do that same for them. This bond allows you to overcome obstacles and reach a level of connection that is unimaginable.

Take Action!

First of all, when it comes to relationships, remember that you are the key. The better your relationship with yourself, the better you're going to be able to have quality relationships with other people.

What are your relationship goals? Be specific!

Is your approach to dating and relationships a healthy one?

How can you improve your communication?

What can you do to build trust?

Put this book down and take action now!

Contribution

Now that you are beginning to grasp all the great concepts and ideas of self-mastery and what it entails, there is one final step left take. There is one more piece of uncharted territory that you must venture into. Once more, you must dig down deep within you and tap into that bigger and better side of you that wants out. You must extend beyond yourself, and utilize the power of contribution.

The fact is, that no matter how much success you achieve in your personal or professional life, you will never be one hundred percent happy or fulfilled unless you are contributing and adding value to other people's lives. There are countless amounts of people who have focused themselves entirely on making **their own** life better. These are the same people who go to sleep at night feeling like something is missing, and who wake up in the morning despite all the success they've achieved, and still do not feel content with their life.

Then you have people who throw the pendulum in the opposite direction. They focus their entire life on giving to others. As good and as respectable as that is, they too feel unhappy about their life. That is because, similar to the case of self-love, these people want to give and give and give. Yet they have never taken the time to contribute to themselves. They've never taken the time to add value to their own life. Therefore, again they end up giving that which they do not have.

One of the most important parts of this that you must understand is that the more you work on yourself, the more you improve who you are, the more you add value to yourself and the more value you are going to be able to add to other people. The more thoroughly you understand yourself, the more thoroughly you are going to be able to understand other people. The more you care about and love yourself, the more you will be able to care about and love other people. The more you value and respect your time, the more quality time you'll be able to give to other people. Remember, you can't give any of those things, unless you have them.

We all have different passions in life. We are all very different people and we all have different purposes to our lives. Yet despite all of our differences, I believe that we all have a fundamental need to give back. I believe that giving truly is the secret to living. It's really no mystery, think about a time when someone contributed to you. Think about how you felt. If you believe that no one has ever contributed to you, just take a moment to imagine what it would feel like for someone to do such a thing.

Let's look at the other side. How about a time when you contributed to somebody else. How did that make you feel? How do you think it made the person you were contributing to feel? Let us take things even a step further. When someone else contributed to you, or when you contributed to somebody else, think about the people that were observing those acts of kindness – people you may not have even been aware of. How do you think it made them feel to see people going beyond themselves and giving to someone else? It is said that just by observing an act of kindness, the quality of a person's life can significantly change.

Think about a time of giving. They say it is better to give than receive. Couldn't that be true all the time? Not just at the holidays or at special events? What if you adopted that is your personal motto? How do you think that would change your life? And how greatly do you think that would change other people's lives? We tend to think that holidays and special events are the only times that we can give. Why couldn't you give in some way shape or form every day?

It is said that random acts of kindness can greatly change the world, and I believe that one hundred percent. However, I also believe that intentional acts of kindness, acts of kindness that are deliberate, are the ones that not only have the most impact, but those are the ones that I believe can change the world the most. When you make a commitment to make a conscious and deliberate contribution to a group of people, or even just one person, the impact you create causes a positive ripple effect that echoes on until the end of time.

I want to make a special note here. That is, regardless of where you are in your life, regardless of how much success you have, or how much money you have made, if you are willing, there is always a way to contribute. You might believe that you don't have anything to give. Or you might believe that you don't have enough to give. Let me tell you something, no matter what your situation is in life, you always have something to give.

The thing is, deep down I believe that we are all heroes. My personal definition of a hero is not someone who saves people. When you save people those people will always need saving. A real hero in my definition is someone who empowers people. Make them better than who they were, so that ultimately they can rise up and save themselves. Whether you want to believe it or not, you my friend are a hero.

Now that you realize that part of who you are is a hero, then what comes along with being a hero is a moral obligation. Just as much as you have a moral obligation to yourself to make your personal life as good as it can be, you also have a moral obligation to others to help them make their lives as good as they can be. Whether you know it or not, you have talents, skills, and abilities that can help other people make their lives better.

The fact of the matter is that there is someone out there who needs you. It might be a friend, family member, or a coworker. It could also be someone you don't even know. The fact remains that there is someone out there who needs you not tomorrow, not next week, not next month, but they need you right now. Now, I'm not saying your entire life should revolve around helping others. I know it can be a challenge to get even your own life in order. I am not asking you to become the next Dalai Lama, or Mother Teresa.

If that is what your goal is in life, then I support you one hundred percent and I believe in you. I know that if you really want to, you can be one of the greatest forms of change this world has ever seen. However, don't think for one second that even the smallest contribution won't make a difference. One person's contribution is no better or worse than someone else's. Giving in any way shape or form is good.

Begin to even just get curious about how you can make a contribution. Start to think about what your skills, talents, and abilities are. Get creative, and realize that even you as you are right now have something to give. There are so many different ways that you can contribute. Here's a list of just a few to get you thinking.

You can:

- Volunteer your time

- Become a mentor

- Donate money to a charity

- Give food to a food shelf

- Donate some clothes to the Salvation Army

- Make a new friend

- Volunteer your time at a retirement center

- Spend more time with your friends and family

- Join the Big Brother Big Sister program.

- Adopt a child

- Teach a class

- Share this book with a friend

It is up to you to find out which method of contributing fits you the best. If nothing in that list interests you, then I challenge you to get creative and find a way that you can contribute. Start to tap into some of that possibility thinking and use it to find a positive and powerful way to give back. Remember, it's okay to start small. It is getting into the ritual of contributing that matters. You'll find that the more you do it, the more you'll want to do it. You will be inspired from there to create new and better ways to give back.

Remember, contribution does not mean you have to give away money. In fact, I believe that money is the lowest form of contributing. Let me repeat that - giving money is the LOWEST form of contributing. It happens to be the easiest and quickest, which is why so many people find it attractive. But the truth is, contributing your time and your love are the greatest gifts you have to offer. Think about it, by giving a man money, you simply feed him for a day. But imagine what you can do beyond that. By teaching him how to fish, you can feed him for a lifetime. By inspiring him, motivating him, and loving him, you feed more than his need to eat. You nourish his heart and soul. Now **THAT** is real power. That is real contribution.

If you are willing to look, you can see the results of great contribution all around you. If you are willing to look, you can see how few have impacted many. I want you to join that movement, but more than that, I want you to get to a state where you want to become part of that movement.

I am asking you to look inside yourself, and find the hero that is there. I am asking you find a sleeping giant of contribution within you, and wake it up. Do whatever it takes to get to a place where you want nothing more than to improve the quality of your own life and the life of others. Do this and the joy and abundance will flow through your life forever.

The reason that I'm asking you to do this is because one of the people that is out there who needs you the most is me. I need your help, because I know that as much as I would like to, I can't help everyone. Although I know that by writing this book, by helping you improve your life and getting you as excited about contributing as I am, then maybe you can reach some of the people that I wouldn't otherwise be able to.

The purpose of the human existence has nothing to do with what or how much we acquire. Truly, at the end of our life none of it will matter. Moreover, the true aspiration of the soul is to leave this world knowing that we have made some impression upon the people of this world and its future.

It's all about raising your level of personal understanding and the understanding of life and then being able to translate that through some type of expression so that it can make an impression on and influence the generations to come. It's the images of strength and genius that spark the greatest power and ability in mankind.

Consequently, planting the seeds of wisdom, industry, and human potential are that which become the foundation for a new and better generation.

I wrote this book with the goal of changing the world. Even though I know if only one person reads this book and changes their life, then I've made a difference. The thing is, you can call me greedy, but I want to make more of a difference than that. I know that if that one person who reads my book decides to go out and make a difference in some way, even if they only contribute to one other person, then that one person's life becomes better. Now that means two people's lives have been impacted in a positive way. It can potentially go on forever in that way.

Will you help me? I want you to stand up and say yes. I want you to stand up and say yes because you are on the way to making your life better and the lives of other people better. I want you to really do this. I want you to stand up right now and say yes. This is not about getting excited. This is about getting determined. Stand up tall and proud and say yes!

You know, everyone is so afraid of death. But guess what. If you spent your time giving back to your fellow man, you would create an echo effect that would go on for the rest of time. If you truly want to live forever, find a way to give back and it will be so.

Take Action!

How can you adopt a new and empowering mindset of contribution?

In what ways would you like to start contributing?

What will your greatest contribution be?

Remember: Contributing is not about money. In fact donating money is the lowest form of contributing. Donating your time and your love are the greatest gifts you have to offer the world. How will you share them?

Put this book down and take action now!

Conclusion

By now you should understand that your life changes when you do. Out of the three keys I have outlined here to achieve maximum personal power, any and all of them have to do with making a change in who you are. As you continue forward on your journey of life, you will face many challenges, trials, and tribulations. Yet the biggest barrier that you will ever face is yourself. Truly, your ego, your self-doubt, and your lack of motivation will be some of the greatest forces that will hold your greatness prisoner.

The more responsibility you take for yourself and the results of your life, the more the excuses about why your life is not the way it should be will disappear. The more you can focus on and master the three keys to personal power, the more your quality of life will increase. Not only that, but the more you can increase your personal power. The more you will shift and revolutionize yourself from your greatest enemy to your own greatest hero.

Like magic before your eyes, you will see your own life transform. With a continuous dedication to improving the quality of your own life and other people's, all of your pain and inner conflict will cease to exist. You will see life through new eyes and you will experience it through a new body. Your dreams will begin to change. You will no longer dream about the same things. That is because slowly but surely the aspects of your life that you hoped, and wished, and prayed to change and become better will change and will become better.

Through my life experience, I've found there are two types of pain. The first type of pain is a pain that you feel when you are not growing. It is the pain you feel when the bigger better, ultimate-self within cannot get out. This is the kind of pain that can make life feel unbearable.
The second type of pain is growing pain. There is no doubt that growing pains are uncomfortable. Yet they are powerful because they are evidence that in some way you are getting

better. They are proof that you are doing what is necessary to overcome your fears and doubts, and transcend into a life full of power and certainty, one that is full of happiness and fulfillment.

The fact of the matter is that no matter what, you are going to feel pain and that's just how it is. The glory is that you can choose which type of pain you want to experience. Do you want to continue living your life in a way where you are living below where you are truly meant to live and remain stuck in your puny comfort zone – the comfort zone that is really more of a prison than anything else? Or, would you rather, for the first time in your life, rise up and make a total resolution to become who you are meant to be and feel the glorious pain of progress?

Aren't you sick and tired of being sick and tired? Aren't you curious to find out how amazing your life can be? Don't you want to experience life with more passion and color? Don't you really honestly deserve it?

Your life changes when you do. Don't wait, don't be afraid, and do not hesitate to take the first step. There is no doubt that time is your most valuable asset. Which means that time is definitely not going to wait for you to get going.

Know that you have the power and the resourcefulness to get started right now. Along with the skills and insights from reading this book, you have everything you need to transform your life. At the end of your life you will have most certainly experienced pain. However, whether you look back on your life with certainty that you lived, loved, and laughed to your greatest potential is up to you. Go forth, be great! And remember to live, love, and laugh...everyday. Long live the revolution.

Take Action!

Throughout this book, you have heard references to my life-coaching clients. As you know, my passion is helping people live the life they truly deserve. I honestly hope that through this book I have been able to help you revolutionize your life. I can only imagine the richness and fulfillment you will be able to attain. And no matter how much that is, I hope it is more than you ever thought possible. You really do deserve the world.

You and I have come a long way since the warning in the beginning of this book. As I sit here, I imagine you exuding this radiance that comes from this amazing journey you and I have been on together. The adventure is far from over, however. I know now that you are ready and able to move forward and handle anything that comes your way. Now you know how to have clarity, and self-love, as well as the tools you need in order to create the life you truly deserve. You now hold the three keys to personal liberation. Take this moment to stop and think about how powerful you feel. Now you are free.

To your success,

Shannon

Special Bonus Offer

As my free gift to you, I have created a companion video series called Life Transformations. This is a four day video e-course that I have put together to highlight some of the strongest points in this book, along with a few other great ideas not mentioned here. To claim your free gift, visit the website below!

www.321lifecoach.com

Get in Touch!

As your coach, I would love to help continue to serve you in any way I can. If you would like to hire me as your coach, have me speak at your event, or work with me in any other fashion, you can get in touch with me directly via email or through my website.

Shannon@321lifecoach.com
www.321lifecoach.com/homepage

22775274R00193

Made in the USA
San Bernardino, CA
20 July 2015